Addiction, Change & Choice

The New View of Alcoholism

by

Vince Fox, M.Ed., CRREd.

See Sharp Press • Tucson, Arizona • 1993

For information contact See Sharp Press, P.O. Box 1731, Tucson, AZ 85702-1731.

Fox, Vince.
    Addiction, change & choice : the new view of alcoholism / by Vince Fox ; introduction by Albert Ellis ; foreword by Jack Trimpey. – Tucson, AZ : See Sharp Press, 1993.
    248 p. ; 23 cm.
    Includes bibliographical references and index.

1. Alcoholics – Rehabilitation. 2. Alcoholism – Treatment. 3. Alcoholics Anonymous. 4. Rational Recovery.

ISBN 0-9613289-7-5   362.29286

first printing – December 1993
second printing – August 1995

Cover by Clifford Harper. Printed with soy-based ink on recycled, acid-free paper by Thomson-Shore, Inc., Dexter, Michigan.

All human despair is the result of resistance to change.

— CONFUCIUS

Contents

Introduction (by Dr. Albert Ellis) 1

Foreword (by Jack Trimpey) 3

Preface 5

1. Heavy Drinking: Its Historical Context 11
personal and social aspects; as cultural norm; as means of social control;
religious aspects; as coping mechanism

2. Alcoholism: Definitions & Opinions 16
traditional (NCADD, AMA, Jim Christopher, Claudia Black, Mark Keller,
Bill Wilson/AA); nontraditional (Claude Steiner/Eric Berne, *Black's Law Dictionary*,
Jack Trimpey, American Psychiatric Association, Herbert Fingarette, Morris
Chavetz); exploratory (World Health Organization, *Webster's New World
Dictionary*, Charles Bufe, *Encyclopedia Britannica*, U.S. Supreme Court, Arnold
Ludwig)

3. Polarization: Us vs. Them 26
traditionalists vs. nontraditionalists; *ad hominem* attacks; withholding of information
from clients; *Controversies in the Addictions Field*

4. The Objective: Personal Autonomy 33
dependence and interdependence; addiction defined; nature vs. nurture; recovery
defined; the function of addictions

5. Alcoholics Anonymous: Essence & Functions 40
what AA is *not* (cult, charitable group, business); what AA *is* (fellowship and
organization); communal AA (not-for-profit support groups); organizational AA
(Alcoholics Anonymous World Services, Alcoholics Anonymous Grapevine, Inc.,
etc.); institutional AA (AA and for-profit treatment); AA as identity transformation
organization; AA as charismatic healing group; AA as modified temperance
society; AA as quasi-religious society; "Big Book" terminology; AA and God

6. Alcoholics Anonymous: Effectiveness 61
ineffectiveness of AA; "Comments on AA's Triennial Surveys" document; refusal to
acknowledge alternative programs

7. The Forces & Direction of Change 73
academic (current research); cultural; economic (reluctance of insurance industry
to continue to pay for 12-step treatment); legal (challenges to coerced attendance
at AA); professional (involvement in alternative programs)

8. The Independent Self-Help Programs 82
Alcoholics Victorious; Calix; Jewish Alcoholics, Chemically Dependent Persons, and Significant Others Foundation; Men for Sobriety; Moderation Management; Secular Organizations for Sobriety; Women for Sobriety

9. Rational Recovery Systems Network 108
purpose of RR; personal worth; behavior, responsibility & disease; social aspects of RR; dependence & interdependence; matching; professional advisors; one life at a time; addictive voice recognition training (AVRT); a few specifics about RR; RR's effectiveness

10. Traditional Recovery Management 136
failure of 12-step treatment; the search for profit; treatment methods shown to be effective, but not commonly employed in the United States; ineffective treatment methods commonly employed in the United States

11. Nontraditional Recovery Management 146
Rational Recovery & Vestibule Inpatient Program (VIP); guidelines for differential diagnosis; common problems in VIP; clinical protocol; outpatient followup

12. Non-Institutional Recovery 166
through private therapist; through self-help group; through "bottomed out" instant decision; through "maturing out"

13. Short Topics 175
adult children of alcoholics; AMA; Antabuse; bashing; bottoms; children's books; codependency; AA as and as not a cult; denial; detoxification; employee assistance programs

14. More Short Topics 197
ethics, treatment centers and the law; genetic predisposition; lapse and relapse; moderate, controlled and social drinking; NCADD; organized religion and addictions; privacy, confidentiality, computers, and victims; RR and other addictions; THIQ; transactional analysis; 12 steps re-ordered

15. The Future 218
predictions: end of the "drug war"; contraction of AA; expansion of AA; merger of WFS, MFS and RR; addiction activities by mainline religions; help for courts and probation officers; new national perspective on addictions; emergence of American Council on Alcoholism; increased professional educator involvement; chiropractic and naturopathic involvement; new, nontraditional magazine

Appendix 225
sources of information and help; educational format of Rational Recovery; ACLU article text; definitions of alcoholic and alcoholism by the author

Bibliography 231

Index 237

Addendum to Second Printing 248

Introduction

This is a remarkably good book on problem drinking. It briefly but comprehensively covers the most important issues in this complex area and does so in a courageous, hard-headed, open-minded, and yet highly personal manner. It honestly advocates alternative and nontraditional approaches to alcoholism treatment and, especially, exposes the problems of Alcoholics Anonymous and the other traditional approaches. But it is factual and fair, and makes more points on both sides of controversial issues than any other book that I have examined on this important subject.

Vince Fox's book, moreover, is both theoretical and highly practical. Its wealth of historical details on problem drinking and the organizations that try to deal with alcoholics is profound. But it also includes a great deal of material on psychotherapy and self-help that can be immensely useful to addicts. Following the principles of rational emotive behavior therapy (REBT) which I started to use and promote in 1955, and which is a core philosophy of Rational Recovery, *Addiction, Change & Choice* beautifully lives up to its title by showing its readers exactly how they can choose to stop drinking and how they can change the emotional disturbances that usually help drive them to alcohol and other addictions. Like Jack Trimpey's *Small Book* and my own book with Emmett Velten, *When AA Doesn't Work for You: Rational Steps to Quitting Alcohol,* Vince's work presents the REBT self-help program in a highly understandable, no-nonsense-about-it manner. As he notes, several other good books, such as those by Phillip Tate and William Knaus, cover this territory too. But Vince's book is one of the best.

Read it and see for yourself. But watch it! Rational emotive behavior therapy shows you that you largely disturb yourself and thereby drive yourself to addictive and other self-defeating behaviors; and no matter how and why you first started to do so, you are still doing so today. These are important insights to acquire, as this book demonstrates. But all the insight in the world isn't enough to help you change. No. Only work and practice—yes, *work and practice*—will enable you to *use* your insight. So carefully read—and often re-read—this book; and *work and practice* at using its valuable lessons.

—Albert Ellis, Ph.D., President
Institute for Rational-Emotive Therapy
45 East 65th Street
New York, NY 10021-6593

Foreword

Addiction is costly—in dollars, in suffering, and in human lives. In the last two decades, addiction to alcohol and other drugs has become the United States' number one domestic problem, and along with it a giant industry has grown which provides remedial services. Nearly every community has agencies, hospitals and support groups for those struggling with addictions, and the cost of these programs in health care dollars is very high. But only a few people, perhaps ten percent, are helped by all that is done, and the cost to the unhelped is extremely high. It is tempting to conclude that addiction is simply a monstrous problem, and that even our best efforts will produce poor results. But even though it seems that the addiction care system has grown in response to the explosion of addiction, and what is needed is more of the same type of addiction care, it is also possible that the American way of looking at addiction and of responding to it are, in part, responsible for what some call the "national epidemic."

One critical link in the addiction care system is dissemination of information about the nature of addiction and recovery. The belief that addiction is a *disease* that renders one powerless, and the idea that one must adopt religious/spiritual attitudes and attend meetings for life in order to recover, seem as American as apple pie. But are these ideas supported by facts? And do they provide a coherent, effective way to solve the problem of mass addiction? Or is it possible that we are spreading the "germ" of addiction through the very means we have chosen to solve the problem?

Vince Fox has been in the trenches for many years pondering these and other prickly questions, preparing the very important book that you are about to read. This highly informative book takes you from the beginnings (in the 1930s) of American-style addiction care with the advent of the religiously oriented 12-step program of Alcoholics Anonymous, through the unfortunate period (1960–1990) of near-universal acceptance of the disease concept of alcoholism, and into a brighter future in which addicted people will have many choices as they embark on their separate paths to recovery.

In addition to his literary pursuits, Vince Fox has been a tireless activist devoted to helping America grow out of its myopic vision of addiction and recovery. I came to know Vince in 1989, when I received a letter from him bearing the letterhead, "Addictions Roundtable." He wrote as the founder of the group, a fledgling organization of people seeking a better understanding of addiction. He said he had just read *The Small Book*, and was elated. "Rational Recovery is what is needed," he wrote, "and I hereby disband Addictions Roundtable and raise the Rational Recovery banner. Here is a check for $100 for whatever purpose will advance the cause." Since that donation, Vince Fox, in his deeds and creativity, has become a very important person in the history of American addiction care—as a community leader, as a national spokesperson and board member for Rational Recovery, as a researcher, and as a group facilitator for RR in Indianapolis. Now, as the author of *Addiction, Change & Choice: The New View of Alcoholism,* he has significantly advanced the cause of democracy in addiction care.

Read and enjoy this wonderfully written book about addiction. Be entertained by Vince's home-spun wit, and be fascinated, as I was, by his ability to express complex ideas in simple terms. When you have finished, you will know more about addiction and recovery than many who have been in the field for years. With your new view of alcoholism and addiction, you will be in a position to speak about change and choice from a broad foundation of knowledge.

—Jack Trimpey
President, Rational Recovery Systems, Inc.
Founder and Executive Director, Rational Recovery Self-Help Network
P.O. Box 800
Lotus, CA 95651
(916) 621-2667

Preface

I am deeply committed to helping those addicted to alcohol and/or illegal drugs, and have devoted a large part of this book to the concept of personal change and how to achieve it. In Jeremiah 13:23 you will find, "Can the Ethiopian change his skin, or the leopard his spots?" Yes and yes, any time, any day. Jeremiah was a loser, a quitter, and a pessimist. The major premise of this book is that alcoholics and drug addicts want and have a right to a happy, productive life, and that that objective is realistic and achievable.

Two old sayings declare that "what goes around, comes around," and "the more things change, the more they stay the same." The sayings are more old than wise. Things are changing rapidly in the addictions field, and many ideas and practices are not going around but going away. Professionals have been hampered by the heavy hand of the past, and alcoholics and other addicts have often been the pawns—and sometimes the victims—of "experts" more concerned with maintaining the status quo than adapting to the realities of a changing world.

We would agree, I think, that change is better effected by peaceful evolution than by violent revolution. In this book I propose *accelerated* peaceful evolution in the form of a partial synthesis of traditional and nontraditional approaches to the prevention, understanding, and management of addictions problems.

We have begun to realize that the traditional approach to the problems associated with chemical dependency has indeed worked—but not as well as we once thought it did. Although it has provided many benefits, it has not come near to solving the problems of drug and alcohol abuse. Change is no longer an option for those who have long dominated the field of addiction services; it is a requirement for survival. Those who resist change—those who are complacent or defensive—will fail; those who adapt will flourish.

Many traditionalists acknowledge the limited success of their time-tested approach to the prevention and solution of addiction problems. They know that decades have gone by during which billions of dollars of private, state, and federal funds have been spent on a problem that hasn't been solved. Fortunately, the majority of traditionalists are intelligent and conscientious people who recognize the need for fundamental change, or at least the inclusion of new ideas, in their time-tested programs.

But change, personal or institutional, is never easy. We make it harder by the way we think. We get set in our ways and we accept on blind faith ideas provided by "authorities," rather than subject those ideas to careful scrutiny and our own good judgment. We tend to perceive things in terms of absolutes, as right or wrong, hard or soft, black or white, genetic or behavioral. Common sense suggests that there is usually—but not always—a middle ground between such extreme positions.

If personal change is difficult, institutional change is excruciating. Rules, regulations, policies, procedures, and bureaucracies are integral parts of institutional management, but they can, and often do, become mechanistic and dehumanizing, both to the servers and those served. Like all too many Washington bureaus, institutions tend to perpetuate themselves even as their usefulness declines. They get big and old and fat and slow and rigid. Hospitals and, to a lesser extent, free-standing treatment centers, are like that too. They resist even internally generated change, and they detest the thought of change suggested by "outsiders," or by their own customers (patients).

But there is another way to get the job done. Increasing numbers of the "New Guard" voice their ideas on the lecture circuit and on national talk shows. They write books and offer new solutions to the many problems that plague the addictions field. Cooperation between the two parties is needed; neither faction can do the job alone. Each needs the other. Addicts need both of them.

The ideas of traditionalists and nontraditionalists are compatible to a limited extent. They agree, for example, that total and permanent abstinence from addictive substances is the best approach. To a large extent, however, the two factions are incompatible. Traditionalists offer a program based on notions of sickness and incurable disease, meetings for life, and a required relationship with a "Higher Power," that is, God. They insist that addicts are *powerless* and therefore, dependent. Nontraditionalists insist that drinking too much is a simple maladaptation, a learned behavior that can be unlearned. They claim that addicts are *powerful,* and they say that although religious and spiritual values can be helpful in the recovery process, they are not *essential* to it, and for the most part are private issues.

New Guard thinkers contend that the Old Guard is like a withered flower in a winter garden. They are certain that the flower needs nourishment and that the seeds of transformation are within it. The New Guard wants to harvest those seeds and plant them in more fertile ground.

But the Old Guard is digging in and preparing to defend its time-honored ways. It insists that the new ways are unacceptable, even dangerous; and it rightfully resists the scathing criticisms and aggressive tactics of some members of the New Guard. While non-traditionalists insist that the traditional approach is *all wrong*, the traditionalists argue that their position is *absolutely right.* Both factions are at fault; the truth lies between the two, but not necessarily in the middle.

I spent eight years as a traditionalist and member of A.A., followed by ten years as a nontraditionalist. As an advocate of mental health, I champion and encourage new ideas, but I also respect and appreciate the efforts and ideas of those who cling to the comfort and familiarity of the old ways.

While this book is not an anti-A.A. diatribe, I occasionally take traditional ideas to task, as I do some of the tenets promoted by nontraditionalists. In other words, I have tried to make this book more constructive than destructive.

One more thought about change. Futurist Alvin Toffler, in his *Powershift* (1991) says, in reference to the breakup of the nuclear family, ". . . everything else is changing . . . All of the systems in society are moving from uniform to diverse." In the fourth century B.C.E.[1] the Chinese philosopher and teacher, Confucius, wrote, "All human despair is the result of resistance to change." Personal change is usually a slow and painful process—and worth it. Professionals in the addictions field know that all change involves risk, but they must now realize that taking a calculated risk is better than colliding with a brick wall.

You have a right to know why I devoted two years of my life to writing this book. I wrote it for *you*, because you are a person of intrinsic worth who deserves respect and a good life. And I wrote it for those who have dedicated their lives to caring for those of us who were, or are, drinkers and druggers. I wrote it because I want to change the world—at least that dark corner of it trashed by broken bottles, twisted lives, and dirty needles. This may be the world in which you now live; it was the world in which I once did.

There is another reason, a personal one. As a young man I studied to become a Jesuit priest and a university professor. I did achieve a teaching fellowship at two universities, but that didn't last. At a critical point in my life I chose to drink rather than pursue my life's objectives. I spent most of my working life at a bench in a glass shop. But you will find no horror stories about my life in the pages you are about to read. Some 15 years ago I said it all to my therapist, Cindy Zeldin. I came, she saw, I conquered. [Thank you, Cindy.] I have no need to say those things again, and you have no need to hear them. Garbage is still garbage, and there are only two things you can do with it: learn from it and throw it out. This book is my life's objective. It is the expression of a priesthood never known and a professorship never achieved. Beyond that, this book is a pursuit of that golden thread of truth that weaves the sublime thought of the Periclean age of ancient Athens into the central theme of the New Testament: the concept of *justice*. That's as personal as I'm going to get. This book is for you; it's not about me.

About problems: A friend once said, "A problem is like a great diamond with many facets; you must look through each facet into the heart of the diamond and there you may or may not find the answers to the problem, but you will at least understand the questions." She was right. In this book I have tried to understand the questions and have attempted to answer a few of them.

About the style of this book: There are two ways of saying the same thing:

Style One:
A sufficiency of painstakingly accumulated empirical data indicates that a certain species of simian primates are devoid of caudal appendages.

Style Two:
Some monkeys have no tails.

This book is written in Style Two.

ACKNOWLEDGEMENTS

My thanks to the great thinkers in this field: Albert Ellis, Max Maultsby, Stanton Peele, Archie Brodsky, Mary Arnold, Herbert Fingarette, Don Cahalan, Jeffrey Schaler, William Wilbanks, Jack Trimpey, Lois Trimpey, Chaz Bufe, Stan Katz, Aimee Liu, Bill Knaus, Philip Tate, Ken Ragge, Jim Christopher, Eric Berne, Jean Kirkpatrick, Jeffrey Brandsma, Roger Vogler, David Burns, Ruth

Engs, Ernest Kurtz, Wayne Bartz, Claude Steiner, Don Goodwin, Bill Wilson, Arnold Ludwig, William Miller, Robin Room, and many others. Each of these has created parts of what I have organized and presented. Occasionally, I have added an idea of my own.

My special gratitude to Chaz Bufe, editor, publisher, critic, and friend. Without him, and without the love and patience of my best friend (and wife), Lucia, I could not have written this book. They were "enablers," as it were. Thanks also to Lynaea Search for a fine editing and copy editing job. Above all, my thanks to the hundreds of former heavy drinkers whom I have known and who have shared with me and taught me. My gratitude to Lucia Brown Fox who read the original manuscript and offered helpful suggestions. I accept full responsibility, however, for every word in this book.

I have generally avoided the use of titles and academic credentials when citing works in this book. Such things can skew the judgment of the reader—in a positive or negative way—toward the arguments presented. Let the words stand on their own merits.

A special note to the reader. We are all familiar with the campaign for a "Drug Free America," and we are accustomed to the phrase "alcohol and other drugs." Neo-prohibitionists, ardent conservatives, and many writers and lecturers promote—deliberately or casually— the use of these unfortunate phrases. But logic and common sense do not support their unqualified use. A "Drug Free America," obviously, would be an America without aspirin, Pepsi Cola (caffeine), or prescription drugs. And the phrase "alcohol and other drugs" is misleading. Through "guilt by association," it places alcohol in the same category with heroin, cocaine, and other dangerous and illegal drugs. The phrase should read "alcohol and *illegal* drugs," thus conveying its actual meaning and intent. Thus, I will not use the phrase "alcohol and other drugs" in this book. [Incidentally, I have no association, formal or informal, with the beverage industry.]

And from a man as much catholic as Catholic, the words of Jesuit priest and paleontologist Teilhard de Chardin: "In this arrangement of values, I may have gone astray at many points. It is up to others to do better."

---

1. B.C.E: Before the Common Era, a notation gradually replacing the more familiar B.C., Before Christ.

1

Heavy Drinking: The Historical Context

Many books in the field of addiction studies begin with a detailed history of how humankind has used and abused alcohol and (sometimes illegal) drugs. This book is not one of them.[1] In this chapter, however, you will find a brief historical overview of chemical use and abuse and the lessons to be drawn from it.

First, we usually think of drinking as a personal choice and an enjoyable activity; and, for the vast majority of people, it is. *Excessive* drinking, however, is *never* an exclusively personal act because it affects the person as a member of society, and because it adversely affects the lives of others. Heavy drinking, often termed problem drinking (drinking that produces problems), is therefore a personal/social phenomenon.

Second, drinking patterns reflect our cultures—the way we live and why we live that way. In Italy and France, drunkenness is considered uncivilized and a serious breach of good manners, and in Israel, excessive drinking is viewed as no less than a social barbarism. But in other parts of the world—Mexico, Ireland, and Spain, for example—the ability to drink excessively is often regarded as a proof of "manhood." In the United States attitudes vary, even regionally, toward heavy drinking as an acceptable mode of behavior. For example, it is tolerated more in the Northeast than in the Bible Belt or in conservative Utah, where even mild drinking may prompt frowns and harsh words—and compliance with socially prescribed modes of behavior.

Social psychologists and historians show deep concern about a third aspect of alcohol consumption. They seem to agree that alcohol has often been used as an instrument of social control, as in 19th-century England where "penny gin" was provided in large quantities to factory workers who were thereby enervated and prevented from organizing in defense of their rights.

Historians also report that organized religion has played an important role in controlling the consumption of alcohol. Western Churches, especially those with Christian or Islamic traditions, have always tried to limit or to prohibit the use of alcohol by invoking divine authority. To a degree, that technique has worked, as it does today in Iran and among religious fundamentalists in the United States. The sanctions are always the same: the risk of God's anger and the peril of everlasting hellfire. The threat of punishment serves as a deterrent, of course.[2] (It seems to me that being condemned to eternal life in a fiery furnace is a rather high price to pay for a night on the town.)

History also teaches that people do whatever it takes in order to survive. The story of every Western country is filled with accounts of times in which life was so wretched for so many that millions of people sought relief through alcohol or drugs. That is exactly what happened during the mass migrations from Europe and Asia to the United States during the early twentieth century. Legions of hopeless and helpless people fled from oppression, poverty, war, and the injustices inherent in societies based on class or caste. In doing so, they experienced devastating personal, family, and social dislocations. They found themselves castoffs in the promised land. At Ellis Island in New York Harbor and at Angel Island in San Francisco Bay, they were numbered, tagged, herded like cattle. Some of them scrapped their dreams and drew a liquid curtain between themselves and the crushing realities of the new world.

Those desperate millions did what many soldiers in Vietnam did: they drank, drugged, and somehow survived. In his *Diseasing of America*, Stanton Peele recounts the history of many U.S. soldiers in Vietnam who used narcotics and became addicted, but who, after returning home, gave up their addictions. Peele remarks, "Thus, Vietnam epitomizes the kind of barren, stressful, and out-of-control situation that encourages addiction"[3]

When I was younger, I thought that people were weak and not very smart. In time, I learned that most people are strong and intelligent, but often fragile in the face of frightening conditions beyond their control. It is not surprising that so many people abuse alcohol and use illegal drugs in today's tension-filled, fast-paced world. It is surprising that more of them don't.

Another insight provided by historians and social psychologists regards the forces of change, their nature and speed, and how changes, especially rapid ones, affect us. The problem, it seems, is not the quality of change, but the quantity of change to which people are exposed in a given period.[4] When many changes occur over a short period people can be overwhelmed, especially if they lack information, choices, and problem solving skills. It is then that they often go to pieces, or go to war. They may spend, eat, work, drink, drug, or love too much. They may develop a neurosis or psychosis. They may join cults, gangs, a terrorist group, the Republican Party, or otherwise seek order in their lives. They may vent their frustrations in ways that are personally destructive and socially disintegrative. Although people are highly adaptable, there seems to be a limit beyond which the lonely and the defenseless can no longer tolerate prolonged and strenuous adjustment. Beyond that point they may "maladjust"; they begin, in puzzling paradox, to self-destruct, even as they cling to humankind's universal and paramount value—survival.[5]

Dealing with rapid change is a modern problem. Futurist Alvin Toffler tells us that the agricultural age lasted 10,000 years, the industrial age 300, and that the information age—which has only begun—has brought with it changes which will overshadow all changes that have gone before.[6] Your great-grandchildren, at your present age, if somehow thrust back into our world, would no doubt perceive it as a strange and primitive place.

How many of us are still apprehensive about computers, and secretly long for the days of the old-fashioned typewriter and the once-familiar card files in neighborhood libraries? Today, in a village on the Outer Banks of North Carolina, there lives a woman who in 1903 rode with her mother in a horse-drawn carriage to witness the first flight of the Wright brothers at Kitty Hawk, and who, only a few decades later, switched on a box filled with complex electronic circuitry and watched an astronaut step from a spaceship onto the surface of the moon. No longer able to cope with change, she survives it, surrounded by treasured artifacts from the past. In one weathered hand she clasps a yellowed photo album, and in the other hand a water glass filled with Wild Irish Rose. Her doctor—an understanding fellow—told her that an occasional sip of wine would be good for her. "Doctor's orders," she says, "Good for my health." It probably is.

The final conclusion that may be drawn from the history of alcohol consumption is that societies consistently view drinking, light or heavy, in simplistic terms. The temperance movement in the United States fulminated against alcohol itself as the problem, against "demon rum." The clergy decreed that drinking was a sin, and few would question those somber men of dark cloth. Today we are told that alcoholism is a disease, or a learned behavior, or a genetic inheritance, or a bad habit. We continue to look at alcoholism as a single dot on a pointillist painting rather than a cluster of multi-colored dots on a large canvas. It's always been like that, and we moderns have done little to improve the picture. We continue to simplify, polarize, dichotomize, and hold inflexible positions on the cause of, and solutions to, problems associated with drinking and drugging.

But things are changing and improving. Hundreds of scholars, researchers, and practitioners have revealed the achievements and the mistakes of the past and have provided useful information with which we can improve the present and plan for the future. Names such as Trimpey, Bufe, Dorsman, Tate, Ragge, Schaler, Cahalan, Burns, Katz, Tessina, Kaminer, Velten, and Barrett were probably not in the computer system of your public library a few years ago. They are now.

The past is bitter; let's hope that the future will be brighter. We can and must learn from the past; we dare not repeat it. In the field of addictions, we are still divided into armed camps, and we continue to play war games and word games. These games are played for high stakes: the chips are the lives of millions of people—also called addicts. There are better games to play, those of the "win/win" type. That conviction is at the heart of this book.

A question: If you were teaching a class of 50 randomly selected addictions professionals and asked them to write the definition of the word *alcoholism*, what would you expect to see? In Chapter 2 you will find a non-scientific survey in which that enigmatic word, "alcoholism," is examined by experts, all of them nationally or internationally recognized figures in the field of addiction studies. You may wish to stop for a moment and write out your own definition of "alcoholism" before turning the page.

---

1. Three of the best are 1) Kurtz, Ernest. (1979) *Not-God: A History of Alcoholics Anonymous.* Center City: Hazelden; 2) Cahalan, Don. (1987) *Understanding America's Drinking Problem.* San Francisco: Jossey-Bass; and Peele, Stanton. (1989) *Diseasing of America: Addiction Treatment Out of Control.* Lexington, MS: Lexington Books

2. Yes, but not much of one. In the days of Charles Dickens public hangings for stealing a loaf of bread or for pickpocketing had to be curtailed because the event attracted so many pickpockets.

3. Page 150.

4. This is an underlying theme of Toffler's *Future Shock*.

5. Survival, but not just survival. Viktor Frankl (of the Third Viennese School of Psychiatry) would add "survival, with meaning." People, he has said, can literally *will* themselves to live or to die, depending on whether they assign a meaning to their lives. (The perfect example, perhaps, may be found in that poignant masterpiece "La Strada" in which Zapatto's companion willed not to live, and died quietly in her sleep.)

6. I recommend Toffler's *Third Wave* to all serious students of addiction, and especially to professionals who can profit immensely by the author's panoramic insights and vision. *The Third Wave* is the second book of a trilogy composed of *Future Shock* (1970) and *Powershift* (1990). May I also recommend his *Previews and Premises*.

2

Alcoholism: Definitions & Opinions

"Words are the most powerful drug used by mankind."
—Kipling, speech (1923)

"We would have a great many fewer disputes in the world if words were taken for what they are, the signs of our ideas only, and not for things themselves."
— Locke, "Essay on Human Understanding"

The field of alcohol studies is littered with words that are casually used and vaguely defined. Lewis Carroll, in *Alice in Wonderland*, wrote, "When I use a word . . . it means just what I choose it to mean—neither more nor less." This chapter deals with one of those words. But first, a word about words.

Words are not realities, but language symbols about realities. They enable us to transmit and receive ideas, ideas about abstractions like liberty and love, or material objects like plastic and polar bears. Words are written or spoken interpretations of things, but that's all they are. In the field of addictions, words have been endowed with a reality they do not and cannot possess, since they are no more real than your reflection in a looking glass, or in the mirrored panels of an amusement park.

This chapter is devoted to one word, *alcoholism*, a potentially useful word, but one that has often been employed not only to express thinking but to manipulate thought. Alcoholism is a word that, like a garden tool left out in the rain, needs to be cleaned up and sharpened—or discarded and replaced. A few of the many definitions of this bewildering term are listed in the pages that follow. Not one of them is universally accepted.

The "definitions" that follow could be more accurately termed *opinions.* You may find some of them confusing. I did. "Alcoholism" may turn out to be nothing more than a word in search of a definition, an idea to which a consensual meaning will one day be assigned. (My definition may be found in the Appendix of this book.) For the sake of convenience, I have classified the 18 "definitions" given as traditional, nontraditional, or exploratory.

The traditional position includes the disease notion, genetic influence, loss of control, personal powerlessness, and—most important—dependence upon a "Higher Power." Recognition of, acceptance of, and cooperation with this "Higher Power"—generally defined as God—are deemed *essential* to the attainment and maintenance of sobriety. This position is held by medical or quasi-medical associations such as Alcoholics Anonymous (A.A.), The American Association of Addiction Treatment Providers (the AAATP), The American Medical Association (AMA), The National Council on Alcoholism and Drug Dependence (NCADD), The American Hospital Association (AHA), and others. The position held by traditionalists is the prevailing standard—although no longer the unquestioned standard—pertaining to the causation and management of problems related to chemical dependency.

Fundamental to the traditional position is the disease concept of alcoholism.[1] The disease concept is generally understood in terms of Bill Wilson's 1939 definition of alcoholism as a "spiritual, emotional, and physical" "illness."[2] Traditionalists assert that this disease can be arrested but not cured. It follows that the traditional position is that alcoholics should maintain total and permanent abstinence from alcohol. (As previously indicated, nontraditionalists, for the most part, share that conviction, but for different reasons.)

The nontraditional perspective is very different: it centers on heavy drinking as a learned behavior that can be changed. It focuses on social and cultural influences, psychological factors, personal capability, personal responsibility, and on an array of possible physical and genetic influences. It asserts that heavy drinking can produce disease, but is not in itself a disease.

The exploratory group holds a third position. Here we'll find definitions that are more descriptive than prescriptive—careful and cautious interpretations concerned as much with unanswered questions as they are with questionable answers.

Out of a pool of 40 or so definitions/opinions I selected 18, ordered them in groups of three, and labeled them Traditional, Nontraditional, or Exploratory. All of them were written by respected people in the field of addictions: researchers, professors, psychiatrists, psychologists, mental health practitioners, self-help leaders, and social workers. You will undoubtedly recognize many of them, agree with some of them, reject others, and wonder about a few. The categorization of quoted material is necessarily based on human judgment, and is, to that extent, subjective. Let the words, unencumbered by the credentials and titles of their authors, now speak for themselves.

1-A) **Traditional:** By The National Council on Alcoholism and Drug Dependence (NCADD):

Part 1: (Initial statement, 1972). Alcoholism is a chronic, progressive and potentially fatal disease characterized by tolerance and physical dependency or pathologic organ changes, or both—all the direct or indirect consequences of the alcohol ingested.

Part 2: (1990) (Written jointly by The National Council on Alcoholism and Drug Dependence and ASAM—the American Society of Addiction Medicine.) Alcoholism is a primary, chronic disease with genetic, psychosocial, and environmental factors influencing its development and manifestations. The disease is often progressive and fatal. It is characterized by continuous or periodic impaired control over drinking, preoccupation with the drug alcohol, use of alcohol despite adverse consequences, and distortions in thinking, most notably denial.[3] (Note departure from the 1972 statement relative to qualification of the progressive nature of alcoholism and the inclusion of *denial* as a symptom of the defined disease.)

1-B) **Nontraditional:** By Claude Steiner and Eric Berne:
Alcoholism is neither incurable nor a disease.[4]

1-C) **Exploratory:** By The World Health Organization (WHO):
Alcoholics are those excessive drinkers whose dependence upon alcohol has attained such a degree that it shows a noticeable mental disturbance or an interference with their bodily and mental health, their interpersonal relations, and their smooth social and economic functioning; or [those] who show the prodromal (warning) signs of such developments.[5]

2-A) **Traditional:** By the American Medical Association:
(1956, December 29): The medical treatment of alcoholism is
rapidly becoming more important in accomplishing recovery for
this disease.
(1966, November 28-30): A reaffirmation of the 1956
resolution.
(1987, June 21-25): RESOLVED, That the American Medical
Association endorses the proposition that drug
dependencies, including alcoholism, are diseases.[6]

2-B) **Nontraditional:** By *Black's Law Dictionary*, 5th ed., 1979:
The pathological effect (as distinguished from physiological
effect) of excessive indulgence in alcoholic liquors. [Pathological:
that is, the diseased condition or structural and functional effects
produced as a result of "excessive consumption"]

2-C) **Exploratory:** By *Webster's New World Dictionary of the
American Language; Second College Edition:*
The habitual drinking of alcoholic liquor to excess, or a diseased
condition caused by this.

3-A) **Traditional:** By Jim Christopher:
Science has established that alcoholism is a physiological disease
predetermined by heredity. Alcohol is a selectively physically
addictive drug . . .[7]

3-B) **Nontraditional:** By Jack Trimpey:
[The words] "alcoholism" and "alcoholic" are folk expressions. . . .
I will use the term "alcoholic" to refer to people who believe they
are powerless over their addictions and act accordingly, and to
those who call themselves "alcoholics." They are practicing the
philosophy of alcoholism, just as Catholics practice the philosophy
of Catholicism. I prefer the correct term "alcohol dependence" to
describe the problem of persistent, heavy drinking. . . [8]

3-C) **Exploratory:** By Charles Bufe:
[Of Alcoholic, Alcoholism]: Since the terms were invented over
100 years ago, a great variety of definitions have been offered, and
there is still no uniformity of opinion among the "experts" about
what constitutes alcoholism nor about what constitutes an
alcoholic. The safest thing that can be said is that definitions are
largely arbitrary and can (and do) change over time.[9]

4-A) **Traditional:** By Claudia Black:
> The alcoholic is a person who, in his drinking, has developed a psychological dependency on the drug alcohol coupled with a physiological addiction. . . . They are people who neither have the ability to consistently control their drinking, nor who can predict their behavior once they start to drink.[10]

4-B) **Nontraditional:** By The American Psychiatric Association (ASA) (DSM-III-R): Note: The word alcoholism is no longer used as a subject heading in the third edition of the familiar DSM-III-R (Diagnostic Statistical Manual, Revised). It lists Alcohol Dependence (Section 303.90, p.173) and Alcohol Abuse (Section 305.00, p.173) in its stead. It observes that abuse can lead to dependence.

Patterns of use.
> There are three main patterns of Alcohol Abuse or Dependence. The first consists of regular daily intake of large amounts; the second, of regular heavy drinking limited to weekends; the third, of long periods of sobriety interspersed with binges of daily heavy drinking lasting for weeks or months. It is a mistake to associate one of these particular patterns exclusively with "alcoholism." Some investigators divide alcoholism into "species" . . . [such as the] so-called gamma alcoholism . . . that is common in the United States and conforms to the stereotype of the alcoholism seen in people who are active in Alcoholics Anonymous . . . [and that] involves problems with "control."[11]

4-C) **Exploratory:** By *The Encyclopedia Britannica:*
> [The] repetitive intake of alcoholic beverages to such an extent that repeated or continued harm to the drinker occurs. . . . Alcoholism may be viewed as a disease, a drug addiction, a learned response to crisis, a symptom of an underlying psychological or physical disorder, or a combination of these facts. The cause of alcoholism is equally uncertain. It has been viewed as a hereditary defect, a physical malfunction, a psychological disorder, a response to economic or social stress, or sin.

5-A) **Traditional:** By Mark Keller:
> I think [alcoholism] is a disease because the alcoholic can't consistently choose whether or not he shall engage in self-injurious behavior–that is, any of the alcoholism drinking patterns. I think of it as a psychological disablement.[12]

5-B) **Nontraditional:** By Herbert Fingarette:
Heavy drinkers [alcoholics] are people who have over time made a long and complex series of decisions, judgments, and choices of commission and omission that have coalesced into a central activity. . . . Instead of viewing heavy drinkers as the helpless victims of a disease, we come to see their drinking as a meaningful, however destructive, part of their struggle to live their lives.[13]

5-C) **Exploratory:** By The United States Supreme Court (1988):
. . . apparently nobody understands alcoholism . . . it appears to be willful misbehavior.[14]

6-A) **Traditional:** By Alcoholics Anonymous and Bill Wilson (delivered at the National Clerical Conference on Alcoholism convention, April 21, 1960):
We have never called alcoholism a disease because, technically speaking, *it is not a disease entity*.[15] (emphasis added) For example, there is no such thing as heart disease. Instead there are many separate heart ailments, or combinations of them. It is something like that with alcoholism. Therefore we did not wish to get in wrong with the medical profession by pronouncing alcoholism a disease entity. Therefore we always called it an illness, or a malady—a far safer term for us to use.[16]

6-B) **Nontraditional:** By Morris Chavetz:
Alcoholism is drinking too much too often. It is permitting alcohol to play an inordinately powerful role in a person's life.[17]

6-C) **Exploratory:** By Arnold Ludwig:
There is no general agreement about the nature, cause, or treatment of alcoholism. What is an alcoholic? Where does one draw the line between problem drinking and alcoholism, between alcohol abuse and alcohol dependence? Is alcoholism one disorder or a collection of different disorders? Is it a moral failing, a bad habit, or a disease? Do alcoholics have distinctive personality features? Is alcoholism hereditary or learned? Does excessive drinking represent a symptomatic expressing of an underlying conflict or is it the primary problem itself? Which treatment approach, if any, is most effective? Who is best qualified to help? . . . In the absence of facts, opinions and beliefs tend to prevail.[18]

Concerning the quotations listed above:

• Most of definitions presented are written in highly
qualified terms.

• Many were comprehensive, leaning toward description in the
vein of alcoholism as a "bio-psycho-social" phenomenon.
They are not precise and prescriptive—a credit, perhaps, to
their authors.

• None of those quoted refer to the "spiritual" element in
Bill Wilson's definition of alcoholism. Since A.A. is the
cornerstone of traditional thinking, this omission represents
a major anomaly—or, perhaps, an emerging trend.

• A number of authors seem to defer to authority and present
their definitions as articles of faith in prestigious
organizations such as the AMA and the NCADD. Thus, to
avoid needless repetition, it was possible to eliminate
quotations from persons such as Mark Gold, Nan Robertson,
and James Milam, et al., since they say much the same
thing, even in the same way.

• Some of those quoted state that they simply don't know, as
in the cases of Ludwig, Bufe, and the Supreme Court.
(They also suggest that no one else knows.)

• A large number of those who define alcoholism as a disease
do so in terms of its associated behaviors and the
consequences of those behaviors.

• The issue of personal responsibility is addressed only by
those classified as nontraditionalists. (The implication of the
disease concept seems to be that the alcoholic is initially a
victim, but is subsequently responsible for his or her own
sobriety. In traditional circles, and specifically in A.A.,
personal responsibility is assumed to require sustained
dependence on the *higher* power, God.)[19]

• One would expect all persons and organizations related to
the medical industry to be in agreement with one another.
Not so. For example, *Preventive Medicine* and *Stedman's*

Medical Dictionary (neither quoted) deviate into the non-traditional camp. Others seem to waffle by including elements of both traditional and nontraditional concepts in their definitions, or they define the term in a loose manner that allows for extensive interpretation.

<u>Conclusion</u>: Effective communication is almost impossible in a field plagued by the lack of consensus concerning the key concept, alcoholism/alcoholic. The variety of "definitions" suggest confusion and lack of direction in the field of alcohol studies. Bluntly, things are in a mess. (But things are—finally—getting better.)

The next chapter may be the most important one in this book because it attempts to eliminate some of these misunderstandings by depolarizing the positions now held by opposing factions in the field of addictions. Please read it carefully.

---

1. Many people assume that what is termed a *disease* is scientifically determined within set parameters and through laboratory testing. This is not always the case. The determination is often made by voice vote within a committee designated by the American Medical Association, as in the case of "alcoholism" as a disease. (Members of many self-help groups feel that they know what a disease is: "Sure, a disease is anything the doctors and hospitals think they can collect insurance on.")

2. It's interesting that Wilson's definition of this *illness* included emotional and spiritual aspects. The disease notion is usually discussed only in its physiological aspect. The other two components mentioned are often ignored or given lesser consideration. Wilson's emphasis was on the *spiritual* aspect.

3. National Council on Alcoholism and Drug Dependence *Facts on Alcohol Related Birth Defects.* (Revised May, 1987). (The same definition appears in dozens of the NCADD's publications.)

4. Steiner, C., with Foreword by Berne, E. (1971). *Games Alcoholics Play: An Analysis of Life Scripts.* New York: Ballantine Books. (Front matter, unnumbered page).

5. This definition appears in several encyclopedias and in many medical dictionaries.

6. AMA "determinations" are made by voice vote, a concert of opinion, as distinct from a conclusion based on scientifically compiled data as, for example, taken from laboratory tests.

7. Flyers received from SOS and in each of Christopher's books, with only slight alterations of wording. I could not find the exact location of the comment quoted, but it was written by Christopher.

8. Trimpey, J., with Introduction by Albert Ellis (1989). *The Small Book: A Revolutionary Alternative for Overcoming Alcohol and Drug Dependence.* New York: Delacorte. (p.5).

9. Bufe, C. (1991). *Alcoholics Anonymous: Cult or Cure?*, with introduction by Albert Ellis. San Francisco: See Sharp Press. (p. 96).

10. Black, C. (1982). *It Will Never Happen to Me.* Denver: M.A.C.

11. *Diagnostic and Statistical Manual of Mental Disorders*, 3rd. ed. (pp.172-175).

12. Keller, M. (1972). "On the Loss-of-Control Phenomenon in Alcoholism." *British Journal of Addiction,* Vol. 67 (pp. 153-166).

13. Fingarette, H. (1989). *Heavy Drinking: The Myth of Alcoholism as a Disease.* Berkeley, CA: University of California Press. (p.102).

14. A comment made during the 1988 proceedings of the Supreme Court during the Traynor vs. the Veterans Administration by the Chief Justice. The NCADD, the AAATP, the AMA, and other medical lobbies exerted considerable influence in this case. Reported in *Time* and many other magazines.

15. *Entity* is defined in Webster's *New World Dictionary* as "the essence of something, apart from its accidental properties." Wilson's addition of this word is superfluous at best, sophomoric at worst. It adds nothing to the meaning of the sentence.

16. Wilson's statement will come as a shock to many. It stands, however, as written. I found it in a footnote on pp. 22-23 of *Not-God*, by Ernest Kurtz. (The book was Kurtz's doctoral dissertation at Harvard, and was published in 1979 by Hazelden Educational Materials.) In Section III, p. 343 of his "Notes on Primary Sources," Kurtz took great pains to document what he undoubtedly recognized as a startling— and to many a disturbing—revelation. It was here that he gave the date (April 21, 1960) and added, "Cited: NCCA, pagination from the transcript. An edited version appears in the NCCA Blue Book 12: 179-205."

Is it possible that Wilson was a nontraditionalist? Yes, but only in the narrow sense of not viewing alcoholism as a physiological disease. In most other areas he was the quintessential traditionalist; he promoted the loss-of-control notion, for example, and he postulated that alcoholism was an incurable but arrestable "malady" or "illness." In the quotation, Wilson addresses only his perception of the physiological aspects of alcoholism as a disease, as the italicized portion of the quotation indicates. His fundamental conviction, however, was that alcoholism is a *spiritual* disease in the metaphorical sense. On page 44 (1976 ed.) of the Big Book he describes alcoholism as ". . . an illness which only a spiritual experience will conquer," and affirms that position on page 64 with, "When the spiritual malady is overcome, we will straighten out mentally and physically." Throughout the Big Book he refers to alcoholism as an illness, malady, sickness, allergy, and craving. A.A. literature generally refers to alcoholism as a "physical, mental (or emotional), and spiritual disease," and shares with Wilson the conviction that the defining issue is spiritual.

The question of alcoholism as a physiological disease is treated gingerly by A.A. as an "outside issue," in accord with its tenth Tradition. Hospitals and treatment centers, however, tend to emphasize—understandably—this aspect of the "disease" of alcoholism. (Insurance companies, it seems, are loath to pay for "spiritual" remedies.)

17. Chavetz, M.E. "Alcohol and Innocent Victims," in *The Wall Street Journal,* March 5, 1990, p. A14.

18. Ludwig, A.M. (1988). *Understanding the Alcoholic's Mind: The Nature of Craving and*

How to Control It. New York: Oxford University Press. (p.3).

19. Many references in the Big Book clearly indicate that the alcoholic's personal responsibility takes the form of a decision to "turn it over," i.e. to become dependent on a *power* (Power) greater than her/him self. The following references (among many others) seem to substantiate that view:

Page 24 "We are without defense against that first drink."

Page 25 "He has commenced to accomplish those things for ourselves that we could never do by ourselves."

Page 45 "[The book's] main object is to enable you to find a Power . . . that will solve your problem."

Page 50 "This Power . . . accomplished . . . the humanly impossible."

Page 84 "We will suddenly realize that God is doing for us what we could not do for ourselves."

Page 99 "[The prospect's] . . . recovery is not dependent upon people. It is dependent upon his relationship with God."

3

Polarization: Us vs. Them

The escalating conflicts between traditionalists and nontraditionalists have produced results that are harmful to those in need of care and to those who provide it.

Among traditionalists, there are few differences of opinion on addictions issues. That's also true, but to a lesser extent, among nontraditionalists. Each camp tends to view itself as right, and the other —the "opposition"—as wrong. Each camp has dug its trenches deep and defends its positions vigorously, often by attacking the other camp. Their differences of opinion have not been and cannot be resolved by such tactics. Nevertheless, decent, intelligent people continue to affront one another, and continue to present arguments that are often subjective and sometimes offensive.

There is no need for this kind of thing. It's unkind, impolite, and counterproductive. Both sides are wasting time and energy that could be spent in more productive ways: exchanging information and ideas, for example. Both sides share a common goal, their dedication to those in need, and (with exceptions) the conviction that total and permanent abstinence is the key to success. With that much in common one might expect harmony and cooperation, but that's not the way it is.

For example: In August 1988, the journal *Alcoholism & Addiction* published a review of Herbert Fingarette's book, *Heavy Drinking: The Myth of Alcoholism as a Disease.*[1] *Alcoholism & Addiction* has long advocated traditional views on alcoholism and treatment, and it was no surprise to read its tough review of Fingarette's book. But Scott Neil, its editor, dipped his pen in sulfuric acid and hurled it like a barbed spear at a gentle, scholarly professor emeritus with whom he happened to disagree. The tough review was OK; what was not OK was the author's *ad hominem* attack on Fingarette, a former consultant to the Supreme Court and to the World Health Organization, and a distinguished professor and scholar with an international reputation. For example, Neil wrote, "Fingarette is a very dangerous man. His writing is extremely convincing to semi-literate readers . . ." Fingarette, dangerous? And "semi-literate readers?" To impugn the intelligence and literacy of readers is a violation of the 11th Commandment: Be courteous. Remarks of the type quoted do little to foster harmony and cooperation among those in the addictions field.

Neil is not alone; his nontraditional counterparts have had a few nasty things to say about traditionalism and A.A. Even Jack Trimpey of Rational Recovery has been harsh at times; and Jean Kirkpatrick, of Women For Sobriety, although somewhat ambivalent about A.A., can, at times, be ruthlessly critical of it. James Christopher, founder of Secular Organizations for Sobriety, wrote a book in which he vents a seething anger against A.A.[2] He asserts, for example, that A.A. promotes "an oppressive cultist atmosphere."[3] He becomes a little oppressive himself when he described the principles of A.A. as the "ravings of religionists," and disdainfully refers to A.A.'s tenets as "the party line."[4] In a subsequent book Christopher refers to "religious superstition of the kind often found in A.A."[5] Why so angry? We're not talking sex and politics here; we're trying to solve addiction problems. We can't do that by attacking people, but we can do it by discussing their ideas with them and by seeking common ground.

Those are but a few examples of prevailing attitudes. They are no longer exceptions to the rule of peaceful coexistence; *they have become the rule.*

The spiritual/religious issue seems to be the major point of contention. Many, and perhaps most, of the nontraditionalists (Wm. Miller, Reid Hester, and Ruth Engs are notable exceptions) fail to recognize the legitimacy of A.A.'s spiritual underpinnings.[6] The fellowship of A.A. considers its spiritual tenets *essential* to the achievement and maintenance of sobriety and the achievement of a new life. A.A. has a right to its spiritual plank; it is, after all, a program of its own design. But there are other programs (reviewed in Chapter 8) that do not use this approach. Although A.A. does not attack them directly, it insults them by ignoring them. The A.A. slogan, "It's our way or the highway," reflects neither an open mind nor a compassionate attitude toward those who find the A.A. program unsuited to their needs.

If nontraditionalists hurl spears, traditionalists build walls. There are few innocent parties in the conflict. It's time to break the spears and tear down the walls. Fortunately, there are solutions.

Example: Nontraditionalists canceled their subscriptions to the *Grapevine* (A.A.'s monthly magazine) long ago, and they open the Big Book only to take from it quotations that can be hurled like poisoned darts at the "opposition." They could renew their subscriptions to the *Grapevine*, attend an occasional A.A. meeting, and at least keep up with the changes (yes, there are some) in progress in A.A.

Example: Traditionalists could read *The Small Book* before judging it.[7] They could refer those who come to A.A., and find the 12-step program unsuited to their needs, to other programs. When asked about such programs, members of A.A. normally respond with a non-answer: "Keep coming back." They could alter their interpretations of the Traditions which supposedly preclude cooperation with other self-help groups. They could acknowledge that recovery from alcoholism, under the banner of *any* organization, is not an outside issue, but an area of common ground to which no organization has an exclusive right or privilege.

Traditionalists and nontraditionalists read only books and magazines that affirm their own views. "Have you read A.A.'s Big Book?" "Sure." "How about Rational Recovery's Small Book?" "Never heard of it." But Rational Recovery has been featured or mentioned at length in over 100 magazines and newspapers (*The Washington Post, Newsweek, The New York Times,* etc.). *The Small Book* is on the shelves of almost every library in the United States, and is in stock at almost all major bookstores. The founders of Rational Recovery, Jack and Lois Trimpey, have appeared on dozens of radio and TV shows, and five national TV talk shows. RR has meetings in over 700 cities in all 50 states, all Canadian provinces, Australia, and six other countries (October, 1993). Yet even traditionalist professionals sometimes claim that they have never heard of RR, or SOS, or Calix, or JACS, or AV, or MM, or WFS, or MFS—all recovery organizations with national bases, six of them with international extensions.[8]

Both parties practice segregation; their conferences are exclusive of one another. Neither traditionalists nor nontraditionalists invite each other to submit manuscripts for publication. A pro/con format on given issues could be enlightening to both parties because it would reduce friction and promote understanding. Would Scott Neil consider such a format in *Alcoholism & Addiction?* (That's a question *and* an invitation.). RR could invite an A.A. speaker to its national convention, and A.A. could extend a similar invitation to Women For Sobriety. That kind of reaching out could be done, and should be done. We need to build bridges, not fortresses.

But those bridges will never be built by people who have attended a *single* A.A. meeting and afterwards raged about all that "God stuff." Did they not understand, or were they so rash as to judge the A.A. program on the basis of *one* 90-minute meeting? And how many traditionalists have said of RR, "They're a bunch of atheists . . . they even think you can go back to social drinking." (The debate rages, but nontraditionalists enjoy an advantage: they have usually experienced and/or are knowledgeable about both approaches. Traditionalists tend to be far more insular.)

As the generals of the New Guard plan strategy, deploy their troops, and stockpile ammunition, the once-complacent members of the Old Guard circle their wagons in anticipation of further attacks from those whom they regard as impatient, aggressive, and wrong—*absolutely* wrong. The New Guard, in turn, looks upon these battle-scarred veterans with an impatience tinged with arrogance, even contempt, and often regards traditionalists as mulish defenders of the status quo, barricaded behind worm-eaten bastions built on sandy foundations of false premises and faulty logic.

Have you read *Controversies in the Addictions Field*, edited by Ruth Engs? The American Council on Alcoholism (ACA) was aware that Engs had been promoting an open pro/con format on major issues in an effort to mitigate tensions in the addictions field. It offered to become the sponsoring organization for a book that would serve that purpose, and asked her to serve as its editor. She accepted, compiled the book, and wrote its introduction.

Professor Engs provided recognized authorities in the addictions field with an opportunity to air divergent views on issues such as the nature of drug dependency and the influence of genetics and environment, as well as their perspectives on prevention, intervention, education, and treatment. She was shocked by what she found when she, as editor, approached authors of national reputation for contributions to her book. In the introduction she writes (slightly paraphrased for the sake of brevity):

> As a researcher and educator who has investigated drinking patterns for almost twenty years, I have become deeply concerned over increased polarization between different factions in the field during the past decade in the United States, and to a minor extent in Canada. I am concerned that this hostility has not only led to disharmony and discord, but has, even more importantly, prevented workable solutions to alcohol and other drug abuse problems in North America. As part of this accelerating conflict, conferences and

publications have been forthcoming with only *one* side of a particular issue being presented, usually promoted as the sole way to solve a problem. Individuals with dissenting viewpoints have not been encouraged or even invited to partake of these forums. Consequently the previous publications and conferences have all been one-sided . . . The mark of a scholar and a scholarly publication is to be tolerant of differing viewpoints and to ensure that all sides have an open forum for presentation . . .

Sadly, I talked with some potential authors who did not agree with or believe in the concept of an open forum and debate. Some had punitive attitudes towards individuals or groups who had opinions or values different than their own. Some were even hostile to the concept of this book. I am distressed by the attitudes of these individuals, all of whom are very well known in their specialty areas. I regret that they declined to participate.

Here are some of their reasons:

1) There was only one point of view or only one right way to solve the problem, and the individual was appalled that anyone could have a different opinion.

2) The American Council on Alcoholism (ACA) [sponsoring organization], as an organization, receives funding from individuals associated with the alcoholic beverage industry.

3) The ACA receives funding from the treatment industry, which would not want to be associated with anything even remotely connected with the alcohol beverage industry.

4) When given the name of certain authors who had agreed to write chapters, other invited contributors felt that these authors should not be given a forum because of their "dangerous," or "non-academic," or "out of date" viewpoints, and, furthermore, did not wish to be presented in the same book with them. I was amazed by these attitudes. Certainly, in academia all attitudes and ideas are [in theory–Ed.] welcome for discussion in an open forum. [But *not*, apparently, in the addictions field.]

Engs was obviously astounded at these attitudes and the intensity with which they were expressed. It led her to comment that such fixed positions "contribute to increased division and hostility rather than to efforts to look for compromise and workable solutions to problems in our field." In the final paragraph of the *Controversies* book she states:

> . . . We must begin to start listening to each other. We must start to work together by openly discussing our differences if we are to solve the alcohol and other drug abuse problems in our culture today.

It is ironic that in the "no man's land" between the opposing factions we find a multitude of individuals—alcoholics and addicts—to whom both camps are fervently devoted.

It's easy to praise tolerant attitudes and a willingness to adapt to new ideas, but it's easier to resist them. Traditionalists have become accustomed to power, position, control, private grants, tax dollars, and unquestioned acceptance. They have institutionalized an idea and built bureaucratic and organizational walls around it. Sociologists observe that institutions share two related traits: an inordinate resistance to change, and a tendency to self-perpetuate. The human factor is there, too; institutions are less abstractions than they are collections of people, and people have jobs to protect, mortgages to pay, and shoes to buy for their little ones. Change is often promising, but always threatening.

Nontraditionalists, however, insist on change—*now*. They contend that the ideas of the '30s no longer apply in the '90s, and must be immediately abandoned. They marshall their facts objectively, but sometimes present them subjectively. You have heard unqualified statements to the effect that "A.A. is dogmatic and provincial" and "treatment centers don't work." One statement is an allegation and the other, a generalization. That's not the way good thinkers present arguments and facts. And some of the schemes cooked up by members of the New Guard are like potato soup that lacks seasoning. And potatoes. It's time to call a truce—before war breaks out. It's time to break bread together and talk it over.

---

1. Neil, S. (1988). "The Fingarette Fallacies." *Alcoholism & Addiction*, Vol. 8, No. 6, 17–19.

2. Christopher, J. (1988). *How to Stay Sober: Recovery Without Religion.* Buffalo, NY: Prometheus Books.

3. Page 29.

4. Page 40.

5. Christopher, J. (1989). *Unhooked: Staying Sober and Drug-Free.* Buffalo, NY: Prometheus. (p. 22)

6. I will propose later in this book that most of those who advance the A.A. program have only a shallow understanding of its spiritual aspects. I have attended hundreds of A.A. meetings over many years and have talked with large numbers of A.A. loyalists. Not once did I hear spirituality addressed in terms other than the usual "A.A. is a spiritual program" and "Anonymity is the basis of our spirituality." Such statements must be construed as allegations, not explanations, since no attempt is made to explain their meaning.

7. In Indianapolis, Indiana there is a virtual smear campaign against Rational Recovery. The word is: "Yeah, I've heard of them. They're a bunch of atheists and they favor controlled drinking." Cherished ignorance, it would seem, is but a half-step away from maliciousness.

8. Ignorance of alternative (to A.A.) self-help programs is understandable in the general population, but is not defensible among professionals. It is the duty of professionals to keep up with changes occurring in the field so as to be of maximum service to their clients.

4

The Objective:
Personal Autonomy

Addicts normally achieve personal autonomy via a four-step process: (1) They start from a position of general dependence, which develops into (2) a specific form of dependence, called addiction,[1] followed by (3) recovery—the extermination of that addiction, followed in turn by (4) the achievement—often a re-achievement—of personal autonomy. The attainment of this goal is the hallmark of a full adult—a person who is responsible, informed, self-disciplined, and, as a result, well adjusted and happy.

In itself, dependency is not a bad thing; we are all dependent on each other in many ways—a condition called "interdependence." The early hunters and gatherers depended on each other as much as today's plumber depends on a surgeon to remove an appendix, or a surgeon depends on a plumber to clear a clogged drain.

Addicts, however, are dependent to an unrealistic and unreasonable extent. They depend on other individuals, a group, or a substance. When the consequences of that dependence become unbearable they often seek help, and are then told that they are diseased and powerless and must accept a substitute dependency—a support group, a God, sponsor, or some other *external* source of guidance and power. How ironic it is that so many therapists promote dependency as a way of life to clients whose greatest need is independence.

Beyond a certain point, interdependence—which is necessary and normal—often becomes unbalanced, unhealthy, and self-defeating dependence when it becomes one sided, that is, when it loses its characteristic mutuality. The addict doesn't lose control over his life; he gives it up. The overly dependent person makes decisions that, to at least some extent, allow him or her[2] to avoid pain, change, and personal responsibility. These decisions are reflected in character traits such as compulsiveness, passive-aggressive or antisocial tendencies,[3] inappropriate or mismanaged anger,[4] and narcissism, all of which promote addictions and inhibit recovery, as pointed out by Stan Katz and Aimee Liu in *The Codependency Conspiracy*.[5] Overdependence may thus be understood as an attitudinal and behavioral problem as well as a maladaptive regression toward a childish (not child-like) way of managing reality. This type of dependence is an acquired, self-imposed limitation that diminishes the full adult and inhibits the natural process of maturation. Thus, *addiction may be understood as a dependency-based behavior, practiced as a way of life.*

In contrast, the full adult is relatively independent and maintains *internal* control. As William Glasser (of Reality Therapy) points out, such an individual meets her personal needs without interfering with the needs of others and without being overly dependent on them. When dependence becomes a problem that seriously affects the quality of a person's life (heavy drinking, for example)—and therefore affects the lives of others—it is called an addiction.

But there are two schools of thought about addiction. In one camp are those who lean toward genetic and physiological causation and/or influence (nature); in the other camp, those who perceive addiction in functional, behavioral terms (nurture). Both factions recognize addiction as an umbrella concept that pertains to things we do (such as heavy drinking[6]) that are harmful to self and others. In his book, *More Revealed*, Ken Ragge provides a good working definition of addiction as "the continual repetition of a normally non-problematic behavior to self-destructive excess."[7]

Definitions such as Ragge's are generally acceptable to advocates of both the "nature" and the "nurture" positions, most of whom also agree that an "addiction" to a behavior like shoplifting, sometimes called a "process addiction," is similar to, yet different from, an addiction to a substance such as alcohol, nicotine, or cocaine. Both schools of thought are championed by responsible people who usually state their views fairly and objectively. Still, we have with us an either/or crowd, some of whom are *absolutely* certain that addiction is physiologically based, and others who are just as certain that addiction is a willful behavior, conditioned by, but not determined by, psychosocial and cultural influences. Neither position can be justified without qualification on the basis of available information.

The "nature" school claims that addiction is the result of a genetically inherited *predisposition* toward certain behaviors. This school declares that some people may be especially vulnerable to the biochemical effects of alcohol, and that after one drink they become unable to control further consumption, though its advocates seldom claim that neurological, metabolic, or genetic factors *cause* addictive behaviors. Researchers qualify their findings and submit them in the form of hypotheses or theories. Their research has often been misinterpreted, in spite of the many disclaimers and qualifications attached to it.[8] Those who advocate this school of thought, however, rarely discuss, and seem to studiously avoid, the issue of personal responsibility relative to that *first* drink; and they tend to absolve drinkers of all responsibility once that drink has been taken.[9]

The "nurture" school claims that addictions are essentially *functional*—that is, that they are learned behaviors that do what a person wants them to do. The members of this school claim that addictions are not the tools of pleasure, but maladaptive coping techniques that enable a person to either manage or avoid reality. In P. Perrin and Wim Coleman's *New Realities* we read:

> Many health professionals now concur that addiction does not necessarily begin as a self-indulgent search for pleasure without responsibility. To the contrary, it may be a failed attempt [to achieve] a legitimate goal. [Thus, people are not judged; their judgment is.][10]

Another segment of this school, well represented by David Hawkins, Director of the Institute for Spiritual Research in Sedona, Arizona, and Andrew Weil, professor of addiction studies at the University of Arizona, tends to agree that "substance abusers are seeking wholeness." Lee Jampolsky, author of *A Course in Miracles* (attitudinal healing), would agree: "Addiction is the result of some form of external searching that can really be seen as a form of spiritual search." There is some truth there, but a search which is often endless and fruitless can easily transform itself into a neurosis, which, as Carl Jung said, is always a substitute for legitimate suffering. Scott Peck, author of *The Road Less Traveled*, concurs: ". . . the attempt to avoid legitimate suffering lies at the root of all emotional illness."[11] Albert Ellis and Jack Trimpey would add: the search for truth (reality) often involves erroneous conclusions based on misinformation (e.g., the debunked notion of "one drink, one drunk"), or a simple lack of information.

In summary, the "nurture" or functional school of thought centers on addiction as a behavior and way of life (Fingarette's "central activity") focused on the adaptation to or avoidance of reality. A vocal minority within this school suggests that addictive behavior may also be understood in spiritual terms; namely, as a personal search for transcendence, connectedness, and wholeness.

The problem is not complicated; *addictions don't work*, regardless of the reasons for them or the rationalizations attached to them. When it becomes clear that an addiction is not achieving its intended goal, and when it becomes obvious that the consequences of maintaining an addiction are greater than its perceived benefits, it becomes desirable to get rid of it. The change, the process of getting rid of an addiction, is called *recovery*, usually understood in the sense of recouping one's losses or overcoming a problem, as in recuperating from an illness.

Recovery at its best, however, is much more than that. It's a springboard, an opportunity to transform one's life—not just by getting rid of something but by adding something. In Alcoholics Anonymous, the term "dry drunk" is applied to a person who has stopped drinking but hasn't "worked" the program in such a way as to achieve a new set of values expressed in a way of life. A.A. is right; recovery is more than not drinking or not using. [Editor's Note: The term "dry drunk" is probably most often employed by A.A. members as an epithet useful in the verbal bludgeoning of apostates and critics.]

Recovery, therefore, is more than "getting over" something like depression, or an injury from an accident, or heavy drinking; recovery is the elimination of a major obstacle that has impeded the achievement of full personal *autonomy*. Any dictionary or thesaurus will confirm that the word *recover* has a distinctly positive meaning. In WordPerfect 5.1, eleven synonyms are provided for that word; three of them suggest physical repair of the body (convalesce, heal, and recuperate), but eight of them sound a more positive note. They are: improve, rejuvenate, reclaim, recoup, regain, repossess, rescue, and retrieve.

Ray Hoskins, in his book, *Rational Madness: The Paradox of Addiction*, writes:

> The pattern of change in recovery is one of moving from fear-based *Survival Consciousness* . . . This is not a major change in the direction in a person's development, but rather, the continuing of a developmental process [toward full autonomy] which has been slowed or halted by addiction.[12]

Tina Tessina, in *The Real Thirteenth Step*, goes even further. She explains, "An addiction is any process over which we are powerless,"[13] and quotes Anne Wilson Schaef (in the same paragraph!) who says that, "An addiction is anything that we are not willing to give up."[14] Both agree, however, that addictions serve a function, that is, they *do* something: they provide us with a dark cave in which to hide. They deflect our attention away from our anger, pain, depression, and confusion. Those who want to achieve full adult status cannot do so by living like hermits in dark caves. When therapists work with clients who have drink-related problems, the drinking is usually perceived *as a symptom of the real problem.* Symptoms are not to be confused with causes. Therapists try to help clients realize that it's vital to get to the root problem, and that the maintenance of an addiction will impede or preclude the solution to that problem.

Addiction, then, may be seen as a chosen mode of behavior, often based on a lack of information and faulty judgment. It is usually accompanied by a measure of self-indulgence based on lack of personal discipline in at least one area of life. (Weak moral character is *a* factor, but not the most important factor, in addictive behavior.) There is a common perception that addicts are just children who never grew up; as we have seen, however, the maintenance of an addictive habit suggests only a lack of *full* maturity, rather than the total absence of it. Addiction is thus a negative concept, the evidence of something we don't have—the fullness of life.

It is in the attainment of full maturity that we achieve the fourth step, *autonomy.* The first two of the Buddha's Four Noble Truths deal with the pain and suffering in life. By refusing to face this part of our lives, he wrote, we diminish and sometimes destroy the joy and beauty of simply being alive. Orestes, a character from Greek mythology, would agree; he said, "Often, the test of courage is not to die, but to live." He was referring to autonomy, the graduate status of the full adult, self-disciplined and self-directed. Personal autonomy is the hallmark of a person who has learned to treat reality as an ally rather than an adversary, a person who, as Scott Peck advises, welcomes the natural flow of problems because in solving them further growth is achieved.

That's the four-step progression. From dependence, to addiction, to recovery, to autonomy. The achievement of personal autonomy is not easy, but you can stand it and you're worth it. It brings rewards far beyond mere "recovery." You can change now, later, or never. It's up to you. If you need help, it's available, and much of it is free.

In Chapters 5 and 8 of this book you will find information about the many self-help support programs available to you. In Chapter 9, you will find a detailed discussion of Rational Recovery Systems Network, a program that incorporates the cognitive-behavioral constructs of Albert Ellis, adapted and tailored to the needs of persons who believe themselves "alcoholics," or who have been saddled with that degrading and meaningless term.

One self-help support program stands out above the rest, Alcoholics Anonymous. It is a fellowship that has been lavishly praised and, more recently, severely criticized. It is a fellowship seldom recognized for what may well be its greatest accomplishment: it gave birth to the modern self-help movement in the addictions field.[15] It gave the rest of us permission, by example, to help one another. It is the proximate parent of the other eight self-help groups for alcoholics and other addicts. The Preamble of A.A. tells us a little something about that venerable fellowship:

> A.A. is a fellowship of men and women who share their experience, strength and hope with each other that they may solve their common problem and help others recover from alcoholism . . .[16]

There's more to it than that. What is the essence of A.A., and how well does it work? That's what the next chapter is all about.

---

1. The etymology of a word is often revealing. In this case, the root word is from the Latin *addicere,* an active verb, meaning "to give assent." Webster adds "to give (oneself) up to some strong habit."

2. The English language has no appropriate gender-neutral pronouns. I will try to avoid all sexist language throughout this book.

3. Often a catchall word, "antisocial" is used here and throughout this book as that which tends to fragment or disintegrate a society as distinct from that which integrates and preserves it.

4. S. Peele, A. Brodsky, and M. Arnold, in *The Truth About Addiction and Recovery,* discuss the subject of mismanaged anger as a precursor to addictions on pp. 287-290. The notion of resentment is often discussed at self-help meetings, but in its full-blown form resentment becomes anger, that, when mismanaged, often triggers addictive behavior.

5. Katz, S.J. and Liu, A.E. (1991). *The Codependency Conspiracy: How to Break the Recovery Habit and Take Charge of Your Life.* New York: Warner Books (p. 93). Katz and Liu credited Emil Chiauzzi ("Breaking the Patterns that Lead to Relapse" in *Psychology Today,* December 1989, pp. 18-19).

6. The phrase "heavy drinking" is generally associated with the consumption of alcohol. However, thousands of substances can be ingested into the body that can cause chemical imbalance resulting in physical and psychological addiction. A friend of mine once drank a case of 12 oz. Pepsi-Colas every day. He became addicted to it, decided to quit, and did. He said that quitting his soft drink was an experience very similar to that associated with quitting alcohol.

7. Ragge, Ken. (1991). *More Revealed: A Critical Analysis of Alcoholics Anonymous and the Twelve Steps.* Henderson, Nevada: Alert! Publishing. (p. 47).

8. The classic example is E.M. Jellinek's treatment of the disease issue in his *The Disease Concept of Alcoholism* (1960). Jellinek's extensive qualifications of his work have been almost totally ignored by traditionalists, some of whom actually refer to alcoholism as "Jellinek's Disease." H. Fingarette comments at length on this matter in his *Heavy Drinking*.

9. The "chemical trigger" effect has been thoroughly debunked by controlled testing of subjects under laboratory conditions. See Fingarette's *Heavy Drinking* Chapter 2, and his 25 references, pp. 46-47.

10. Perrin, P. & Coleman, Wi In *New Realities*. (Sept./Oct. 1987).

11. Peck, S. (1978). *The Road Less Traveled: A New Psychology of Love, Traditional Values and Spiritual Growth.* New York: Simon and Schuster.

12. Hoskins, R. *Rational Madness: The Paradox of Addiction.* Blue Ridge Summit, PA: Tab Books, 1989. (p. 163)

13. Tessina, T. (1991). *The Real Thirteenth Step: Discovering Confidence, Self-Reliance, and Autonomy Beyond the 12-Step Programs.* Jeremy P. Tarcher: Los Angeles.

14. Schaef, A.W. (1987). *When Society Becomes an Addict.* San Francisco: Harper & Row.

15. Later we will discuss the progenitors of the self-help support movement, the Washingtonians and the Oxford Group Movement (Moral Re-Armament). A.A. is the immediate ancestor of the self-help movement in the United States.

16. From an issue of the *A.A. Grapevine.* The preamble may be found in dozens of A.A. pamphlets. It is read at the opening of every meeting of Alcoholics Anonymous.

5

Alcoholics Anonymous: Essence and Functions

No book on alcoholism is complete without a discussion of Alcoholics Anonymous (A.A.). In this chapter I focus on three aspects of A.A: 1) its *essence*—what it *is*; 2) its *functions*—what it *does*; and 3) its *philosophical underpinnings.*

A.A. has been called a religion, a spiritual program, a cult, a temperance movement, and a spiritualism society, but A.A. is essentially what it claims to be: a fellowship of men and women who share a common problem and who seek to achieve and maintain sobriety by helping themselves and supporting one another. Many people have pronounced it an abysmal failure, but others have claimed that it is the best thing since sliced bread. However effective A.A. may be, few would declare it either an unqualified success or a total failure. Its advocates claim that it is a spiritual fellowship, but others insist that it is a religious organization. Allegations and accusations abound, though some interesting facts are also known—but not widely.

What you are about to read is neither an endorsement nor a condemnation of this venerable fellowship. In this chapter, you will find the facts that are available, the opinions of many responsible and recognized authorities in the addictions field, and a few of my own observations. I hope that the information and comments that follow are more objective than those extended toward A.A. by either its promoters or detractors, many of whom offer only anecdotal evidence, allegations, and unqualified personal opinions in support of their positions.

Before we consider what A.A. *is,* let us determine what A.A. *is not.*

Is A.A. a cult? No, because it does not conform to established criteria that define an organization as a cult. For example, A.A. is not authoritarian, nor is it given to the exploitation of its members or to violence against them. (Chapter 13 treats the cult charge in depth.) In his *Alcoholics Anonymous: Cult or Cure?*, Charles Bufe measures A.A. against 17 criteria which identify cults.[1] To the question "Is A.A. a cult?" he answers, "No, though it does have dangerous, cult-like tendencies."[2]

Nor can A.A. be termed a neo-prohibitionist society, because its total abstinence position applies only to its own voluntary (in part) membership. Certainly, A.A. is not a religion in the manner of the Catholic or the Lutheran faiths. Some people have called it a social club for misfits. Not so. Had such people attended even one A.A. meeting, they would have seen that, although A.A. is indeed a separatist society (as are the Elks, Lions, Eagles, etc.), it is also a benevolent mini-community within the larger community.

Is A.A. a charitable organization like the Salvation Army or Goodwill? Obviously not. A business, then? Again, no; A.A. is a not-for-profit 501(C)3 corporation. A.A. is not a missionary society either. It is not zealously dedicated to a world-changing agenda; it caters only to those who avail themselves of its services or who are mandated by the courts to attend its meetings. That's what A.A. is not; what A.A. *is*, is less obvious—but let's try to see.

First, A.A. is a fellowship of *people* who have endured a common experience and who share a common vulnerability and a common goal. A.A. is a support group first, a self-help group second. (The distinctions between these two will be detailed in Chapter 12.) Members of A.A. support one another, and are encouraged to avail themselves of support from a *Higher Power*. But members of A.A. are also expected to help themselves, as indicated by the familiar saying, "Read the Big Book and go to meetings," and by a statement often heard at meetings, "Today I choose to remain sober, by the grace of God and the fellowship of Alcoholics Anonymous."

The people of A.A. have not only a program, but a mission that is stated in A.A.'s twelfth Step: "Having had a spiritual awakening as the result of these steps, we tried to carry this message to alcoholics, and to practice these principles in all our affairs."

The message is indeed carried. Many people assume that A.A. gains members solely by word of mouth. Word of mouth may account for a large percentage of its membership, but A.A. attracts fewer members that way than from sources outside of A.A. that funnel prospects into it. A.A. is a dumping ground for many social agencies (the courts, for example), and a useful tool for others, such as the thousands of treatment centers which use Communal A.A. as an extension of their in-house A.A. programs.

The twelfth Step message is also carried through the organizational structure of A.A.[3] Members like to say that A.A. has no structure and no organization, in keeping with A.A.'s ninth Tradition which is essentially a proscription against organization.[4] It's obvious, however, that any large organization (fellowship) must have structure in order to exist, certainly an organization that claims two million members and lists outlets in over 100 foreign countries.[5] A.A.'s structure is certainly not as tight as that of, say, IBM, but it is real and functional. A.A. loyalists downplay this aspect of their fellowship, but no organization with the national and international outreach of A.A. could long survive without a sound and effective structure. A.A's structure may be described as having three aspects.

Communal A.A. is the first of these. It is the A.A. we all know, the gatherings in church basements of people helping one another and seeking answers to common problems. They talk and listen, give "leads" (short monologues), and share intimacies. They consume doughnuts by the megaton and drink coffee that makes your teeth itch, and they smoke a lot. (There are some smoke-free meetings.) They read the "Big Book" aloud to each other at meetings. They have discussion meetings in which members don't really *discuss* ("crosstalk" is seriously discouraged), but offer individual comments, mini-monologues so to speak, on a variety of subjects. In A.A. some find a home away from home, but most of those who try it leave it after a short visit, as will be shown in the next chapter. A.A. is free, but at every meeting the hat is passed, and the monies collected are used for operational expenses, local and national.

The second part of A.A. is its structural aspect. Let's call it **Organizational A.A.** Although individual A.A. groups enjoy a healthy degree of autonomy, they neither seek nor want independence from Organizational A.A.—which is basically the General Service Office (GSO) of Alcoholics Anonymous, Inc., which oversees its two totally owned subsidiaries, Alcoholics Anonymous World Services, Inc., and Alcoholics Anonymous Grapevine, Inc. (Organizational A.A.'s total income for 1991 was $12,352,341, and its total expense was $12,134,691, leaving an excess of income of $217,650.)[6] Its staff operates out of modern offices equipped with state-of-the-art computers. It manages a multitude of tasks, such as keeping track of sales, salaries, contributions, payments of royalties and writers' fees, insurance, professional and institutional relations, film development, conferences, and foreign literature assistance. Organizational A.A. operates a multi-million dollar publishing empire that sells over 158 items, including but not limited to books, pamphlets, brochures, charts, public service announcements, and tapes for radio and TV. It also handles budgetary matters, policy decisions, office management, legal problems, personnel, special staff appointments (liaison functions), purchasing, public relations, correspondence, etc.

The reality is that A.A., in its organizational aspect, does not conform to the popular perception of a loosely knit "Mom and Pop" operation; it is a multi-million-dollar, multi-national organization with considerable outreach and influence. All of that is neither good nor bad; it's simply information that can correct misconceptions about, and provide perspective on, this venerable fellowship.[7]

That brings us to the third part of A.A., a part which is "unofficial" but highly functional and vital to the interests of A.A. Let's call it **Institutional A.A.**

One day, back in the '70s, came thieves skilled in alchemy, the art of changing base metals into pure gold. They took the "money" and ran, and with that money—the 12-step program—established treatment centers and hospitals that appropriated the A.A. program, put a price tag on it, and offered it for sale in institutional settings. Communal and Organizational A.A. painfully adapted to what they could not (and did not even attempt to) control, but in time both developed a love/hate relationship with the thieves.

Communal and Organizational A.A. watched as multitudes of their misbegotten children sold at sky-high rates what they had always given away—and continue to give away—so freely. In supreme irony, however, the acquisitive ways of the wayward offspring are now encouraged, and even catered to, by the parent—A.A.'s General Service Office. It continues, always *unofficially*, to "cooperate but not affiliate" with Institutional (commercial) A.A.

But what is it that Institutional A.A. is selling? When A.A. loyalists say (of A.A.), "It works!", they are referring to its ability to effect personal change, and that change may be understood by detailing the four basic functions of A.A's 12-step program. A.A. is *first*, an Identity Transformation Organization (ITO); *second*, a Charismatic Healing Group; *third*, a Modified Temperance Society; and *fourth*, a Quasi-Religious Society. Let's take them in order.

A.A. is an Identity Transformation Organization (ITO). Credit Professors David Rudy and Arthur Greil with their brilliant description of A.A. as an ITO.[8] (I will, at times, expand on and deviate from their analysis when it seems appropriate to do so.) Rudy and Greil explain the process by which a novice in A.A. is encapsulated within its structure and protected from outside influences. Within that shelter, the novice finds camaraderie and discovers a whole sphere of personal and social activity. Here, the alcoholic—separated, and sometimes alienated from the larger society—finds social acceptance, but this acceptance is conditioned on allegiance to the group and conformity to its expectations. The subordination of personal ego to the "group conscience" is expected, and identification with the group anticipated.

New members are nurtured and parented, and their problems are simplified and focused. Here, often for the first time, the newcomer finds himself embraced as "one of us." He is praised, hugged, and listened to. He is told that he is OK and he begins to experience a sense of self-esteem, of being a real person after all. As a sense of "institutional awe" is generated, members modify and then identify their interests and goals with those of the group. A Hyde to Jekyll transformation takes place under the protective wing of the fellowship where the novice, having become a regular, finds unaccustomed approval in a warm and welcome place. He has a sponsor who functions as a mentor, guide, and parent figure. Life becomes centered on self and the fellowship. Cahalan agrees,[9] as I do, with David Doroff, who labels the process "therapeutic regression."[10] In her book, *I'm Dysfunctional, You're Dysfunctional,* Wendy Kaminer provides this telling insight: "Self-help is usually a misnomer for 'how to' programs in identity-formation."[11] But nothing is free, and there are house rules.

Don't drink, go to meetings, and read the Big Book. *Believe,* and don't ask questions that can't be answered by over two hundred slogans such as "Utilize, don't analyze," "Take the cotton out of your ears and put it in your mouth," and "Let go and let God." The A.A. program is one of indoctrination, not education. As they say in A.A., "KISS!," an acronym for "Keep It Simple, Stupid!" The statement is ill-advised, impolite at best, and offensive at worst. People seeking self-esteem don't need to be called stupid.

A.A. is a Charismatic Healing Group. Bill Wilson probably considered himself a charismatic, that is, a person divinely inspired. The account of his conversion experience (detailed in Endnote #12) would certainly suggest that. He felt that he had been healed, but considered himself only an instructor in the ways of healing rather than a healer as such. He dedicated his life to encouraging others to follow the path that he had taken, the path that had been provided to him by the "God of the Preachers." Wilson was convinced that the God who had healed him in Towns Hospital was available to all alcoholics.[12] Wilson's destiny, as he saw it, was to put powerless people in contact with an all-powerful God. Wilson is still revered within the fellowship as a distant, ghostly guru whose words are quoted with a finality usually reserved for sacred scripture.[13]

A.A. is indeed a charismatic healing group, and the healing that takes place within it is of a special kind. It's a form of displacement; the attitudes and values that prompted drinking are displaced by a new set of values based on a relationship with a Higher Power. This *Power* (obviously God) is also the Great Enabler and giver of a great gift, the gift of power to those who are otherwise powerless. The *power* is more loaned than given; it remains the property of the loaner and must be earned daily in order to be retained. The healing process seldom occurs in a miraculous moment, as Wilson pointed out. It is more often gradual, something to be nourished, and once achieved, maintained.[14]

A.A. knows that healing is a process, not a product, and it knows how to sustain that process. It does so with the help of rites and rituals, such as "birthday parties," and the use of tokens (chips) to commemorate significant periods of sobriety. Sociologists Max Weber and Emile Durkheim, among others, stress the importance of ritual as essential to the maintenance of the group and the fulfillment of its mission; and in A.A. there are many rites and rituals. For example, it is *de rigueur* at meetings to say "My name is _____ , and I'm an alcoholic." A set preamble and two prayers (the Serenity Prayer, by Rev. Reinhold Niebuhr, and the Lord's Prayer) are incorporated into the format of virtually all A.A. meetings. There are midnight candlelight meetings. Language is codified: "Let go and let God," "Easy does it," and "One day at a time" are three of the many "passwords" that function as verbal handshakes among regulars. Cohesion is thus generated as the group wisdom is validated. These rites and rituals have a special significance for all members of A.A.—they serve not only as guidelines for living, but as reminders of what has been learned.

At a given stage of development, the cocoon that once held the novice captive opens and releases a butterfly—a new person, self-aware and at one with her or his group. The larger, more threatening community is sometimes forsaken and a commitment made to a constricted version of it, the mini-world of A.A. There, in that comfortable and comforting world, the fully committed acolyte is guaranteed a place forever. Full recovery never happens and recovering never stops, but the healing goes on.[15]

A.A. is a Modified Temperance Society ("modified" in the sense that it appeals to a specific segment of the population). A.A. is a "temperance" (abstinence) society to the extent that it serves to reduce or eliminate the consumption of alcohol on the part of those who are called, or who call themselves, "alcoholics." Historically, A.A. is but one of many organized efforts to reduce or eliminate the consumption of alcohol in the United States, and although A.A. is not a temperance society in the crusading sense of a Carry Nation, it serves a similar purpose.[16] (The *primary* purpose of A.A. is to encourage its members to accept a spirituality based on God-related concepts, a set of values expressed as a way of life. Abstinence is seen as a necessary means to that end.) It is no coincidence that the Volstead Act (Prohibition) was repealed in 1933 and A.A. established in 1935. Those inclined toward both religion and alcohol were ready candidates for membership in A.A., and substantial remnants of the anti-alcohol coalition remained in a society in which zealous evangelism was almost as popular as sin. (I lived through those years, and, having been threatened once too often with the "good news" of the preachers, chose the lesser of the two evils: sin.)

   A.A. is a Quasi-Religious Society. After a penetrating and well documented inquiry concerning a possible religious component in A.A., Rudy and Greil state:

> Thus, it would be quite appropriate to characterize A.A. ideology as essentially *quasi-religious* [emphasis added] in character. We do not mean that A.A. is a religious entity. . . . We mean that a tension between sacred and secular is an integral part of the A.A. program."[17]

"Quasi-religious?" Rudy and Greil use the adjective *quasi* to suggest "as if," in a sense or manner, seemingly, or in part. The authors offer a cautious compromise rather than a firm conclusion Others are more explicit. Ernest Kurtz, for example, examines the spiritual and religious content of A.A. in *Not-God*, originally his 1979 doctoral thesis at Harvard. The next few pages of this chapter contain a synthesis of some of his ideas, along with observations of my own based on independent research.

   Alcoholics Anonymous is often called the "father" of the self-help movement for heavy drinkers in the United States. It isn't. A.A. may be considered a distant descendant of the Washingtonian Society, a temperance group that flourished in the 1840s and 1850s. A.A. is linked by a visible thread to that Society, an organization rooted in Pietist and Protestant evangelical thought. Bill Wilson, aware of the Washingtonian experiment, was influenced by it and disenchanted with it. He encouraged members of A.A. to avoid the four major flaws that he perceived in the Washingtonians: 1) a policy of self-promotion through advertising; 2) exhibitionism to the point of grandiosity, coupled with a competitive stance and an unwillingness to cooperate with other organizations in their field; 3) the dissipation of effort in fruitless controversy and divergent aims (such as the abolitionist movement); and 4) "Refusal to stick to their original purpose and so refrain from fighting anybody." (Some tenets of A.A. —though not certain of A.A.'s current positions and practices— clearly reflect these reactions to the Washingtonians.)[18]

Thus, the relationship of A.A. to the Washingtonian Society, although something of a historical accident, is one that involves a similarity of purpose but a contrast of method. Despite Wilson's claim (in *A.A. Comes of Age*) that he knew little about the Washingtonians, the fact is that he knew quite a bit about them, as indicated above. A.A. shared with the Washingtonians a common religious core of thought, but the two groups used different methods to carry that thought to the heavy drinkers of their respective periods.

The religious foundation of A.A. was *intimately* related, as child is to parent, to the Oxford Group Movement (not related to Oxford University or John Henry Newman's Oxford Movement),[19] which flourished in the 1920s and 1930s, of which Wilson said, "Our debt to them . . . was and is immense."[20] The connection between the Oxford Group Movement and A.A. is described in detail by researcher Charles Bufe in his book, *Alcoholics Anonymous: Cult or Cure?*

Kurtz reviews the immediate history of Pietist thought in the Washington and Oxford groups and relates them to the precepts of Alcoholics Anonymous.[21] I go a step further and link his observations with the original Pietist movement in Germany. The two efforts dovetail nicely into an explanation of the theological underpinnings of Alcoholics Anonymous.

Pietism was a 17th- and 18th-century religious movement introduced in Protestant Germany by the Rev. P. J. Spener (1635–1705) as a reaction against the Lutheran Church of his day, a church which he perceived as rigid and formalistic. He balked at its coldness, its intellectualism, and its focus on style rather than substance. He resisted its rigid traditions entombed in a rock-hard bureaucracy. He was repelled by its austere doctrine and inflexible dogma, and was troubled by a bitter irony that he perceived: humankind, he felt, had been separated from God by the Church.

Spener launched Pietism, a God-and-Bible-based form of experiential Christianity. It promoted a devotional relationship to God and a loving attitude toward fellow humans. His tenets were highly subjective and expressed with extreme emotion. Pietism's core concept was that there was but one tie which held members of a community together—a common love of the divine Christ as depicted in the synoptic gospels of the New Testament.[22] Pietism was an early amalgam of modern "New Age" spirituality and ancient New Testament theology. It rejected the concept of a distant and wrathful God and promoted a belief in a close and kind God, personally perceived and experienced.

Pietists contended that people were *powerless* in themselves, but that salvation was available through a power beyond themselves: God. Any Pietist with a drinking problem could have written A.A.'s first Step, "We admitted that we were powerless over alcohol—that our lives had become unmanageable." The Power in A.A. is not within A.A. or its members; it is greater than either and external to both. Pietism quickly spread to Scandinavia, Switzerland, England, and the United States. But it faded away (circa 1850) because of its lack of structure and its exaggerated emphasis on individualism and emotionalism.[23] Its leaders failed to understand that human projects need some structure and cannot manage long without it.

A.A.'s insistence on humility as the basis of spirituality posits the self as hopeless and helpless, self-serving, and deceptively self-reliant, until such time as a relationship is established with a helpful, all-serving, and totally reliable Other. This is the God of the Pietists and A.A., a God devoid of institutional trappings, organizational impediments, and pontifical pronouncements. Kurtz refers to it as a God who is *felt,* personally perceived, tailor-made and manufactured to suit individual needs. The Pietist God and, to a lesser extent, the Higher Power of A.A. conjure the image of a warm and fuzzy God, a God who is concerned, loving, and available—a God with a carrot in each hand and a stick in neither.

Alcoholics Anonymous promotes the traditional God of the New Testament, and at the same time (but with less enthusiasm) encourages the recognition of a more personal God, a God of one's own design and perception. A certain deference is paid to the personal god ("God, as you understand *Him*"), but the traditional, patriarchal God is the preeminent God of the Lord's Prayer, recited collectively at the end of almost every A.A. meeting. However defined, both Gods, as it were, are the source—the ultimate and the only source—of Power.

There is a second link between Pietism and Alcoholics Anonymous. It's called *evangelicalism.* Kurtz states, "The heart of evangelicalism consists in the announcement of salvation as a gift from God."[24] Members of A.A. often speak of themselves as God's people, his *chosen* people. The first evangelists announced salvation from sin (and ultimately, death), just as A.A. proclaims the good news of salvation—with God's help—from alcohol.

Empirical evidence seems to confirm Kurtz's observations. Outsiders are consistently impressed with the strong religious tone—as distinct from the euphemistic "religious flavor"—of A.A. meetings. The 12 steps listed on page 59 of Wilson's book (1976 edition) mention God or an equivalent seven times. Wilson prefaced his list of steps with this significant statement: "But there is One who has all power—that One is God. May you find Him now!"[25] Here it seems that the word power (small p) coupled with capitalized *One* and *God* in the same sentence produce a balanced equation. The semantic games devised to define this Power as something other than God usually confuse rather than clarify the issue.

May we then conclude that A.A. is a religious program? It's not that simple. There is no Yes or No answer to the question. I propose that A.A. is, in part, religious, but much depends on how you define the word *religion*, a virtually undefinable term. Certainly, there are many religious activities in A.A., but that does not make A.A. a religion any more than prayer in a public school makes that school a church. A Supreme Court Justice once commented that he didn't know what obscenity was, but that he could recognize it when he saw it. Perhaps it's that way with A.A and religion; we can intuit, and often recognize in a non-analytical way, that which is not amenable to ready definition.

In general, I agree with the comments by Kurtz on religion and spirituality in A.A., but I must go even further. A.A. makes an enormous mistake in masking its manifest religiosity in exclusively "spiritual" terms.[26] This subterfuge attenuates its integrity, denigrates its spirituality, and undermines its credibility. I sometimes think that A.A. neither understands nor appreciates its own spiritual/religious character. It does an inadequate, even appalling, job of explaining its position on this vital issue. A.A. has never delved into the treasure chest of its own spirituality. Its simple, even simplistic, declaration that "A.A. is a spiritual rather than a religious program" is an allegation, not an explanation.[27] And to say that "humility is the basis of our spirituality"—and to stop there—is akin to explaining World War II by saying, "We had a big fight with Germany." It must be admitted, however, that the achievement of the virtue of humility is something to be proud of.

A.A. also inherited a tradition of anti-intellectualism and anti-professionalism from Pietism. Not only does A.A. display that attitude in the spiritual/religious realm, it *extends* it to disciplines such as psychiatry, psychology, and medicine. (Kurtz, a close friend of A.A., soft pedals this issue.) In almost every A.A. meeting, one hears demeaning and often caustic remarks about professionals (especially psychologists and psychiatrists) proffered by individuals uniquely unqualified to make them. Many professionals, nevertheless, continue to accept and promote A.A. even as they are insulted by its members. Other professionals, more respectful of their legitimate and hard-earned academic credentials and experience, resent A.A.'s judgmental negativism. They realize, but seldom admit, that A.A.'s anti-professional and anti-intellectual posture serves only to keep it on the cutting edge of 19th-century thought.

The more important issue, however, is the matter of religion and spirituality in A.A., and on that subject it would be well to let A.A. speak for itself. It has done so eloquently in the 12 steps and in the Big Book. I reviewed the terminology used in the Big Book, and came up with some interesting results, detailed below.

Big Book Terminology

The purpose of this section is to shed light on whether and to what extent Alcoholics Anonymous is a religiously oriented organization. It is based on the assumption that one can judge the subject matter of the Big Book (or any book) by examining the vocabulary it employs.[28]

I've confined my study to the 164 pages of actual text in the Big Book, plus its 20 pages of preliminary matter, recording only those words and phrases usually listed in dictionaries of religious terms, and which I deemed to have a theological or religious significance as used in context. I did not record similar terms found in the 43 personal stories that follow the text, and which comprise over two-thirds of the book, because these personal narratives do not reflect direct input from A.A. co-founder Bill Wilson.[29] When common nouns such as maker, one, and presence, were capitalized, and thus given special significance, I recorded them and tabulated the frequency with which they were used. For example: the word *power*, when used to suggest personal capacity or capability, was not recorded. However, the word *Power*, when capitalized and used in reference to an entity above and beyond the human, was listed.

Finally, I categorized the terms used, combined them when appropriate, and tabulated the frequencies of each. The results of that study follow.

TERMINOLOGY—FREQUENCY

1) Amen—1
2) Biblical References (or paraphrases thereof):
    a) Been raised from the dead—1
    b) Faith without works was dead—3
    c) Peace on earth and good will to men—2
    d) Take up their beds and walk—1
    e) We were born again—1
    f) Thy will be done—1
    g) Love thy neighbor as thyself—2
3) Bless/blessed—2
4) Boss Universal—1
5) Brotherhood of man—1
6) Christ—1
7) Church—3
8) Congregation—1
9) Creation—1
10) Creative Intelligence—2
11) Creator—11
12) Denomination—2
13) Devil—1
14) Divine—1
15) Director—1
16) Employer—1
17) Faith—26
18) Father, Father of Light—2
19) God and God-associated words: God, Godly, God-given, God-conscious, God of Reason, God's, God-sufficiency, God's Universe, All Powerful God—174
20) Personal pronouns relative to God, with first letter capitalized:
    a) He—23
    b) His—11
    c) Him—24
    d) Himself—1
    e) Thee—2
    f) Thy—1
    [Total of Items 19 and 20 = 174 + 62 = 236]
21) God, as we understood Him—3

22) Great Reality—2
23) Higher Power—3
24) Heaven—1
25) Maker—1
26) Maker, as we understand Him—1
27) Meditation—4
28) Minister—2
29) Miracle, miraculous—13
30) Moral, moral teaching, moral inventory, moral psychology—6
31) New Land—1
32) Omnipotence (said of God)—1
33) One (said of God)—1
34) Ordained—1
35) Power, greater than myself, yourself, ourselves, themselves, himself—8
36) Pray, prayed, prayer—11
37) Presence, of Infinite Power and Love, of God,
        of Power of God—4
38) Priest—2
39) Providence—1
40) Religion, religious—33
41) Saint (said of Dr. Silkworth)—1
42) Sin—1
43) Spirit, of the Universe, of Nature, Realm of—10
44) Spiritual—108
45) Supreme Being—1
46) Theological—1
47) Universal Mind—1

OTHER SIGNIFICANT WORD CLUSTERS

1) An Alcoholic as:
        a) Problem drinker—4
        b) Abnormal drinker—2
        c) Sick—3
        d) Deranged—1
        e) Psychopath—1
        f) Manic-depressive—1
2) Alcoholism as:
        a) Illness—15
        b) Malady—5
        c) Sickness—1
        d) Allergy—4
        e) Craving—2
3) Archaic or dated terms:[30]
        a) Wet brain—2

b) Nip of the wringer—1
c) Whoopee parties—1
d) John Barleycorn (liquor)—2
e) Our women folk—1
f) Men, as head of the house—3

Although open to interpretation, these findings seem to speak for themselves. During its early years, A.A. found it politic to distance itself from organized religion, and with good reason. But times change, and the appropriate and understandable caution exercised by A.A.'s founders is no longer imperative. If A.A. is a religion, or at least "religious," let it be said; it is nothing to be ashamed of. The Big Book seems to define itself, as do the 12 steps.

———————————————

The *essence* of A.A. cannot be grasped without a thoughtful review of its 12 steps. The steps are a program for personal change, concerned—*but only incidentally*—with abstention from alcohol. The ability to abstain from the use of alcohol is viewed, as mentioned earlier, not so much as an end in itself but as a gift from God contingent upon the acceptance of a new and God-centered life. The powerless person, whose life has become *unmanageable*, cannot achieve durable sobriety on his or her own, as A.A. has stated. He or she simply lacks the power—as in "powerless." Therefore an external power, a *Higher Power*, is required.

The determination of the nature of this Power is of paramount importance, not only in order to understand the process of personal change within A.A., but because this determination will have an enormous impact on the future of addiction care—especially professional and institutional services (including probation and prison)—in the United States.

The Higher Power concept in A.A. can be understood as the complete "Other" in whose fullness a person can participate.[31] Theologically, this corresponds to divine grace, an infusion of God-life into human life, in order to achieve a new life, devoid of alcohol. Thus it seems that there is no room in A.A. for those who acknowledge their limitations and have learned to deal with them through the exclusive use of human resources.

The few A.A. meetings for agnostics[32] (concerned with the use of *human* resources) are only adulterated A.A.; those who attend them, as Trimpey points out in his *Small Book*, find themselves riding in the back of the A.A. bus. "Agnostics meetings" are nothing more than entry-level A.A. meetings, designed as stepping stones to a higher plateau. The barely restrained intolerance of Chapter 4 ("We Agnostics") confirms this. Nonbelievers often find that chapter condescending to the point of insult. A.A.'s Higher Power, this "God as you understand *Him*" (emphasis added), is clearly not a lamp post or a door knob (options often proffered in A.A. meetings in reference to the second Step—"Came to believe that a Power greater than ourselves could restore us to sanity"), nor can it be, in view of A.A.'s Steps 3, 5, 6, 7, and 11:

3) Made a decision to turn our will and our lives over to the care of God *as we understood Him.* (emphasis A.A.)

5) Admitted to God, to ourselves, and to another human being the exact nature of our wrongs.

6) Were entirely ready to have God remove all these defects of character.

7) Humbly asked Him to remove our shortcomings.

11) Sought through prayer and meditation to improve our conscious contact with God *as we understood Him,* praying only for knowledge of His will for us and the power to carry that out.

How can a being, one greater than ourselves, to whom we can turn over our lives and will, to whom we confess (admit) our wrongs, a being able to remove our character defects and shortcomings, and to whom we pray for guidance, be—by any stretch of the imagination—an *inanimate* object such as a door knob or a lamp post? The Steps describe an *animate* entity who is benevolent, all-powerful, forgiving and caring. These are not the traits of door knobs and lamp posts; they are the traits of a supernatural being "greater than ourselves." The Steps identify that being. It has a gender; it is *He*, the personal pronoun with a capital H, used throughout the Big Book. Bill Wilson, who regarded doorknobs and lamp posts with the same detachment as you and I regard them, was more candid. He knew what "a Power greater than yourself" really means: ". . . it means, of course, that we are going to talk about God."[33]

It's possible, however, that the power-full doorknob phenomenon can be explained away. It has been described as a "bait and switch" tactic—doorknobs and lamp shades now, God later. But there may be another explanation. The objective may be to promote the idea that the rescuing Power is *anything other than the self*—that the person is indeed powerless, and that, until enlightenment comes, any substitute for self-power will do. After enlightenment, conversion, and acceptance, the temporary pinch-hitting "gods" may be discarded, the real God accepted, and the Lord's Prayer finally said in earnest.[34] A.A., however, offers no explanation for the bizarre notion that a doorknob is capable of doing anything other than performing its mundane mechanical function.

Bill Wilson was, in my view, a "God-ridden" man, but while writing the Big Book (with major input from an ad hoc committee of friends) he bowed to pressures from Hank P. and Jim B., who insisted that there was "too much God" in the 12 Steps. Then too, a Catholic priest had forbidden two of his flock to attend A.A. meetings because he perceived those meetings as competitive religious gatherings. Wilson reluctantly, but wisely, compromised. He knew that his program "had to remain attractive to the temperamentally non-religious while it avoided giving offense to the personally religious."[35] He wanted to avoid dissension with organized religions. His grating experiences with A.A.'s immediate parent, the Oxford Group, had taught him the benefits of diplomacy. Words of compromise may be found in *Alcoholics Anonymous Comes of Age*:

> In Step Two we decided to describe God as a "Power greater than ourselves." In Steps Three and Eleven we inserted the words "God as we understand Him." From Step Seven we deleted the expression "on our knees." And, as a lead-in sentence to all the steps we wrote these words: "Here are the steps we took which are suggested as a Program of Recovery." A.A.'s 12 steps were to be *suggestions* only (emphasis Wilson).[36]

The intent seems to have been to mask God, and rename Him. Kurtz observes, "The explicit theism of Alcoholics Anonymous witnessed clearly that its founders believed that the fundamental reality was 'God.'"[37] Others thought so too. Kurtz references 23 researchers in support of his conclusion:

> Over the years, other careful students—among them diverse sociologists, psychologists, and anthropologists have . . . clearly and consistently intuited the key to the program and the fellowship of Alcoholics Anonymous somehow to be "religion." For all the problems inherent in the connotations of the term [religion], such diverse unanimity cannot be ignored simply because of A.A.'s own insistence that it is "a spiritual rather than a religious program."[38]

To classify a program as religious, spiritual, or both is to assume that generally agreed upon definitions of religion and spirituality exist. But, unfortunately, such definitions don't exist. People usually respond to questions about the meaning of spirituality and religion by giving qualified answers in the form of opinions. They show laudable discretion in doing so. They admit that they don't *know* and seem to sense that no one else knows either.

As Judge John Shabaz ruled in the 1984 Wisconsin case, *Granberg V. Ashland County:*

> "Alcoholics Anonymous materials . . . and the testimony of the witness established beyond a doubt that religious activities, as defined in constitutional law, were a part of the treatment program. The distinction between religion and spirituality is meaningless, and serves merely to confuse the issue . . ."

---

1. Bufe, C. (1991). *Alcoholics Anonymous: Cult or Cure?*. See Sharp Press: San Francisco [now Tucson, AZ]. (pp. 92-102). Note: Bufe's work is a thorough and objective presentation of criteria that can be applied to any organization to determine whether it is a cult.

2. Page 101.

3. At the forty-second annual meeting of the General Service Conference of Alcoholics Anonymous (April 26-May 2, 1992) a report was read to the assembled body by Owen J. Flanagan and Company (Certified Public Accountants) as part of the Final Report titled *The A.A. Message in a Changing World* (p. 63). In that report Flanagan and Company denote The General Service Board of Alcoholics Anonymous as the parent company, holding two totally owned subsidiaries: Alcoholics Anonymous World Services, Inc. and Alcoholics Anonymous Grapevine, Inc., as of December 31, 1991. (The combined operations of these organizations were presented in the usual format: assets, liabilities, salaries, et al.). This kind of structuring is not at all unusual in a corporation the size of A.A., and is necessary for reasons pertaining to taxes and general management functions.

4. Ninth Tradition: "A.A., as such, ought never be organized; but we may create service boards or committees directly responsible to those they serve."

5. The population of A.A. is unknown and can only be estimated, as A.A.'s 1992 "Final Report" indicates (p. 28). That report estimates its United States population, as of January 1, 1992, at 1,079,710 plus an additional 1,040,411 members scattered throughout Canada, correctional facilities, in countries other than the United States, and so on. A.A.'s definition of a member as "anyone who wants to quit drinking" is not really amenable to statistical manipulation, and is so encompassing as to be meaningless. It may be compared to a definition of a fish as "anything that swims," such as a frog, an alligator, Rover the dog, or your significant other. Since A.A. generates and interprets its own statistics, it is possible that the data it presents,

and its interpretation of that data, may be optimistically skewed. Those whom A.A. recognizes as "alcoholics" are those who have accepted its definition of an alcoholic as a person who is "spiritually, emotionally, and physically diseased."

6. Some qualification is needed here. The 1992 A.A. "Final Report" shows (p. 58) that in 1990 only 54.5% of the combined U.S. and Canadian groups contributed to G.S.O with an average per person contribution of $3.43. The 1991 figures showed a decrease from 54.5% to 51.6% of groups contributing, with a decrease of 40 cents per person, down from $3.43 to $3.03. In this category the total 1990 group contribution was $3,771,496, against the 1991 figure of $3,543,804—an approximate 2% decrease in monies contributed. Many interpretations of this phenomenon could be made.

7. Much interesting information about A.A. may be found in its 72-page 1992 "Final Report" which can be ordered from World Services Inc., P.O. Box 459, Grand Central Station, New York, NY 10163. It is identified as Item M-23 and costs $2. It is described as **"Confidential; for A.A. members only,"** but is obviously available to anyone who wants it. It was first distributed at A.A.'s forty-second annual meeting, held at the Holiday Inn Crowne Plaza, New York, NY, April 26 through May 2, 1992. A revealing document, worthy of close review.

8. Rudy, D.R. and Greil, A.L. (1988). "Is Alcoholics Anonymous a Religious Organization?: Meditations on Marginality." In a revised version of a paper presented at the annual meeting of the Society for Scientific Study of Religion, 1985, Savannah, GA. *Sociological Analysis*, 50:1 41-51.

9. Cahalan, D. (1987). *Understanding America's Drinking Problem: How to Combat the Hazards of Alcohol.* San Francisco: Jossey Bass.

10. Doroff, D. (1977). "Group Psychotherapy in Alcoholism" in B. Kissin and H. Begleiter (eds), *The Bibliography of Alcoholism. Vol. 5: Treatment and Rehabilitation of the Chronic Alcoholic* (p.237). New York: Plenum.

11. Kaminer, W. (1992). *I'm Dysfunctional, You're Dysfunctional.* Reading, MA: Addison-Wesley. Note. (p.6). An exceptional book. Recommended reading.

12. Wilson's experience may have been induced by belladonna (see note, below), a manifestation of his personal instability, or a pivotal moment of spiritual enlightenment in the manner of a Paul, Dante, Pascal, Augustine, or dozens of other well-known people. We simply don't know. His own account of that experience (in *Alcoholics Anonymous Comes of Age*) can be interpreted several ways. After that experience, however, Wilson became and remained a "God-ridden" man.

   Note: belladonna is a poisonous European plant of the nightshade family, and the source of atropine, used to relieve spasms (as in withdrawal from alcohol) and to dilate the pupil of the eye. It is probable, and can be almost assumed, that Wilson underwent delirium tremens in Towns Hospital. Interpretations of Wilson's experience at Towns Hospital often seem to reflect the prejudices—pro or con—of the interpreter concerning Wilson and A.A. For a description of Wilson's treatment at Towns Hospital, see *A.A. The Way It Began*, by Bill Pittman (1988). Seattle: Glen Abbey Books (pp. 163-169).

13. Bill Wilson, co-founder of A.A., was the first among equals. The less equal co-founder was Dr. Bob Smith, a proctologist (there is no end to the jokes about that lowly profession), generally referred to as "Dr. Bob." It seems that when leaders

emerge in pairs, one of them becomes the shadow of the other.

14. This is the primary thrust of Wilson's Appendix II (on spirituality). Many early members of A.A. lived in expectation of that "miraculous moment" of the kind Wilson experienced in Towns Hospital. He admonished them that the process was seldom sudden and was more akin to ". . . what the psychologist William James calls the 'educational variety' because it develops slowly over a period of time."

15. Erich Fromm wrote (1941, in his *Escape from Freedom*) that the rise of democracy set us free politically, but that it gave birth to a society in which the individual feels alienated and dehumanized. There is a counterpart to that with life in A.A. The individual is no longer alienated, but is, to a degree, diminished by merging the self with the group, accepting its tenets without question, and identifying with it. For example, A.A. refers to a "group conscience"; obviously, there can be a consensus within a group, but there is no such thing as a "group conscience."

16. Born Carry Amelia Moore, Carry Nation (1846-1911) was an eccentric agitator for temperance. She used a hatchet to break up beer barrels, whiskey bottles, plate glass windows, and human heads. A first class nut.

17. Op. cit., p. 49.

18. Ernest Kurtz details this issue on pp. 116-117 of *Not-God*, and refers to Wilson's *Grapevine* article (AAGV 2:3, August, 1945, published one year before the publication of the Traditions. In that article, Wilson listed the four "flaws" of the Washingtonian Society, that is, differences in approach and procedure, from that which he envisioned for a still nascent A.A. *The Grapevine* carried 12 articles on the Washingtonian Society between 1945 and 1976. Kurtz reports (p. 292), "Further, the Washingtonians have been kept before A.A.'s attention over these years by Professor Milton Maxwell, currently an A.A. trustee, whose deepest scholarly treatment appeared as 'The Washingtonian Movement,' QJSA [*Quarterly Journal of Studies on Alcohol*], Vol. 11, pp. 410-451 (1950)." The result of A.A.'s early views on the Washingtonian program produced, in large part, its tenth Tradition: 'Alcoholics Anonymous has no opinion on outside issues; hence the A.A. name ought never be drawn into public controversy.'" There are now many reasons for A.A. to reconsider its 47- year-old position, but the tenth Tradition is now solidly grounded, and—in any case—A.A. is disinclined toward adaptation to changing conditions.

19. Ernest Kurtz distinguished between the "Oxford Group" and the "Oxford Movement" in a footnote on page 9 of *Not-God*. He explained that the *Oxford Group* (circa 1920–1940) ". . . was a non-denominational, theologically conservative, evangelically styled attempt to recapture the impetus and spirit of what its members understood to be primitive Christianity." *The Oxford Movement* (circa 1801–1890) "was a late nineteenth-century, strongly liturgical movement within Anglo-Catholicism [Episcopalianism] toward Roman Catholicism." The organizations do not relate one to the other.

20. *Alcoholics Anonymous Comes of Age*, p.73.

21. Kurtz, op. cit., pp. 179-182, 191, 247-248.

22. From the Greek, meaning accounts presented from the same or similar points of view—here, the gospels of Matthew, Mark and Luke.

23. A.A. is making the same mistake today and may suffer thereby Emotionalism is a heavy component of A.A., as evidenced in meetings which highlight

"drunkalogs" or "birthday parties."

24. Kurtz, op. cit., p. 179.

25. "Big Book," p. 59.

26. Even Frank Reissman, Director of the National Self-Help Clearinghouse in New York, admits that A.A. has a strong religious character (not "flavor"). Reissman seems to incline favorably toward A.A. and may, indeed, be one of its many "unofficial" spokespersons.

27. For further reading into this fascinating facet of A.A., see W.R. Miller's and M. Edwards' (1990), "Spirituality: The Silent Dimension in Addictions Research." This monograph was presented at the annual Leonard Ball Oration, Melbourne, Australia, May, 1990. (The authors include 31 references in support of their thesis.) Note: Miller is a professor of psychology and psychiatry at the University of New Mexico, and Edwards is a visiting professor attached to the National Drug and Alcohol Research Centre, University of New South Wales.

28. As I studied the text of *Alcoholics Anonymous* I noticed, and have included, certain clusters of words that are not especially germane to the understanding of A.A. as a spiritual/religious fellowship, but which you may, nevertheless, find interesting.

29. Of 575 pages in the Big Book, 391 of them (68%) are devoted to personal narratives.

30. This is the language of the 1930s and was commonly accepted in its day. The opening phrase in Chapter 9 ("Our women folk . . . "), and words and phrases like it, are not acceptable to the modern reader. Sexist, dated, and unfamiliar terms inhibit communication and are out of place in today's world. (Reference Miller and Swift's book *The Handbook of Nonsexist Writing*.) Strangely, women in A.A.— specifically those who choose to remain in A.A.—seldom object to language of this type. A.A. has updated some of its material, but refuses to amend the text of the original Big Book, and generally treats it with a reverence usually reserved for the Bible—which has been revised several times.

31. The term "other" with a capital O is used frequently in theological circles to refer to God by another name. Theologians tend to use a battery of esoteric terms; for example, one of them defined spirituality as the "flight of the alone to the Alone." Mystics may understand that sort of thing, but most of us don't.

32. Not necessarily "agnostic" in the formal definition of that term. "Agnostic" is often used as an umbrella term pertaining to anyone who has not accepted the A.A. program in toto. Such groups are almost certainly few in number. In Indianapolis, Indiana, for example, a city of about one million people, there is no such group. Information concerning the numbers of such groups and their populations is not published by A.A. They do exist, however, but there are probably less than 25 or so throughout the United States. I hereby ask A.A./GSO, the NCADD, or any other "unofficial" representative of A.A. to publish information concerning such groups.

33. Big Book, p. 45.

34. On the East Coast the idea of a temporary substitute God is often taken lightly, almost tongue-in-cheek. In Indiana, however, and in other Bible-thumping states, they don't even smile when they tell you that your Higher Power can be a chair or

a mail box.

    The name of Jesus is invoked with enthusiasm at many A.A. meetings, especially in Bible Belt areas. Wilson, however, commented (Big Book, p. 11), "To Christ I conceded the certainty of a great *man* (emphasis added)." Wilson judged the teachings of Christ as "most excellent," but added, "For myself, I had adopted those parts which seemed convenient and not too difficult; the rest I disregarded." Is that statement supercilious, arrogant, or what? I am not a Christian, but to speak of Christ, Buddha, or Mohammed in such a way seems sophomoric and inexcusable to me. Wilson seems to have reduced the Christian triune God (Father, Son, and Holy Spirit) to Father and Spirit. That's a major theological revelation from a man who was never exposed to Theology 101. Christians, however, whether in or out of A.A., seem unoffended by this crass assessment of the teachings of Jesus.

35. Kurtz, page 176.

36. p. 167

37. Op cit., pp. 184-185

38. Ibid., p. 176

6

Alcoholics Anonymous: Effectiveness

When we say that something is effective, we usually assume that everybody knows what we mean. We also assume the existence of a standard against which effectiveness can be judged, and we further assume that we have the means of measuring performance against that standard. In the area of addictions one finds little consensus, few standards, and no measuring tools other than "length of sobriety" (a "non-behavior"), that is, not drinking over some period.

None of that, however, was known to the editor of the *Mensa Bulletin,* who in December 1989 phoned me with a special assignment. He said that he had heard that A.A. was a good outfit, but that it was not as successful as many assumed it to be. Would I do an article on the subject? Yes.

This chapter is a revision of that article, which was titled "Alcoholics Anonymous, Reputation and Performance: Challenge and Choice" and published in the *Mensa Bulletin: The Magazine of American Mensa* in May 1990. In December 1990 it was reprinted in *The Journal of Rational Recovery* (JRR), and again, in April 1991, in *Freethought Today.* An updated version was published in abridged form in the March/April 1992 issue of the JRR.

At a meeting of Alcoholics Anonymous the speaker recommends its program with a ringing declaration, "It works!" True, *but how well does it work?*

Several prestigious organizations seem to know, having endorsed A.A. enthusiastically. Among them are the National Council on Alcoholism and Drug Dependence, The American Medical Association,

The American Hospital Association, and the American Association of Addiction Treatment Providers. They certainly ought to know, but do they? Let's take a closer look.

First, is the performance of A.A. commensurate with its reputation? A definitive answer would require facts, but *facts* about A.A. are as scarce as hen's teeth. We can, however, make some judgments by exploring the extent to which A.A.'s members have fulfilled their mission "to stay sober and to help other alcoholics to achieve sobriety." Given the lack of verifiable information from A.A., the question of performance must be referred to scholars and researchers. Is A.A. an effective organization? Here are some answers:

U.S. News and World Report of November 1987 featured an article, "Coming to Grips with Alcoholism," in which it estimated the number of "alcoholics" in the United States at 10.6 million, and A.A. membership at 676,000. That works out to a membership of 6.4% of total potential members. There are extenuating circumstances, of course, but with the benefit of a 52-year near-monopoly (as of 1987) in its field, that performance—judged by *any* standard—is inadequate.

Of those whom A.A. does reach, the *U.S. News* article continued: ". . . outside researchers—A.A. is reluctant to let them in [!]—believe that perhaps four out of five people who go to A.A. meetings soon drop out." That's a conservative estimate. My opinion is based not only on knowledge gained from years of study and hundreds of contacts, but on personal experience as a former member of A.A. A.A. regulars know about this come-and-go membership problem; they call it A.A.'s "revolving door."

Let us pause to acknowledge the merits of A.A. I've mentioned four approving organizations (there are others), and I know from experience that A.A. is dedicated and conscientious. The question, however, remains: Is it effective? Does it get the job done?

No, says Herbert Fingarette, professor emeritus at the University of California, and former consultant to the United States Supreme Court and the World Health Organization. In his book, *Heavy Drinking*, he states, "It is well known to everyone actively engaged in the field . . . (that) the A.A. program of recovery is simply not acceptable or attractive to the majority of people suffering problems of heavy drinking."

No, says Arnold Ludwig, professor of psychiatry at the University of Kentucky College of Medicine. In his *Understanding the Alcoholic's Mind*, he observes, "Estimates are that only 5 to 10 percent of the alcoholics in this country use A.A. and of those who recover, only 10 percent do so through A.A."

No, says Professor Stanton Peele, social-clinical psychologist and senior survey-researcher at the Mathematical Policy Research Center at Princeton, New Jersey. In his *Diseasing of America: Addiction Treatment Out of Control*, he writes, "In fact, research has not shown A.A. to be an effective treatment for general populations of alcoholics."

No (qualified), says Donald Goodwin, professor and chair of the department of psychiatry at the University of Kansas Medical Center. In his book, *Is Alcoholism Hereditary?*, he observes, "A.A. is credited with helping more alcoholics than all other treatments combined, [but] . . . there is no way of knowing if this is true, since the kind of careful studies needed to show it have not been done."

No, says Ken Ragge in his *More Revealed: A Critical Analysis of Alcoholics Anonymous and the Twelve Steps.* Ragge devotes a chapter titled "Does it Really Work?" to the question of A.A.'s effectiveness. He references two controlled studies on A.A., both of which produced negative results.[1] He then analyzes the research of psychiatrist George Vaillant of Dartmouth Medical School. Vaillant, author of *The Natural History of Alcoholism*, has produced convincing data indicating that Institutional A.A. is *ineffective.* Vaillant writes (in "The Doctor's Dilemma"), "The best than can be said for our existing treatment is that we are certainly not interfering with the normal recovery process."[2] Vaillant, however, continues to promote A.A. and the traditional approach in the face of his own research.

No, (qualified) says Don Cahalan, professor emeritus of public health at the University of California, Berkeley. In his book, *Understanding America's Drinking Problem*, he states, "It (A.A.) is widely regarded as the most effective avenue for the treatment of alcoholism, although there has been little actual research to bear this out . . . and folklore has it that only about 10 percent of those with the most severe drinking problems ever avail themselves of A.A."

No, says Jerry Dorsman, administrator, researcher, and addictions therapist in Maryland's Cecil County Department of Health, Division of Mental Health. In his book, *How to Quit Drinking Without A.A*, he notes, ". . . only 5 to 10 percent of Americans with serious drinking problems belong to A.A. What's worse, among those who join, only about 12% remain in the program more than 3 years." Dorsman does not document his 12% figure, but most researchers would consider his estimate very optimistic.

No, says Jeffrey Schaler, author, editor, and therapist, writing in *Prince George's Journal* of March 1991. He states: "Many people believe that A.A. is the most effective form of treatment for alcoholism. There is no evidence to support this claim."

No, says Charles Bufe in his well-researched *Alcoholics Anonymous: Cult or Cure?* He presents an especially convincing case as follows: An extrapolation from the 1989 membership survey indicates that in that year A.A. claimed 820,000 members in the United States. At that time there were from 10 to 20 million "alcoholics" (by some definition of that nebulous term) in this country. Therefore A.A.'s membership figure represented only 4.1% to 8.2% of the estimated population of alcoholics. Of A.A.'s 820,000 members, the survey asserted that 29% had at least five years sobriety. ("Success" includes length of sobriety, but may not be fully defined by it.) Using A.A.'s 29% figure as a criterion of success, Bufe calculated an overall success rate of 1.2% to 2.4% relative to the number of alcoholics in the United States, and he went on to estimate that A.A.'s success rate relative to past and present members is at most 2.4% to 4.8%.[3]

Bufe estimates that 50% to 90% of all heavy drinkers investigate A.A. at some time during their drinking careers; this by virtue of the facts that: 1) A.A. is a mandatory part of treatment in 99% of treatment centers; 2) drunk drivers and other alcoholic offenders are routinely sentenced to A.A. in most parts of the country;[4] and 3) the general *perceptions,* popular and professional, that A.A. is successful and that it's the only program available to problem drinkers, results in a large amount of "walk-in traffic" for A.A.

My own position is that the general belief in A.A.'s effectiveness is off the mark, as can be seen by an examination of A.A.'s 24-page body of data and commentary concerning its five triennial surveys from 1977 through 1989. This document is important because it reveals information about: 1) the extent to which A.A. actually retains members over a one-year period; and 2) because it provides a clear indication of the effectiveness of A.A., determined on the basis of periods of sobriety over a period of one year.

The first reference to this now famous "Comments" document (bearing A.A.'s identification number 5M/12-90/TC) was made by researcher/author Charles Bufe in *Alcoholics Anonymous: Cult or Cure?*[5] It is the most revealing and damaging report on A.A. ever uncovered. Significantly, this document is not listed in A.A.'s "Conference Approved Literature." For public consumption, A.A. lists only a single-page 15¢ summary, Brochure P-48, "A.A. Membership Survey," a simple, sanguine exposition of no real value.[6] The "Comments" document, on the other hand—produced for *internal* purposes—reveals significant information. For example:

There are limitations to the data of the surveys. Perhaps most tantaliz-
ing [an interesting word choice] is that the rate at which members
abandon active participation in A.A. can be estimated, but there isn't
a clue as to the causes.[7]

The "Comments" document mentions (three times) that *about
50% of all those who try A.A. leave within 90 days* (!) and that this fact
qualifies as one of "... certain findings" which, it observes, "seem to
call for concern on the part of the Fellowship." Without the infusion
of members from treatment centers and courts (an approximate
45%-plus of membership), A.A.'s guarded "concern" might well have
been expressed in terms of full-blown panic.

In "Comments on A.A.'s Triennial Surveys," the A.A. personnel,
who both generated and interpreted its data, presented even more
shocking information, especially that revealed in Figure C-1, page 12
of that document. But it was difficult to interpret the graph provided. Four qualified people in the field of addictions took a look
at it and came up with observations and possible interpretations, but
no firm answers. Then came George Fish, author and mathe-
matician, who examined the statistics provided by A.A. and the
commentary and interpretation which accompanied them. Fish
studied Figure C-1 (reproduced on page 66) and explained it as
follows. (Fish's conclusions, incidentally, concur with the abbreviated
analysis made by Bufe in *Alcoholics Anonymous: Cult or Cure?*)

On the top left of the graph, 22% and 17% represent the high
and low percent of any number of people who entered A.A. on, say,
January 1 of any year between and including 1977 through 1989,
and who still remained in A.A. after 30 days. (The average is shown
as 19% on the table). To simplify that a little, let's pick a number,
say 100, representing the number of people entering A.A. on the
first day of January of any of the 15 years covered by the survey.
After the first month, Fish explains, 81 of the original 100 have left,
and 19 (19%, the average of the five surveys) remain. At the end of
the first 90 days, 90 of the original 100 have left, and 10% (10
persons) remain. *And at end of any given year (January 1 through
December 31) 95 of the original 100 have left A.A.* Therefore, as A.A.
claims, A.A. works; that is, it retains—and thus presumably fills the
needs of—five of every 100 persons who enter it.[8]

Fish comments: "The A.A. pictured in 'Comments' is a picture of
an A.A. in crisis ..." He also expresses surprise at the age brackets
revealed in the "Comments" document: "Three percent of the
membership is under 21; 56% is between 31 and 50; and 23% of the

Figure C-1 from "Comments on A.A.'s Triennial Surveys":

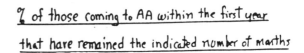

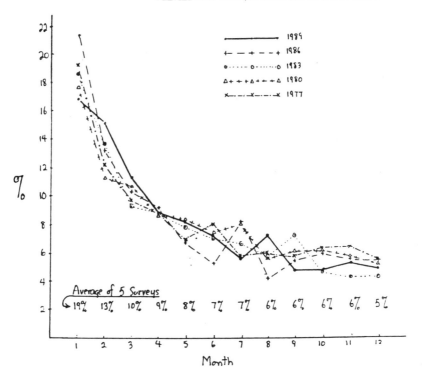

membership is over 50."[9] (Therefore, 79% of the membership is 31 or older). He further observes that 60% of A.A. members were getting outside professional help during their sojourn in A.A., which indicates that credit for recovery by those successful in A.A. must be shared to a large extent with therapists or agencies outside of A.A. This fact does not detract from the merits of A.A., but reflects well on those of its members who recognize that there may be problems in their lives that are reflected in drinking behaviors and causally related to them.

George Fish characterizes the "Comments" document as *disingenuous*; that is, it lacks candor but gives the appearance of simple frankness. He concludes his written analysis with, "As can be seen from this, the picture of A.A. so portrayed is manifestly different from the one it presents to the public."[10]

In general, given A.A.'s near-monopoly of more than 58 years, together with public, private, and institutional support, it would seem that A.A.'s greatest accomplishment lies in the field of public relations rather than in its usefulness to those who suffer drinking-related problems. Nevertheless, A.A. claims that it is successful, that it "works." It does—somewhat, as detailed above.

A.A.'s view of "success," however, needs clarification. Its definition of that highly subjective term is a negative-positive one. It couples non-drinking over some period to a "spiritual awakening." That definition is arbitrary, subjective, and non-quantifiable. What statistician would not burst into laughter if asked to produce a body of information that is methodologically sound, valid, verifiable, and based on data generated and interpreted by an organization concerned with a population of non-drinking and spiritually enlightened "alcoholics." Add A.A.'s definition of an alcoholic as "anyone who wants to quit drinking" (which is like defining transportation as anything with wheels) and you could drive a good statistician to drink.

But what is generally deemed "successful" in the addictions field? There is no agreement on the subject. Length of sobriety—that is, *not* being drunk or high—is a negative and artificial gauge of success, although the cessation of alcohol or drug intake usually produces social, occupational, and health-related rewards. More reliable measures of "success" can and must be devised.[11]

The ineffectiveness of A.A. goes far beyond the "Comments" document or interpretive commentary. And issues of policy and procedure don't cover it either; the root cause of A.A's problems lies in its myopic views and in what may be termed a "meanness of spirit." A.A. may, in truth, even be guilty of a kind of inadvertent homicide, practiced in the name of its conviction that it is *the way*—the one and only way—whereby an alcoholic can achieve sobriety and the good life.[12] That statement is less than a formal charge, but more than a literary device. Please walk for a moment in the shoes of those who entered, then exited, the "revolving doors"[13] of A.A.

Most of them came freely and heroically to face *the* problem at last. They were welcomed warmly and accepted without judgment, and, for a while, were at peace. But soon came a disturbing awareness of an incompatibility between many of their convictions, values, and beliefs, and the tenets of the A.A. program. In moments of dis-

such as

content they wondered aloud and were told "Some people are too smart to make it in A.A.," or "Take the cotton out of your ears and put it in your mouth," or "Let go and let God." Translation: Don't think, believe, and let God and A.A. do it for you. But no one said, "Hey, if our program doesn't fit your needs, let me tell you about some others that might. There *are* eight others, you know." They said, instead, "Keep coming back."

A.A. knows that other self-help support programs exist, but refuses to acknowledge them even when its members ask about alternatives. A.A.'s unwavering response to such queries is to advise questioners to read the Big Book, go to meetings, and "keep coming back." That's not an answer: it's a refusal to answer. A.A. purports to cooperate but not affiliate, and does neither. To pretend ignorance of other programs in the face of a direct question, or to refuse to impart known information, is not only dishonest but often damaging to thousands of people in need. Ignorance of alternative programs is no excuse; only a recent arrival from the planet Zenobica could be ignorant of the fact that there are many programs now available to alcoholics.

In defending its position, A.A. usually cites its sixth and, more often, its tenth Traditions:

Sixth Tradition: An A.A. group ought never endorse, finance or lend the A.A. name to any related facility or outside enterprise, lest problems of money, property and prestige divert us from our primary purpose.

Tenth Tradition: Alcoholics Anonymous has no opinion on outside issues; hence the A.A. name ought never be drawn into public controversy.

When the 12 Traditions were published in April 1946, A.A. had no competition, and it was assumed that its fellowship could and would fulfill the needs of all who approached it. That assumption is no longer valid—if indeed, it ever was. Over the years, hundreds of thousands of heavy drinkers have found A.A. unsuited to their needs and alien to their values. They sought other avenues of recovery, and pioneers such as Jack Trimpey of Rational Recovery and Jean Kirkpatrick of Women For Sobriety established national organizations (see Chapter 8) to meet those needs. These organizations and six others are widely established throughout the United States and in several other countries.[14] Their books are in most public libraries, and hundreds of articles have appeared about them in newspapers and magazines across the country (*The New York Times, The Washington Post, Newsweek, Reason, and many others*).

Yet, to those who ask and are in need, A.A. remains inflexible, mute, and uncooperative, like the lonely king in *The Little Prince* who still "ruled" a world of his own making, oblivious to everything but his own kingdom. The A.A. "king"—its General Service Board— continues to maintain a position that reflects a serious lack of understanding and compassion for those who have tried its program, found it unsuitable to their needs, and are in search of an alternative. As a former victim of this policy, I remain affronted by it in the name of millions harmed by it. That's a polite way of saying that I'm damned well ticked off about it. A.A. is acting in a seriously unethical manner by withholding *vital—as in life and death—* information. The prevailing A.A. policy displays a lack of compassion, honesty, courtesy, and simple decency.

As a result of this rigid policy, countless individuals have left A.A. They left in despair and desperation, weary and worried, wondering what to do next, having played and lost at what they thought was the only game in town. They staggered away toward an empty life, the loneliness of a crowded tavern, a lost job, a failed marriage, an institution, and—sometimes—a cemetery. Their explanations? "The program just didn't work for me," or "I couldn't handle all that God-stuff." And often they protested, "Hell, I'm not *powerless*, and I'm certainly not *diseased!*, and I'm not about to go to meetings for the rest of my life. I just drink too much."

Those are *objections*, not excuses—words of frustration, not of criticism. It's baffling; A.A. is not, for the most part, filled with mean and mindless people, so why this tone of self-righteous fundamentalism, this "My way or the highway" position? Part of the answer lies in A.A.'s hallowed Traditions, rudders that guided A.A. during its early years. But in time those rudders have become anchors. And now they are virtual laws, helpful to some but hurtful to many.

Another part of the answer lies in the abandonment of Bill Wilson's position on alternative therapies by A.A.'s GSO and Board. It was Wilson who said, "Upon therapy for the alcoholic himself, we surely have no monopoly."[15] He would have agreed with a recent statement by Dr. Robert Sparks, president emeritus and senior consultant to the W.K. Kellogg Foundation. The Institute of Medicine of the National Academy of Sciences appointed Sparks to lead a special investigative group devoted to the study of alcohol treatment problems. Speaking for that committee, Sparks said, ". . . no single approach works for everybody . . . The challenge is to match the individuals with the right programs." He praised A.A., then added, "Yet, A.A. is not for everyone." Bill Wilson would have approved; A.A.'s General Service Board would not. The membership seems ambivalent; at meetings one hears "We're not for everybody" *and* "It's our way or the highway."

A.A.'s uncompromising position can be explained in yet another way: change is painful, but when an idea becomes fixed and institutionalized, change becomes not just painful but excruciating, and is often postponed indefinitely. Hence, no change. In increasing numbers, legions of the New Guard look upon A.A. of today with an impatience tinged with anger, tempered by sadness. They regard it as a product of the 1930s, encapsulated in a cocoon, time-warped into a new world, impervious to substantive change, even resistant to survival-sustaining adaptation. A.A., the courageous pioneer of the thirties, became a quaint anachronism by the 1960s and is a veritable antique in the 1990s. It still works, as a Model A Ford "works," but not very well on an eight-lane super highway.

That may help to explain the provincialism of many of A.A.'s adherents, but is of no help to those thousands of disheartened and disillusioned people who, when they departed A.A., resigned themselves to despair, and were labeled failures. Failures? *No. Absolutely not!* They had not failed A.A.—A.A. had failed them. They could not bend far enough, and A.A. would not bend at all. They had come, seen, and left unconquered, but many were bruised and others broken by a rigidity intended as a kindness. A.A. has filled a small niche, and left a large void.

That void is now being filled by eight self-help programs for those with problems associated with drinking, drugging, or both. Three of these groups are A.A.-type quasi-clones (Calix, JACS, and AV), one of them (SOS) defies classification, and four of them are true independents which are basically antithetical to A.A., and divergent from it in both theory and practice.[16] All of them are designed to fill major areas of need such as those of atheists, casual Christians, Jews, women, non-theists, nominal Catholics, humanists, et al. Three of them have emerged as major players: Rational Recovery Systems, Women for Sobriety, and Secular Organizations for Sobriety. They, and the others, exist for the same reason that shoes are made in different sizes.

(An aside: It is unfortunate that some people will label this analysis ["Utilize, don't analyze!"] with that quaint and pejorative term, "A.A.-bashing." That's ridiculous. Logicians abhor the use of terms such as "A.A.-bashing" because they embody a fallacy known as "begging the point," in this case, the assumption that criticism of A.A., however presented, is unjust and invalid. The suggestion that A.A. is less than perfect is often perceived as a vicious attack, but it is known that even sacred cows are sometimes spotted. May I also remind my high strung and hypersensitive critics that the Bible, the United States Constitution, and Webster's Dictionary have been criticized, corrected, updated, amended, and revised.)

Conclusion: All major changes (the Protestant Reformation and the American Revolution, for example) involve reaction to and criticism of that which has gone before them. The status quo always contains the seeds of its own transformation. The problems in today's addictions field may be compared to the unstable condition of stacks of paper, clothing, and oil-soaked rags stored in an unventilated closet. In time, they will generate heat, then smolder, then smoke, then burn—and the question is not *if* but *when*. The "when," I think, is now.

In the dimly lit corridors of the addictions field there is evidence of smolder and smoke, and a little fire too—one that will soon become a conflagration. We are not on the brink of a revolution in the addictions field; it has already begun, and the same forces that produced it now accelerate it. The change may manifest itself as an accelerated evolution or sudden revolution, but nothing can stop it. The forces behind that change are the subject of the next chapter.

---

1. The nature of those studies was such that it's debatable whether the findings could be applied to A.A. in general. See Ragge in bibliography for further details.

2. Page 18.

3. Bufe, pp. 106-108.

4. About 75,000 to 85,000 mandates each year. Exact figures have not been published by either A.A. or the courts, and may, in fact, be unknown to both. The number, however, is substantial.

5. Bufe, op. cit., pp. 106, 107, 113.

6. The single-page brochure, titled "Alcoholics Anonymous 1989 Membership Survey" [Identification No. 150N-1\91 (K) P-48; its cost is 15 cents] and the "Comments" document may be obtained from A.A. World Services, Box 459, Grand Central Station, New York, NY 10163. The 24-page "Comments" document, however, is not listed in A.A.'s Approved Literature list, and is not intended for public distribution. I asked for it, enclosed $2, and with time and persistence managed to get a copy from the New York office.

7. Op. cit., p. 4.

8. No one can prove that A.A. does *not* work, since the terminology is so vague as to be "unfalsifiable." We can only observe the extent to which it *does* "work" that is, the extent of its effectiveness.

9. Update, and the 1992 A.A. survey: Volume 39, No. 4, of *Box 459*, August-September, 1993 (A GSO publication), touched briefly on the 1992 survey. The average A.A. member is now 42 years of age (up one year from 1989); treatment facility referrals are down from 30% in 1989 to 27% in 1992; Box 459 comments that 8% of its membership (about 80,000 members) were *influenced* (emphasis added) by the courts. (*Influence* is a preposterous word choice. In the context of the courts, to "influence" means to mandate, to order—or go to jail. A.A. tends to sugar coat mud pies by manipulating the language.) Again, 7% of the membership was "influenced" by doctors, and "74% of respondents report that their doctors know they are in A.A." Meaningless tripe; it says nothing but insinuates much. The 1992 format differs in some significant aspects from that used in 1989; however, a comparison of the two documents is quite revealing, especially as it reveals actual or possible trends. At the time of this writing only limited information is available from A.A. concerning the results of its 1992 survey.

10. From two personal letters dated February 23, and March 16, 1993.

11. The essence of that measure may be the extent to which a person can function without danger to her or himself or to the broader society. Such a person would be one who is doing more than accommodating to circumstance or operating on the basis of threats and social sanctions; it would be a person who has had a change of values—measured against a former set of values—that produces a problem-less lifestyle. The Life Process Program of Peele, Brodsky, and Arnold would serve to effect this transformation (especially in the area of social skills) and the behaviors that would quite naturally flow from it.

12. A typical member of A.A. will believe this, but deny it. The best possible source of information on this matter comes from those who have left A.A., not those who have chosen to remain in it. This suggests a major area of research which, for the most part, has been neglected.

13. Significantly, a term commonly used in A.A.

14. With the advent of Moderation Management, growing at an amazing rate, there will soon be *seven* others.

15. Also, again in the Big Book, "By no means do we offer it [the book and its program] as the last word on this subject . . ."

16. There is a much-overlooked reason that so many people leave A.A. and join other self-help support programs. It is not just a matter of accepting or rejecting the spiritual and religious components of A.A., but involves a much broader issue. It concerns the rejection of an entire system of thought, including the disease notion, the declaration of personal *incapacity* (powerlessness), the insistence on belief rather than reason, the imposed identification as a permanent "alcoholic," and the injunction that it is necessary to attend meetings for life in order to maintain sobriety. Thus, the entire philosophy *and* program of A.A. is rejected.

7

The Forces & Direction
of Change

"The old order changeth, yielding to new."
— Alfred Lord Tennyson

We have the power to change ourselves and, when we see fit, to change our society. This chapter centers on the forces of change that are currently affecting the field of addictions and that will shape its future. (The next chapter will present evidence of change in a specific area—self-help support programs for alcoholics and other addicts.)

What's happening? And why? What are the forces of change in the addictions field, and how did they originate? These forces are producing shifts in the way we think about, and in what we do about, addiction problems in general and alcoholism in particular. They can be understood as *reactions* to the status quo, and they are positive and constructive in design and intent.

Those who refuse to recognize and adapt to changing conditions will court continued problems; but there is still time for them to gracefully change—and thus survive. When things don't work—whether those "things" are people, presidents, institutions, governments, or addiction care systems—they change to survive or, failing that, they are changed (or discarded) by external forces. I have used the word *revolution* to describe the nature and number of changes occurring in the addictions field, but so far the revolution is slow paced and resisted at every turn. It may be more accurately characterized as an accelerated evolution. It's almost certain that the ongoing changes will bring many benefits, especially economic and therapeutic. For example, professional care may soon become available and affordable not just for those who are affluent or insured, but for all who need it. Even now, persons addicted to alcohol or illegal drugs have a wide range of choices in self-help support groups, but these choices are not yet widely available on the professional and institutional level.

The forces of change listed below will affect you personally, regardless of your station in life and regardless of whether you need care or provide it. These forces may be classified as academic, cultural, economic, legal, and professional.

Academic: We in the United States are an anti-intellectual lot; everybody would like to have a Ph.D., but we tend to scoff at those who have them. We call them "eggheads" and "intellectuals." We perceive academics, professors, and researchers in stereotypical images—out of touch, forgetful, and impractical; we say that Einstein couldn't balance his checkbook (but he could and did). We know that those in academia are often smarter, and usually better educated, than the rest of us, and we also know that some of them regularly provide us with new and important observations and information. The best among them wonder about things that we take for granted, assume nothing, and are curious about everything. They debunk myths and misconceptions, and help us plan a better tomorrow.

In the addictions field, neither the popularity of A.A. nor the pontifications of the AMA faze academic researchers. They realize that the traditional approach to solving problems related to addictions can be valid and effective, invalid and ineffective, or somewhere in between. Researchers tend to be courageous; they take risks in revealing the truth. But many people—accustomed to the old ways—resist their findings. Why? Because truth brings change, and change is always difficult and sometimes costly—though never as costly as error.

A few scholars in the addictions field sized up the situation quite early, among them Arthur Cain, Albert Ellis, Jeffrey Brandsma, Eric Berne, Bill Miller, Claude Steiner, Stanton Peele, and, of course, the irrepressible and brilliant maverick, Thomas Szasz.[1] Their numbers grew geometrically in the late 1970s and exponentially in the 1980s. They, and those now using the information they provided, are restructuring the addictions field.

The most important point of agreement among researchers over the past 20 years is the understanding that the accepted ways of managing addiction problems are seriously flawed and must be changed—the old ways simply haven't worked. The jury is in; it has presented us with a verdict based on a vast amount of research that not merely suggests, but clearly indicates, that the traditional system has not done its job. The conclusion is inescapable: it's time to try something else.

Cultural: Hemingway said it in *The Moon is Down*, a story of the Nazi occupation of a little town in Norway during World War II: "The people *know*," he said, "they always know." The people of the United States know that the addiction-care system, non-professional and professional, has not lived up to their expectations. That's why we have begun to call our institutions to account, and that's why the self-help movement is so strong.

I'm convinced that the people know that there's something fundamentally wrong in the addictions field. They've had a lot of frustrating first-hand experience with the established way of doing things; and while most of them have probably never heard of Peele, Ellis, Szasz, Kirkpatrick, Fingarette, and Trimpey, they would likely agree with their views.

Economic: In the past, the insurance industry naively followed directives issued by the NCADD, the AMA, the AHA (American Hospital Association), and other lobbyists. No longer. More recently it has been pulling back on its coverage of institutional "treatment" for heavy drinking and is aggressively insisting that treatment services be provided on an affordable outpatient basis.

Insurance executives discovered—about 20 years after the fact—that institutional treatment is no more effective than out-patient treatment. Then they discovered the multitude of institutional repeaters, the recidivists, and did a little belated homework: they discovered that *traditional* "treatment," whether inpatient or out-patient, is generally ineffective.[2] Insurance company actuaries, accountants, and executives, have learned to cast a wary eye on the self-generated success figures published by the marketing departments of hospitals and private treatment chains.

Then they were confronted with the AIDS crisis, and with it insurance claims that soaked up premium dollars as dry earth absorbs a summer rain. As potential investment dollars were diverted, insurance executives began to look for ways to save money. They had been looking at the cost of institutional addiction services, and had begun to question the enthusiastic reports of success claimed by providers. Now they have begun to act; for example, many of them have begun to limit coverage. The magic number 28, as in the familiar 28-day hospital stay (at which point insurance runs out), has lost its magic. Many insurance executives now think that 14 is a better number. Some of them think that zero is an even better number.

Predictably, someone would put all the pieces together, think it through, and write about it. Enter George Will, a brilliant and ultra-conservative journalist (with whom I seldom agree). In August 1988, Will wrote an article about the Circle K Corporation, a convenience store chain. He reported that Circle K was denying health insurance benefits to those of its employees who required medical care because of ailments resulting from "personal lifestyle decisions" such as self-inflicted wounds, jumping off mountains in hang gliders, smoking, playing Russian roulette, and yes—alcohol and drug abuse. Have fun, they said, but don't expect the rest of us to bear the financial burden of your risk-filled behavior.

Other corporations have begun to catch on. They know that heavy drinking is not a disease and they have begun to insist that responsibility for "volitional behavior" be placed back where it belongs—on the individual. The best Employee Assistance Programs (EAPs) have become aware of changes in the addictions field and have begun to advise management that alcohol and drug treatment programs that teach the "powerless" notion to employees do little to *empower* them. (See segment on EAP Programs in Chapter 13.) This new wave of corporate thought has no doubt been prompted in large part by economic considerations, but it also happens to dovetail with the conclusions of modern researchers.

The new corporate policies will probably be carried to extremes before those carrying them out realize that many problems associated with heavy drinking are far more complex than the simple notion implicit in the terms "personal responsibility" and "volitional behavior." But the hard-line position taken by Circle K and others has substantial merit and presages things to come.

The usually forward-looking insurance industry has not yet taken the next logical steps: 1) the establishment of national criteria of success against which treatment centers and hospitals must show results; 2) the objective determination of success rates by an agency independent of both the treatment and insurance industries, and mutually contracted by both; 3) the elimination of medical services from 90% of recovery processes; and 4) the honoring of insurance claims from persons (therapists or others) that produce results based on reasonable standards of performance. (And there, insurance people, is a 4-step program which will work, cost less, and enable you to put your premium dollars to work in profit-making investments.)

Staying with the economic forces of change a moment more, it is now known that the Reagan/Bush/Bennett "Drug War" was, and still is, a disaster. When such programs are finally dumped (which seems to be happening now), monies will be available for more productive efforts, such as education, prevention, and low-cost recovery programs. The time is right. We now have a relatively enlightened federal administration, and with the Clinton/Gore team at the helm it is probable that intelligent and practical programs will soon be instituted. The Lee Iacoccas of industry know what's happening, and the insurance companies have finally figured it out. Now, one would hope, state and federal governments will understand (the Veterans Administration already does) and, of course, the people knew it all along. Nothing can withstand the effects of the cumulative pressures mentioned. The entire addictions field will, in the face of these combined forces, either change or be changed. The results will be the same.

Industry will assume a major role in effecting these changes because it is has a heavy financial stake in this issue. As our industrial base shrinks, CEOs (Chief Executive Officers) and managers of EAP programs continue to seek ways to save money; they must do so in order to compete in the world market. They always look at human services first when the financial ax falls, and they've seen a red flag—recidivism. They've become painfully aware that too many employees enter treatment programs only to come out and drink again. Corporate America doesn't like to pour money down the drain once, much less two or three times, and it is finally putting on the pressure. That pressure will produce greater effectiveness by forcing EAPs and treatment centers to revamp their addiction programs so as to produce results rather than promises. Most of them still cling to the 12-step approach (which simply hasn't worked), but look for the more enlightened EAPs to soon reach out to all of the other self-help support programs to solicit their help in solving employee drinking and drugging problems.

Legal: The courts are in a terrible bind. Persons convicted of alcohol-related offenses, especially driving under the influence, are routinely: a) sent to jail; b) mandated to A.A. or Narcotics Anonymous (NA); c) forced into "driver education" programs; or d) forced to seek A.A.-oriented institutional or professional help.

The courts are in a bind because they know the prevailing system has not produced the desired results, but feel that they have few choices available to them. Jails and prisons are not the answer because they don't work and never have. (They often convert amateur offenders into skilled criminals.) Even if the penal system did work, we couldn't afford to build and maintain enough facilities to contain those convicted of alcohol-related offenses. So what happens? A vast number of defendants are assigned, that is, ordered, to attend A.A and N.A.

A.A. calls it "dumping," and doesn't like it, but does nothing about it. Many A.A. members feel that court-mandated persons are disruptive and just don't belong in a fellowship designed as an all-volunteer program. Some A.A. secretaries refuse to sign attendance slips provided to clients by probation officers. And there's a saying, "You can take a horse to water, but you can't make him drink." People forced into A.A. seldom work the program; they go through the motions in a perfunctory and resentful way. They play the game until it's over. Much the same can be said for mandated drivers education programs because, although such programs are educational in part, they also involve a hefty dose of A.A. indoctrination.

I audited two of them, and have talked with dozens of people who have endured them. Those assigned to such programs—even first offenders—are told that they are alcoholics. They deeply resent it, and I don't blame them. The vast majority of those forced to attend such programs are not alcoholics by any reasonable definition of the word. They just got caught. If everyone who ever drove drunk were in a drivers education program or in jail on any given day, there wouldn't be enough people left on the outside to teach them or to guard them.

Treatment centers and hospitals (Institutional A.A.) are more receptive to court assignments. They get paid, either by insurance companies or by taxpayers.

But what if court-mandated attendance is proven unconstitutional on the grounds that A.A. is a religiously oriented organization? As we know, the first Amendment to the U.S. Constitution guarantees freedom of religious choice. Cathy Downs, a third-year law student at Indiana University/Purdue University at Indianapolis, did a research project on the issue of constitutionality of court mandates to A.A. In her thesis, Downs highlights the law as a force for change, and suggests that it holds enormous implications for the future of the treatment industry. She writes:

The Supreme Court has never addressed the issue of court-ordered A.A. attendance directly. [However] five States have addressed this issue or similar issues . . . ranging from forced A.A. attendance in prison to forced A.A. attendance for veterans to receive their government benefits. Most all of these cases have found mandatory A.A. attendance unconstitutional on First Amendment grounds.[3] [The exception: *Stafford v. Harrison.*[4]]

Now the American Civil Liberties Union (ACLU), through its affiliate in Des Moines, Iowa, is co-plaintiff in a lawsuit charging that the TOW (The Other Way) program of the Clarinda Correctional Facility is religiously (A.A.) based. The suit is based on alleged violations of the First, Fifth, and Fourteenth Amendments.[5] It is typical of a number of suits being filed, and I have no doubt that the customary court practice of assigning defendants to A.A.'s 12-step program will be declared unconstitutional in over half the states within the next five to ten years.

In March 1991, Andrew Meacham, Associate Editor for the *U.S. Journal of Drug and Alcohol Dependence,* listed four cases in which defendants assigned by the courts to A.A. challenged the system and won.[6] Another case is pending in Oregon, where a coalition of attorneys headed by John Meyer, Esq. is devoted to the defense of those assigned by courts to A.A. Meacham quoted Ellen Luff of the ACLU who said that nearly all criminal defendants who fight A.A. attendance on religious grounds win, and that similar lawsuits don't even have to go to trial because "the case that it [A.A.] is a religion is so strong."

Concerning the claim that A.A. is a spiritual rather than a religious program, Wisconsin's District Judge John Shabaz said, "The distinction between religion and spirituality is meaningless and serves merely to confuse the issue." The courts are being challenged now and will be, to a far greater extent, in the near future. (Look for activity in Oregon, California, Iowa, then your state, or mine.)

And then what? A snowball effect. Multiple legal challenges will generate a firestorm of activity. The courts will find themselves out of the religion business and will be forced to avail themselves of other resources, such as the eight other self-help programs for heavy drinkers (the subject of the next chapter). A.A. will remain as one of many alternatives, but will no longer be dominant.

It gets even better—or worse—depending on your view. With greater acceptance and exposure, those "other" eight self-help support programs will gain members as A.A. loses them. The availability of the additional programs will be a blessing for judges, probation officers, and defendants. The courts will not only welcome help from such programs, but will encourage them to establish additional chapters. It's a win/win situation.

Probation officers will play a major role in this scenario. They will review each program with each defendant who, in turn, will choose a program compatible with his or her needs and values. The defendant's selection will be subject to the approval of the probation officer, and the defendant will be required to submit proof of attendance at meetings, as is often done now in the case of A.A., N.A., and RR. With the advent of new legislation, defendants assigned to drivers ed. courses will learn about safe driving and responsible attitudes, but will not be labeled "alcoholics" or subjected to religious training or traditional notions about addiction. Then treatment centers and hospitals will go into shock; if they want to get paid, they will be forced to offer the two-track system, that is, the traditional 12-step program *and* (a) non-religious program(s).

There is a high probability of positive results from such an arrangement for three reasons: 1) the effectiveness of A.A. has been shown to be unacceptably low; 2) people work best when options are available to them; and 3) no one self-help support program is, or can be, acceptable to everyone in need of help. Good things are already happening; as an RR coordinator, I have signed many attendance slips, as have dozens of RR coordinators throughout the United States.

Professional: Mental health practitioners, social workers, educators, and private therapists constitute the last of the forces of change. (The 20-member Board of Directors of Rational Recovery Systems is largely composed of such professionals.) These people get much of the real work done, and they know what works and what doesn't. They are educated, conscientious, observant, and hard to deceive. They see the graduates of traditional programs come back again and again, sometimes forced back—two, three, and more times—into the same program that didn't work the first time.

The Veterans Administration is worthy of special mention because of its advanced professionalism in the addictions field. At six of its hospitals, two programs are offered, the traditional 12-step *and* the nontraditional cognitive/behavioral programs. (*Not* in combination, since the two programs are not compatible.) The V.A. is light years ahead of commercial institutions that offer only the traditional 12-

step program, and force—or attempt to force—everyone into the same mold.[7] The enlightened V.A. knows how to save both lives and money. The fact that it is not concerned with the collection of insurance dollars may have something to do with it.

Conclusion: In *The Third Wave,* Alvin Toffler said that the people started to take charge of their lives back in the late 1950s. Then came the glorious decade of the sixties, which had little to do with "flower-children" and hippies with long hair, and much to do with basic change. The 1960s gave birth to a powerful and visible surge of change that eventually produced the accelerated evolution of the 1990s—a revolution in thought, in the dissemination of information, in government, in industry, in institutional management, and in the understanding and handling of substance abuse problems. The next chapter deals with the striking effects of those changes.

---

1. I am convinced that no one in the addictions field may consider his or her education complete without having read Szasz's *Ceremonial Chemistry,* published in 1985 by Learning Publications, Inc.

2. Chapter 9 (Recovery Management) deals in detail with the effectiveness of institutional treatment.

3. Downs, C. (1993). "Court Ordered Attendance: Do Indiana Courts Violate the Establishment Clause?" Unpublished thesis (23-page document, replete with 106 references), Indiana University Purdue University at Indianapolis.

4. *Stafford v. Harrison.* 766 F. Supp. 1014 and 1016 (1991). Appendix II, "Spiritual Experience" (p.569), from A.A.'s Big Book was quoted and, in this instance, the defendant lost the case. Downs comments that other passages in the Big Book are clearly religious, and that A.A. involves many religious activities. She adds that "school prayer is not a religion, but is a religious activity, and the Supreme Court has found this activity unconstitutional." Her shift from the usual approach of attempting to define A.A. as a religion, to an organization that promotes religious activity, is a major development in this area of heated controversy.

5. Article by Jonathan Anderson in "Affiliate Notes," *Civil Liberties* (national ACLU newsletter), Winter, 1992-1993, No. 378. Text of article in Appendix.

6. U.S. District Court in Alaska, 1989; Circuit Court of Queen Anne's County, Maryland, 1989; U.S. District Court in Colorado, 1985; and U.S. District Court in Wisconsin, 1985.

7. The V.A., as of 1992, is conducting a longitudinal five-year study of treatment modality outcomes, comparing the effectiveness of traditional and nontraditional approaches. The study is, in general, comparable to those conducted (1991-1992) by New York and Harvard Universities assessing Rational Recovery's performance vis à vis that of the traditional 12-step program.

8

The Independent Self-Help Programs

"There is no need to feel helpless or get paralyzed by hopelessness. We have the power to make changes if we can join together and raise our voices in unison."
— Ken Keyes, Jr.

In *Megatrends*, by John Naisbitt, one of the world's premier futurists, we discover the roots of the self-help movement.[1] In the introduction to his book, Naisbitt describes each of his ten chapters in capsule form. *Four* of these descriptions, numbered below, pertain directly to the self-help movement in America. Naisbitt comments:

(4) In cities and states, in small organizations and subdivisions, we have rediscovered the ability to act innovatively and to achieve results–*from the bottom up*. (Emphasis added.)
(6) We are shifting from institutional help to more self-reliance in all aspects of our lives.
(8) We are giving up our dependence on hierarchial structures in favor of informal networks.
(10) From a narrow either/or society with a limited range of personal choices, we are exploding into a free-wheeling multiple-option society.

These are revealing observations, with which virtually all futurists agree. Naisbitt continues:

During the 1970s, Americans began to disengage from the institutions that had disillusioned them and to relearn the ability to take action on their own. In a sense, we have come full circle. We are reclaiming America's traditional sense of self-reliance after four decades of trusting in institutional help.

Starting with the Great Depression of the 1930s, we allowed institutions to manage our lives, our health, our education, our finances, and our legal problems. Institutions even provided us with identities. I overheard the following exchange at a computer show: "Who are you?" asked a visitor. A company representative responded, "I'm an IBM programmer."

Eventually, our irresponsibility came back to haunt us. The institutions met some of our needs, often to *their* advantage. Giant bureaucracies, especially those concerned with services, became insensitive to individual needs and ceased to function acceptably. Bluntly, they just didn't get the job done. Institutional services became not only ineffective, but financially prohibitive for many. For example, who could afford a psychiatrist at $100 an hour—almost $2 a *minute*—whatever the need? The medical establishment is a good example of an institution that has mismanaged its mission.[2] The medical industry is in a condition approaching chaos, and the American people are again taking charge of their own lives. They have been virtually forced to do so.[3]

The forces of change outlined in the previous chapter have already produced major changes in the addictions field. The mere *existence* of the "independents," as they have come to be known, represents a significant development in the addictions field. The list below was generated and first published by Rational Recovery Systems Network, the only self-help support organization to have published such a list. (In the *Journal of Rational Recovery*, November/ December, 1990; Vol. 3, Issue 2, pp. 17–18.)

Self-Help Programs for Heavy Drinkers

AA—[1935] Alcoholics Anonymous. Box 459, Grand Central Station, New York, NY 10163. Phone: 212-870-3400. Fax: 212-870-3003. (Traditional)

AV—[1983] Alcoholics Victorious (The Institute for Christian Living.) Westview Business Center, 620 Mendelssohn Avenue, Suite 105, Golden Valley, MN 55427-4351. Phone: 612-593-1791. [A service of Fairview Medical Center.] (Traditional)

CALIX—[1947], The Society. 7601 Wayzata Blvd., Minneapolis, MN 55426. Phone: 612-546-6209. Catholic orientation. (Traditional)

JACS—[1980] Jewish Alcoholics, Chemically Dependent Persons and Significant Others Foundation. 197 E. Broadway, Room M-7, New York, NY 10002. Phone: 212-473-4747. (Traditional)

MFS—[1988] Men for Sobriety. Box 618, Quakertown, PA 18951. Phone: 215-536-8026 and 1-800-333-1606. (Nontraditional)

MM—[1993] Moderation Management. 3230 Alpine, Ann Arbor, MI 48101-1766. Phone: 313-677-0243. (Nontraditional)

RRS—[1986] Rational Recovery Systems. Box 800, Lotus CA, 95651-0080. Phone: 916-621-4374. Voice/Fax: 916-621-2667. (Nontraditional)

SOS—[1985] Secular Organizations for Sobriety. P.O. Box 5, Buffalo, NY. 14215-0050. Phone: 716-834-2922. FAX: 716-834-0841. (Traditional/Nontraditional Hybrid)

WFS—[1975] Women for Sobriety. Box 618, Quakertown, PA 18951. Phone: 215-536-8026, and 1-800-333-1605. (Nontraditional)
(WFS and MFS share administrative facilities)

The dates of origin given above show that in the 39 years between 1935 and 1974 only two self-help groups took form, while in the 18-year span between 1975 and 1993 *seven* additional groups formed—an average of more than one every three years. Naisbitt reminds us in *Megatrends* that the *rate* of change, in this case, the rate at which new self-help support groups have formed, has implications apart from, and sometimes more important than, the nature of the changes that such groups incorporate.

Just as tensions and stresses in the crust of the earth produce yawning cracks on its surface, so have the tensions and stresses between the traditional addiction system and the emerging non-traditional systems produced a visible and widening crack in the addictions-treatment field.

Eight cracks, to be accurate—the eight independents, those "other" (than A.A.) self-help support organizations that have erupted like molten lava from a slumbering volcano. They have formed streams of influence, each finding its own way down the mountain, not as yet converging with the others. What would happen, and *could* happen, if the four nontraditional organizations (and possibly SOS) formed a coalition and worked together? The unstoppable force—new thinking—would collide with the immovable object—traditionalism—and the immovable object would move.

The independents may be understood as reactions to the status quo. That's how Glasser's Reality Therapy, Ellis's Rational Emotive Therapy, and Berne's Transactional Analysis came into being—as reactions against Freudian psychoanalytic constructs. Historically, virtually all actions begin as reactions, either to widespread injustice or to the stultifying inadequacies of the status quo. Essentially, progress is a matter of displacement rather than destruction; but as Picasso said, "Every act of creation is first of all an act of [partial or total] destruction." As the independents emerge, A.A. remains oblivious to the changing world around it. It will soon pay a heavy price for its ostrich-like posture.

Albert Ellis and Emmett Velten make an interesting comment about the development of the new self-help groups on page 80 of *When AA Doesn't Work for You*:

> Secular Organizations for Sobriety, Women For Sobriety, Men For Sobriety, and Rational Recovery would probably not exist if many people did not perceive AA as religious.

I agree in part, but contend that the emergence of new self-help approaches for alcoholics was *inevitable*, due largely to the forces of change previously outlined, including the growing realization that the traditional approach is clearly ineffective. We now know that one size does *not* fit all. The religious content of A.A. *does* drive many away from it, as Ellis and Velten point out, but other planks in the A.A. platform do so even more forcefully. For example, notions about dependence, disease, powerlessness, and the alleged need for attendance at meetings for life are vigorously resisted by the majority of those who enter—and soon depart—through the revolving doors of Alcoholics Anonymous.

Advocates of A.A. claim that A.A. *does* provide for non-believers, through its meetings for agnostics. That's highly questionable. The members of the agnostic groups know that they are viewed condescendingly, as potential rather than full-fledged members of the larger fellowship. The agnostic members of A.A. are an iconoclastic bunch, more inclined to think than to believe. They live in a limbo-land between believers and non-believers, and probably remain in A.A. only because they don't know about other self-help groups. They are not so much a part of A.A. as a renegade band of distant cousins *tolerated* by it. Like black Americans riding in the back of a 1930s bus, they await a new connection down the road, ready to transfer to a recovery program more suited to their needs.

Such programs didn't exist when Arthur Cain and Jerome Ellison examined traditional concepts and practices in the addictions field and found them deficient. Cain created a storm with his 1963 article in *Harper's* (later expanded into a book[4]) and a 1965 article in the *Saturday Evening Post*. (The new *Post* continues to promote A.A., but *never* mentions this article.) Ellison added fuel to the fire in his 1964 article in *The Nation*. The views of Cain and Ellison were promptly dismissed as liberal and outlandish, but their echoes began to bounce back to us in the seventies and eighties and are booming back in the nineties. The American Atheists Addiction Recovery Groups (AAARG) organization was born (prematurely) in 1983 and lived but a few years.[5] A number of other small, nontraditional groups sprang up but could not survive in an oppressive atmosphere. The time was not right.

Now the time *is* right, and eight self-help support programs stand as evidence to that fact. It's important to remember that even those programs that are supplemental to A.A. (Calix, JACS, AV) are independent of and distinct from it. If the performance of A.A. matched its reputation, we would need nothing but A.A., but, as we have seen, this is not the case.

The (A.A.) concepts of single choice and permanent dependence seem peculiarly unsuited to the American ethos. Marilyn Ferguson writes:

> As increasing numbers of people come to a sense of autonomy, they respect the choices of others. At the 1977 Women's Year convention, many debates died away as the audience began to chant: "Choice, choice, choice . . ." Even if you don't want a particular lifestyle or philosophy for yourself, they were saying, you can allow others their options."[6]

Their options, yes, and their rights too. People need and demand choices, a fact which needs no defense. We do not all fit the same mold and we vigorously resent the presumption that we are all alike. People intuitively know that their personal identity and uniqueness are violated by those who insist that "one size fits all."

There is a universal standard in social work and in therapy that one must "fit the program to the client." Since that principle has been consistently ignored by professionals in the addictions field, we the people have undertaken the task ourselves. We decided to self-serve, cafeteria style. Lots of choices, no hassles. The list above—which is still growing—attests to that fact.

(It is a common practice to refer to those "other" programs as "alternatives" to A.A. The implication is that we are comparing a Chevette to a Cadillac, the one distinctly preferable to the other. This characterization is often casual, but always offensive. Each independent program is a separate entity, and as such merits identification as a matter of courtesy and accuracy. The independents *are* alternatives to A.A., but only in the same way that A.A. is an "alternative" to them, and they are to each other.)

I will devote the balance of this chapter to a description of the newer self-help support programs for "alcoholics" and users of illicit drugs. (Alcoholics Anonymous and Rational Recovery are treated separately in Chapters 5 and 6, and 9, respectively).

Alcoholics Victorious (AV): This support group is sponsored by the Institute for Christian Living (I.C.L.) which is a service of Riverside Medical Center, a joint venture of St. Mary's and Fairview Riverside hospitals. Ron Keller, Program Director for the I.C.L., was reported by Kay Urtz in the June 1988 *Catholic Bulletin* as saying that, "I.C.L. works with mainline churches, principally Lutheran and Catholic."

I.C.L. offers counseling services in the area of alcoholism, eating disorders, codependency, abusive relationships, and dysfunctional families. In a February 28, 1993 letter to me, Vernon J. Bittner, Director of the I.C.L., advised that the book *Twelve Steps for Christian Living*, written and distributed by the I.C.L., is comparable to the original 12 steps, but generally "focuses more on the theology of the Twelve Steps." The philosophy of I.C.L. was given as follows:

> The Institute for Christian Living operates on the principle that health is not simply the absence of problems. It is the development and maintenance of a balance between physical, emotional and spiritual factors. Healing is viewed as a life-long process where a healthy life comes from a new way of living in God's presence with the support of God's people.

The first paragraph of I.C.L's Vision Statement (mission) reveals the essence of I.C.L. and AV:

> The Institute for Christian Living is an expression of the healing ministry of Jesus Christ which advocates through counseling and life-style education the utilization of one's unique spiritual and personal faith to promote wholeness.

The Institute claims (as of May 1991) that "more than 200 groups [are] available within various denominations throughout the Twin Cities [St. Paul and Minneapolis, MN] and surrounding states." I.C.L.'s literature, however, lists only 46 groups within Minnesota and an additional 25 groups spread over 11 other States, most of them in the Southwest and Midwest. It explains that "The Twelve Steps for Christian Living" support groups serve as a framework to aid individuals in their personal growth, enrichment and Christian maturity." I.C.L/AV has a seven-step program:

1) I know that I am powerless over alcohol/drug addiction, behavior patterns, and sin . . . and that I cannot overcome it by myself. I believe the healing power of Jesus Christ is available and able to change me.

2) Believing that Jesus can change my life, I commit my life to Him. Dear Father, I know that I am bound to these habits and that they are my gods. I know that your Son, Jesus Christ, died to free me from my sins and to give me new life. . . . I now decide to turn from my sins and to turn to Jesus Christ for salvation. I ask you to forgive me of my sins. I now confess Jesus Christ as my own Lord and Savior. Thank you for the victory that is mine in Christ Jesus over sin. . . .

3) Satan, my real enemy who hates God and what God is doing in my life, may deceive me to believe the desire for alcohol/drugs has returned or that people are the cause of my problems, so I will trust God to keep me from falling. . . .

4) As a Christian, I recognize that I can only grow in a healthy, new environment. Therefore, by the grace of God I will sever friendships that drag me down, while developing new friends. . . . I will attempt reconciliation by admitting my wrong in the situation and make restitution, as necessary. . . .

5) I know that I need to develop wholesome attitudes. I will allow God to change my thinking through His Word by applying it to my life . . . . I will allow the Holy Spirit to take inventory of my life and guide me into all truth. I believe that I will receive a new self image based on God's word, not on my feelings or actions. . . .

6) I will spend time daily talking to God and being honest with Him about my attitudes. I will obey His Word and be thankful daily for my new life. . . .

7) I will share my faith in Christ with others and help them to victory so they, too, can be freed from Satan's web. . . .

The Seven Steps are tailored to the needs of a thoroughly Christian and very religious segment of the heavy-drinking population. AV is, I think, a perfect example of a self-help support group which has oriented itself to a specific segment of the population. AAARG (American Atheists Addiction Recovery Groups), were it to exist today, would be another example of thoughtful adaptation to distinctive needs.

In the I.C.L. Steps we see addiction to alcohol or illegal drugs presented as a sinful activity, but one that can be rectified by adopting the principles of the Institute for Christian Living. I am certain that the majority of addictionologists would agree that the solution to addiction problems (for most people) cannot be reduced to a single-factor explanation (sin) or solution (religion). Although the Institute represents mainstream religion in America in only a nominal fashion, it generally reflects the prevailing oversimplified view of alcohol and drug addiction in the orthodox religious community.

I attended a local meeting of Alcoholics Victorious. The regular members, four in number, carried a Bible and quoted frequently from it. Although they knew little about addictions, they demonstrated a sincerity and determination that was heartwarming. They even tried to convert me, but eventually decided that I was doomed and beyond help.

Calix, The Society: Calix[7] was founded in 1947 as a recovery group for impaired priests, and was formally organized in 1949 in Minneapolis, Minnesota. Growth was steady but very slow until 1974, when Pope Paul VI received representatives of this society in private audience, and formally endorsed its organization.[8] The Society has 69 units spread over the United States, Canada, Scotland, and England. Its influence is, at best, minimal, but it exists and is slowly growing. Members pay dues, attend an inauguration ceremony, celebrate a monthly Mass and breakfast, go on retreats, say daily prayers, and have a professional clergyman (a priest) who acts as their spiritual director. In the December 1992 issue of the *New Covenant*, Bill Fox (no relation to the author) of the Minneapolis headquarters wrote, "The heart of Calix is prayer and the sacraments, especially the Eucharist."

I hesitated before listing the Calix Society as a self-help support organization alternative to A.A. Calix does not announce itself as such, and its literature is ambivalent on this issue. The relationship between the two organizations is friendly, yet distant. Their relationship is also curious, almost peculiar. Calix actively promotes A.A., but is ignored by it as an "outside issue."[9] In a letter to me, the Executive Director of Calix advised:

> We do not consider Calix as an alternative to AA—in fact we encourage and expect all Calix members who are recovering alcoholics to stay with the AA program. We must keep the two programs in their proper perspective, lest we be *accused* (emphasis added) of running a "Catholic AA." We consider Calix as a *supplement.*[10]

Calix assigns to A.A. responsibility for the physical, emotional, and mental aspects of recovery, but "for Catholics something more is needed." According to Mary Costello, columnist for *Chalice*, the Society's bimonthly newsletter, "[Calix is] a place where I could name my God and talk about my devotion to the Blessed Mother." In a Calix pamphlet we find:

> Accordingly, when approached to help someone still bogged down in alcohol, the first effort of a Calix member is to get the suffering man or woman into a detoxification center, a treatment facility, or an A.A. squad. *When, and only when, the recovering person achieves some measure of sobriety is he or she ready for Calix.*

Thus, Calix views A.A. as a kind of way station, a place to begin recovery. But it rejects A.A.'s personalized spiritual program and its flexible concept of a Higher Power in favor of its own doctrine based on the unequivocal identification of A.A.'s "Higher Power" as the second person of the Trinity, specifically Jesus Christ of the New Testament. Calix' stated purpose is threefold, as detailed in its "Credo" (from the Latin, "I believe"), the preamble read at the beginning of every meeting:

> . . . Our first concern is to interest Catholics with an alcoholic problem in the VIRTUE[11] of total abstinence. Our second stated purpose is to promote the spiritual development of our membership. . . . our third objective [is] to strive for the sanctification of the whole personality of each member. . . .

Calix makes no attempt to distinguish the spiritual from the religious. The above Calix statement, referring to the Liturgy, Sacraments, Holy Days, etc., would probably be interpreted by most people as more religious than spiritual. Interesting too, is the fact that Calix refers to alcoholism as an "illness" rather than a "disease."

In summary, Calix is an alternative to A.A., independent of it, supportive of it, and ignored by it. Calix is a religious expression of Catholicism singing in off-key harmony with A.A. Politics and happy relationships aside, Calix is a self-described Apostolate in search of lost sheep that it hopes to bring back to the Church. Calix is a special-purpose, intra-Church missionary society designed to develop the spiritual and religious aspects of its members and to seek out those in need of its services.

Mainstream religion in the United States has been extremely neglectful of its addicted members. In the case of Calix, for example, the Catholic Church has managed to reach only 1,000 of them. Let us say that 5% of its adult population of 43,000,000 (of its claimed total population of 59,000,000) is addicted to alcohol or illegal drugs. Excluding those under eighteen, Calix reaches .00232% of those who might benefit from its services.[12]

This is a typical performance for organized religion in the United States, and it is, in the opinion of this author, a serious failure on the part of Calix in particular, and mainstream religion in general. In the U.S. population there are approximately 6,000,000 Jews, 89,000,000 Protestants, and 59,000,000 Catholics, representing, in total, 62% of the population, or about 115,000,000 adults. Virtually all organized religions in the United States approach the problem of addiction care with the naive and outdated notion that alcoholism is little more than a moral deficiency and/or a sin, a view not in step with modern thinking. In the meantime, the sheep are dying, and although the shepherds care, it is obvious that they haven't done their homework and they aren't paying attention.

Jewish Alcoholics and Chemically Dependent and Significant Others (JACS): The official Jewish position on JACS as a self-help group for alcoholics was presented to me in a letter from Jeff Neipris, dated February 6, 1990:

> Thank you for contacting us. . . . The JACS Foundation is first and foremost an advocacy organization within the Jewish community—educating clergy, Jewish health professionals and the community at large as to the devastating effects of chemical dependency[13] on Jewish family life. We serve as an information clearing-house, speak in the community, put on Awareness seminars, lobby for substance abuse education and chaplaincy training. In particular we are proponents of the efficacy of the 12-step programs, and lobby our synagogues and other Jewish facilities to "open their doors" to traditional A.A. and Al-Anon meetings, etc.

Additionally we hold workshops and Spiritual Retreats for addicted Jews and their loved ones who wish to *enhance the 12-step recovery process from the perspective of Jewish tradition and belief.* Simply put, we are not a self-help program or a "Jewish A.A." No one attends a JACS program to "get sober" or explore any form [of] treatment, alternative or otherwise. The participants at JACS events are, with rare exception, members of the traditional 12-step programs searching for a Jewish connection to their spiritual recovery. I have enclosed some literature. . . . I'm sure that you will agree that JACS does not belong on your list of "self-help" groups.

Regardless of the letter from Mr. Neipris, I have listed JACS as an independent self-help support organization. His position is a good example of the fable about the emperor who wore no clothes. But to appreciate his stance one must first appreciate the Jewish people. Their culture is tightly integrated; they remain defensive to prejudice (especially in the form of "humor" among the intellectually disadvantaged); they are sensitive and private people with high standards of conduct and family values. For them, the designation "alcoholic" is shameful (a *chet*), a departure from essential goodness, and a painful reflection on the entire Jewish community.

JACS operates in 14 states, with a total of 29 chapters, plus two in Canada. Its track record in successfully reaching out to addicted members of the Jewish community is comparable to that of Calix, give or take a decimal point or two. A September 1992 information sheet from JACS states:

JACS is a membership organization of Jews in recovery from the disease of chemical dependency who gather together to connect with other Jews in the same circumstances and with Jewish spirituality. JACS sponsors a wide variety of events addressing these themes.

There is a myth that Jewish country clubs have higher membership fees because income from the sales of alcoholic beverages is less than that of non-Jewish clubs. In an article in *Psychology Today*, psychologist Benzion Twerski[14] dispels that myth. Twerski quotes David Steinhardt as saying, "JACS reports that its programs are overflowing, indicating that a very real problem exists." Of special interest is evidence which indicates that the problem of cross-addiction among Jews is relatively higher than that found in the population at large.[15]

To help you decide the role of JACS in the recovery system, consider JACS' mission statement:

J.A.C.S. supplements and complements existing self-help programs[16] and attempts to help addicted Jews, their families, and the community to integrate Jewish traditions and heritage into the recovery process.

There is a striking resemblance between the positions of the Calix Society and JACS on the subject of self-help and the relationships between their respective organizations and A.A. Both embrace A.A., but maintain a distance from it—Calix by a foot, JACS by a yard. Both proclaim the virtues of A.A., but also insist that A.A.'s generic spiritual/religious content lacks a significant dimension which each of them feels that it can and must provide. The common denominator seems to be: Let A.A. sober them up; we'll take care of their souls. We can, of course, respect the "official" position statements of Calix and JACS without agreeing with either.

Men for Sobriety (MFS): MFS is a self-help support program concerned with growth and change, based on MFS founder Jean Kirkpatrick's statement, "I am what I think."[17] Like its counterpart, WFS (Women For Sobriety), MFS is unique among the self-help support programs in that it is gender oriented. It is sensitive to the fundamental differences between men and women, and it provides a program tailored to the distinctive orientation and needs of men. Other self-help support programs recognize this difference too, and cater to it in a limited way by providing separate meetings for men and for women. Separate meetings, however, operating under a common set of principles, lack the depth and consistency of programs tailored specifically to gender differences. Other programs have not yet fully recognized the merits of the WFS/MFS example.

Mottos often provide major insights into an organization. Men For Sobriety has one: "We are capable and competent, caring and compassionate, always willing to help another, bonded together in overcoming our addictions." MFS' Statement of Purpose is as follows:

1. Men For Sobriety is a Program whose purpose is to help all men recover from problem drinking through the discovery of self, gained by sharing experiences, hopes, and encouragement with other men.

2. Men For Sobriety is a Program for men only. It recognizes men's complex role in today's society and the necessity for recovery from alcoholism through self-discovery, leading to a sense of self-value and self-worth.

3. Men for Sobriety is not affiliated with Alcoholics Anonymous, although members of Men For Sobriety sometimes belong to both organizations. Each organization and Program has its individual purpose and must be kept apart.

4. Men For Sobriety believes that drinking began to overcome stress, loneliness, frustration, or any number of other kinds of harassment. Dependence upon alcohol resulted. This physiological dependence can only be overcome by abstinence. Mental and emotional addiction are overcome with the knowledge of self gained through the Men For Sobriety Program.

5. Men For Sobriety meets weekly. Meetings are led by a Moderator who is thoroughly familiar with the MFS philosophy, central to which is: forget the past, plan for the future, and live in today.

6. Membership in Men for Sobriety requires a desire to stop drinking, a desire for a new life, and a total commitment to the MFS Program.

The heart of the MFS program is revealed in a 1976 brochure which encourages men to overcome the pitfalls of faulty thinking and destructive behavior by learning how to cope with problems in more effective ways. The "how-to" part of the MFS New Life Program is clear and positive:

1. Exchanging information (literature, group members)
2. Positive reinforcement (approval and encouragement)
3. Cognitive strategies (positive thinking)
4. Observation and imitation (imagery)
5. Letting the body help (relaxation techniques, meditation, diet and physical exercise)

A cognitive/learning emphasis pervades the literature and program of MFS. "The philosophy of the Program is that image precedes action. Whatever we think, eventually we act out."[18] Later in that same brochure we read, "*We have the power* (emphasis added) of changing our way of thinking. That means we have a way of changing our life," followed by the highly significant "We are responsible for ourselves and our choices." As a result of this mental health approach, members learn to accept themselves and deal with reality. They declare:

1. I have a drinking problem that once had me.
2. Negative emotions destroy only myself.
3. Happiness is a habit I will develop.
4. Problems bother me only to the degree I permit them to.
5. I am what I think.
6. Life can be ordinary or it can be great.
7. Love can change the course of my world.
8. The fundamental object of life is emotional and spiritual growth.
9. The past is gone forever.
10. All love given returns twofold.
11. Enthusiasm is my daily exercise.
12. I am competent and have much to give others.
13. I am responsible for myself and my brothers.

The responsibility mentioned in the thirteenth acceptance statement (MFS is not a step-program) includes total and permanent abstinence from alcohol and illegal drugs.

The position of MFS on the disease issue is one of mild indifference; it is almost casual in the manner of Jack Trimpey's position: So what? If alcoholism is a disease, don't drink. If it isn't, don't drink. Uncommon common sense.

Men For Sobriety also objects, as do most other independents, to A.A.'s view of itself as the "one and only." The implication of that view is clear: "they" don't work; "we" do. MFS (and the others) do not appreciate being ignored, and thus insulted, by A.A.'s view of them as an "outside issue," a position taken by A.A. supposedly on the basis of its tenth Tradition.[19] MFS, however, in its third Statement of Purpose, takes a courteous and cooperative position toward A.A.

MFS is concerned with the *now* and the *future*, but is willing to learn from the past without dwelling in it. MFS is clearly a mental health program, one in which members consider themselves powerful rather than powerless, and in which they self-direct change.

And spirituality? It is mentioned almost casually in Kirkpatrick's eighth acceptance statement and is seen by MFS as essentially a personal issue. This is yet another contrast between A.A. and MFS: A.A. is distinctly religious in that a relationship with God is seen as essential to recovery. Mental health-oriented MFS views religious inclinations, or lack of them, as personal matters which can be helpful to the recovery process, but which are not essential to it.

Many self-help programs mention (and some encourage) attendance of A.A. as well as their own meetings, as in MFS's statement that "although members of Men For Sobriety sometimes belong to both organizations . . ." *Sometimes*, yes, but I've found in my contacts with several self-help support programs that "sometimes" translates to at most 5% of members. The human mind cannot deal simultaneously with advisements that it is both powerful *and* powerless. People are looking for answers, not cognitive dissonance. Sometimes people do attend separate programs, especially when they're in the first stage of recovery or in the process of switching from one program to another. Before long, however, they make a choice and stick with it, because conflicting ideas are difficult, and often impossible, to live with. The human mind tends to quickly resolve such conflicts through its powers of analysis and decision. Time is a factor too—we only have so much of it to spend on recovery. There are other more interesting things to do in life.

A final distinction between A.A. and MFS is that MFS does not encourage its members to center their lives around recovery. Its members attend one or two meetings a week, as do members of RR and WFS. MFS, again like RR, considers the traditional idea of 90 meetings in 90 days ill advised.[20]

Moderation Management (MM): MM is new (late 1993), and a last-minute addition to this chapter. Although it is a nascent organization, it has already attracted an astonishing amount of support from major figures in the addictions field (Stanton Peele, Jeffrey Schaler, Mark and Linda Sobell, Archie Brodsky, et al.). Its founder, Audrey Kishline, is finishing a manual on the subject of moderate drinking, and has been offered a contract by a publisher.

The design and orientation of MM is clear; it emphasizes education and problem prevention for those who recognize that their use of alcohol has begun to, or may soon, cause problems in their lives. Thus, MM is not intended for that minority of the alcohol-abusing population generally termed "alcoholics," but toward that majority who may be termed "problem drinkers." I am convinced that the Kishline project is a rising star in the addictions field. You'll find more comments on MM in the "Moderate, Controlled, and Social Drinking" segment of Chapter 14.

Secular Organizations for Sobriety (SOS): In 1987, a year after the birth of what was then called SSG (Secular Sobriety Groups), I met Jim Christopher, founder of SOS. He had written an article in the Summer 1985 issue of *Free Inquiry* outlining his problems with A.A., and the response to the piece encouraged him to launch SSG (now

SOS) the following year, 1986. I liked him, supported his efforts, wrote for the SSG Newsletter, and became coordinator for SOS in Indiana. Let him tell you about Secular Organizations for Sobriety (also known as Save Our Selves). From the SOS literature, a collage of sorts:

> What is SOS? SOS is an alternative recovery program for those alcoholics or drug addicts who are uncomfortable with the spiritual content of the 12-Step program. SOS takes a reasonable, secular approach to recovery, and maintains that sobriety is an issue separate from religion or spirituality. SOS credits the individual for achieving and maintaining his or her own sobriety without reliance on a "Higher Power." SOS respects recovery in any form, regardless of the path by which it is achieved. It is not opposed to or in competition with any other recovery programs.[21] It supports healthy skepticism and encourages the use of the scientific method.

The general principles of SOS (taken from its literature):

> 1) All those who sincerely seek sobriety are welcome as members in any SOS Group.

> 2) SOS is not a spin-off of any religious group. There are no hidden agendas, as SOS is concerned with sobriety, not religiosity.

> 3) SOS seeks only to promote sobriety amongst those who suffer from alcoholism or other drug addictions. As a group, SOS has no opinion on outside matters and does not wish to become entangled in outside controversy.

> 4) Although sobriety is an individual responsibility, life does not have to be faced alone. The support of other alcoholics and addicts is a vital adjunct to recovery. In SOS, members share experiences, insights, information, strength, and encouragement in friendly, honest, anonymous, and supportive group meetings.

> 5) To avoid unnecessary entanglements, each SOS group is self-supporting through contributions from its members and refuses outside support.

> 6) Sobriety is the number one priority in an alcoholic's or addict's life. As such, he or she must abstain from all drugs or alcohol.

7) Honest, clear, and direct communication of feelings, thoughts, and knowledge aids in recovery and in choosing non-destructive, non-delusional, and rational approaches to living sober and rewarding lives.

8) As knowledge of drinking or addiction might cause a person harm or embarrassment in the outside world, SOS guards the anonymity of its membership and the contents of its discussions from those not within the group.

9) SOS encourages the scientific study of alcoholism and addiction in all their aspects. SOS does not limit its outlook to one area of knowledge or theory of alcoholism and addiction.

And, a few excerpts from a letter sent to me dated April 1, 1991, from J.W. Cain, Director of Public Relations for SOS:

• SOS . . . does not suggest that one's sobriety be made contingent upon belief in or reliance on a mystical or supernatural force.

• SOS encourages the individual to take responsibility for his/her own sobriety and give himself credit for having stayed sober/clean on a daily basis. [SOS] is a program of Self-Empowerment rather than self-deprecation. . . .

• The Cycle of Addiction is comprised of 1) chemical need, 2) learned habit, and 3) denial of both need and habit. The Cycle of Sobriety employs 1) daily acknowledgement, 2) daily acceptance, and 3) daily prioritization of sobriety as a separate issue.

• SOS does not subscribe to the notion that there is "one right way" to get and stay sober, and encourages membership in more than one self-help organization when and if the individual finds that beneficial.

• SOS does subscribe to and promote the building of self-worth and self-empowerment through sobriety, the notion that a "good" quality of life can be achieved . . . and the concept that self-responsibility frees one from the tenuous dependence on unseen and unproven forces for continuous abstinence.

• SOS is an abstinence program and contends that an alcoholic can no more be retrained to drink normally than a heroin addict, for example, can be retrained to use recreationally. We feel that such notions are absurd and counter-productive.

• We recognize that many find the "disease concept" a useful model and a workable concept. SOS, however, encourages healthy skepticism about any program which limits itself to one view or definition of alcoholism or addiction.

It's been interesting to watch the growth of SOS. In Jim Christopher's first article, "Sobriety Without Superstition,"[22] he expressed anger toward A.A., along with a full statement of personal convictions upon which he would build his organization. His article was well received by *Free Inquiry's* subscribers, and was soon followed by a second. Their combined effect, however, was to produce a storm of controversy in the wider community. How could anyone dare question, much less criticize, A.A.? Christopher dared, and was widely applauded for his efforts. In 1988 Prometheus Books published Christopher's first book, *How to Stay Sober: Recovery Without Religion*, which is used as a manual in SOS.

Christopher claims that alcoholism is a "cellular addiction," a disease based on physiology and genetic inheritance. He stresses the importance of personal responsibility and, above all, the *sobriety priority*: "I have two 'programs' in my life as a sober alcoholic: 1) my sobriety priority, and 2) everything else."[23] The emphasis of the SOS program is on mutual support, as distinct from self-help, although it necessarily includes both. It's a program of exhortation, encouragement, and value-setting. Its overriding emphasis is on sobriety and total and permanent abstinence, on a number-one-priority basis, daily.[24] SOS may also be described, within limits, as a cognitive program.[25]

And its relationship to A.A.?[26] Generally harsh, more so during its formative years than now. Still, in current SOS literature we find A.A. described as a "cult," complete with "Gods and goblins" and a "mystical source" of power. But SOS agrees with A.A. on the disease notion[27] and, like A.A., contends that alcoholism must be contained "one day at a time." SOS, however, emphasizes empowerment and independence rather than powerlessness and dependence on an external source.

Christopher argues that the use of Antabuse[28] makes sense at times; A.A. says No. He also takes the position that prescription drugs (e.g., Librium, a relaxant) serve a good purpose in the detoxification process and beyond, when needed. Again A.A. is far less flexible on this point. SOS endorses the scientific approach to addictions and the cognitive element as vital to its recovery program. A.A. remains spiritual, religious, and belief-based. Crosstalk is just fine in SOS, but not allowed in A.A. SOS does not consider itself the "one and only" program for alcoholics; A.A.—to put it mildly—is self-contained.

In summary, SOS contains major elements of both the traditional and the nontraditional approaches. Like A.A., SOS is essentially a support program. It cannot be described either as a cognitive/behavioral mental health program or a minor variant of A.A. It is, perhaps, best described as a hybrid—a mix of traditional and nontraditional ideas, positioned midway between programs such as A.A., Calix, JACS, and AV on the one hand, and MFS, MM, WFS, and RR on the other. SOS is a simple program in both structure and message, but it is not just a Godless A.A.; it is more of a bridge between traditional and nontraditional approaches to alcoholism. SOS operates under the aegis of CODESH—the Council for Democratic and Secular Humanism, a nonprofit, educational corporation.

Women for Sobriety (WFS): The WFS Program is based on the simple fact that women are different from men in significant ways. The physical differences are obvious, of course, but the fundamental psychic differences between the genders seem *not* to have been obvious to many, including treatment professionals, until Jean Kirkpatrick founded WFS in July 1975 and pointed it out. She said to them: Think! Look! At least, blink. Pretend, if you must, that this "minority" group—we women, 52% of the population—really exist and have special needs of our own.[29]

Jean Kirkpatrick has been a guest on many talk shows and is the author of four books. She has appeared as an expert witness before a U.S. Senate committee on the subject of alcoholism. She has lectured throughout the United States and in France, Austria, Wales, England and Germany. Although I promised to avoid the mention of academic credentials in this book, I hereby declare an exception: Jean Kirkpatrick holds a doctorate in her field (sociology). That's significant in itself, but even more significant is the fact that after a drinking career that outlasted even my own she took her Ph.D. at age 50. That deserves mention. As for her program, here it is in her words:

Women for Sobriety is both an organization and a self-help program for women alcoholics. It is, in fact, the first national self-help program for women alcoholics. Women For Sobriety has been providing services to women alcoholics since July, 1975. The WFS

"New Life" Program grew out of one woman's search for sobriety. (See *Turnabout: Help For a New Life*.) Now hundreds of WFS self-help groups are found all across this country and abroad. The New Life Program is based on a Thirteen Statement Program of positivity—a strong positive approach to life—that encourages emotional and spiritual growth.[30] It has been extremely effective in helping women to overcome their alcoholism and learn a wholly (and wholistic) new lifestyle.

As a Program, it can stand alone or be used along with other programs simultaneously. It is being used not only by women alcoholics in small self-help groups but also in hospitals, clinics, treatment facilities, and women's centers.

The activities of WFS include the establishment of self-help groups and the distribution of literature to women seeking help with problems of addictions. Unfunded by any agency, WFS derives its operational money from group donations, sale of literature, speaking engagements, workshops, and outside donations.

Until the founding of WFS, it was assumed that any program for recovery from alcoholism would work equally well for men and women alike. When it became obvious that recovery rates for male alcoholics were higher than for females, it was argued [by men] that women were harder to treat and were less cooperative than men. WFS maintained, however, that women alcoholics required a different kind of recovery program, a program that was gender-oriented and tailored to their special needs. The success of the WFS New Life Program has validated that observation. Although physiological recovery from alcoholism is much the same for both sexes, psychological and emotional recovery is distinctly different. The New Life Program is directed to these specific emotional needs of the woman alcoholic in recovery. There are an estimated 5,000,000 women [1987] alcoholics in the United States alone. . . . Surely this large number of women deserve a program that speaks to their specific needs in recovery. We know the WFS "New Life" Program does this.[31]

The "New Life" program is based on Thirteen Statements of Acceptance, not to be construed as imitative of A.A.'s "steps," but as a clear departure from them. Here they are:

1) I have a drinking (life-threatening) problem that once had me. (We now take charge of our life and our disease. We accept the responsibility.)

2) Negative emotions destroy only myself. (Our first conscious act must be to remove negativity from our life.)

3) Happiness is a habit I will develop. (Happiness is created, not waited for.)

4) Problems bother me only to the degree I permit them to. (We now better understand our problems and do not need substances as coping mechanisms.)

5) I am what I think. (I *am* a capable, competent, caring, compassionate woman.)

6) Life can be ordinary or it can be great.(Greatness is mine by a conscious effort.)

7) Love can change the course of my world. (Caring becomes all important.)

8) The fundamental object of life is emotional and spiritual growth. (Daily I put my life into proper order, knowing which are the priorities.)

9) The past is gone forever. (No longer will I be victimized by the past. I am a new person.)

10) All love given returns twofold. (I will learn to know that others love me.)

11) Enthusiasm is my daily exercise. (I treasure all moments of my new life.)

12) I am a competent woman and have much to give life. (This is what I am and I shall know it always.)

13) I am responsible for myself and for my actions. (I am in charge of my mind, my thoughts, and my life.)

As a professional sociologist, Kirkpatrick is aware of the importance of group dynamics. Her groups limit themselves to an optimum size of six to eight persons.[32] WFS also suggests attendance at one or two meetings a week, in contrast to the traditional A.A. view that members should attend as many meetings as possible (initially 90 meetings in 90 days).[33]

Moderators for WFS groups are carefully selected, trained, and formally certified (Rational Recovery also does this), in contrast to A.A.'s nonchalant approach. Professional counselors are also welcome in WFS (and RR, but not A.A.) as advisors. Members of WFS are encouraged to seek full independence in the form of graduating from the group, but with the understanding that total abstinence is expected for life.

Kirkpatrick endorses the "disease" concept, but not in the manner of A.A. or the AMA. She writes, "Alcoholism is a physical disorder . . ." and ". . . alcoholism can be viewed as a cell disease." Similar to the SOS position, but not as insistent, nor as demanding as the position taken by A.A., which defends Wilson's definition of alcoholism as a "physical, emotional, and spiritual disease."

Regarding spirituality and WFS—from *Sobering Thoughts* of September 1990:

> We see spirituality as a goal in our recovery. We see ourselves as related to both that which is within and that which is without. . . . It [spirituality] is the working toward the highest realization of ourselves. It is our privilege to recognize the spirit within ourselves as one with the spirit within every atom of being in the universe.[34] We are an integral part of the whole. We can see spirit or Spirit, however the individual chooses to see life and life's relations . . . We must look for a higher, inner life. We must seek to come into conscious touch with the soul of the universe.

On humility, I think Kirkpatrick, in one of her more earthy moments, might say, "Screw humility!" Women have been taught to be second-class citizens, dependent on men, loaded with guilt, forced to suppress feelings of anger and frustration. Kirkpatrick promotes self-worth, positive imagery, equality, potential for growth, and independence. Humility, in Kirkpatrick's view—and I share this with her—is possibly the last thing women alcoholics need. The careful reader of Kirkpatrick's works will sense a seething anger toward the status quo, including A.A. and any other program that consistently denigrates women. She is, however, sometimes surprisingly conciliatory. For example: "Although there are extreme differences between our programs [WFS and A.A.], they are neither mutually exclusive nor contradictory."[35]

In a single-page publication titled "AA and WFS," Kirkpatrick compares the two organizations. Here are some excerpts:

1) AA: Philosophy is to "turn over" our will and our lives.
   WFS: We take charge.

2) AA: Higher Power concept. [God]
   WFS: Emotional and spiritual growth are fundamental.

3) AA: Emphasis on alcoholism. "My name is Jean and I'm an
   alcoholic."
   WFS: Emphasis on recovery. "My name is Jean and I'm a competent
   woman."

4) AA: Keep the past vibrant [alive] in order to stay sober.
   WFS: Put the past behind us to stay sober.

5) AA: Program based on religious philosophy of the Oxford Group.
   [Concerned with powerlessness, continuing moral inventories,
   confession of shortcomings (faults), the making of amends, and
   praying for a source of Power outside of the self]
   WFS: Program based upon metaphysical[36] philosophy—our thoughts
   create our world.

6) AA: A meeting a week for life-time or will be drinking.
   WFS: Once we learn how to cope with the problems of life, we won't
   need a group any longer. [Members can/do graduate.]

7) AA: Emphasis on humility and dampening down the ego.
   WFS: We must *overcome* [emphasis added] humility and learn to find
   ego strengths.

Summary Statement: The common denominator of the independent
groups is one of *disenchantment* with the status quo, and *independence*
from it. The eight independents are, by definition, not clones of
A.A., and each distances itself from it to some significant degree.
Each seeks to tailor a specific program to a certain segment of the
population; none (excepting A.A.) feels that its program is, or even
should be, acceptable to all. The independents are gaining strength
and making inroads in hospitals, treatment centers, among professional therapists, and in the judicial system. They are changing
the field of addictions, conceptually and practically. They are the
wave of the present—and the future.

---

1. An excellent overview of the self-help movement in the United States can be
found in *Helping Ourselves: Social Solutions to Global Problems* (1981). New York: W.W.
Norton. The history of the self-help movement goes far beyond the last few
decades. It is a part of the American ethos–the characteristic and distinguishing

attitudes, habits, and beliefs of an individual, group, or nation. In the history of the United States there are many examples of self-and mutual-help efforts, among them, the cooperative movement, barn raising, bartering, and the communal harvesting of crops.

2. Naisbitt's Chapter 6 is titled "From Institutional Help to Self-help." It gives an excellent account of the origin, development, and future direction of the self-help movement in this country. He concludes that the self-help movement is *not* a passing fad, but a deep-rooted trend–a social shift of major proportions.

3. The thesis that the self-help movement was created by institutional failures was presented by J. Kirkpatrick (among others) in an article in *Alcohol Health Research World* in the Summer 1982 issue of that publication. A copy of that article may be secured by writing to WFS at the address given a few paragraphs below.

4. Cain, A. (1964). *The CURED Alcoholic.* New York: John Day.

5. Bill Talley, its director, later changed its name to Methods of Moderation and Abstinence (MOMA). Talley's organization was very antagonistic toward A.A. It folded in1988 due to lack of acceptance, effective administration, and funds.

6. Ferguson, M. with Foreword by Max Lerner. (1980). *The Aquarian Conspiracy: Personal and Social Transformation in the 1980s*, p. 225. Los Angeles: J.P. Tarcher.

7. *Calix* is the Latin word for chalice. Members are encouraged to accept the chalice, "the cup that sanctifies," in preference to "the cup that stupefies." The chalice is a symbol of the Eucharist, the focal point of the Catholic Mass.

8. Paul VI endorsed Calix on the occasion of its twenty-fifth anniversary in the weekly edition (in English) of the *Editorial and Management Offices of Vatican City* 23, 1974. The official translation from the Latin refers twice to a "higher power," and in neither case capitalizes either word. Paul VI identified that "higher power" in Calix as ". . . the supernatural grace of Jesus Christ, the healing power of his word and of his sacraments."

9. A.A.'s "hands off" policy of today is not congruent with that of its co-founder, Bill Wilson, who on May 15, 1962, wrote a friendly and supportive letter to Gene Trow, at that time president of Calix International. Wilson warmly expressed his appreciation of the support given to A.A. by the Calix Society. Wilson was, I'm convinced, more liberal and flexible than many, and perhaps most, of his present-day followers.

10. Letter to the author, dated November 4, 1988, from R.D. Dickinson, Executive Director, International Headquarters, Minneapolis Minnesota.

11. From a theological perspective, the use of this term in this context is unusual (as in chastity as a virtue), but perfectly acceptable. It is neither a theological virtue (faith, hope, and charity [love]) which has God as its immediate object, nor a Cardinal virtue from the Greek or Christian perspectives. *Virtues* are usually positive, sometimes negative—as in *not* doing something. I know this is not terribly relevant, but thought you might be interested.

12. From the *Statistical Abstract*, based on 1990 census figures. The performance of the Catholic Church, as indicated by Calix membership figures, would be even more dismal if its juvenile population were included in the calculation.

13. Note the avoidance of the term "disease" in this instance. JACS uses the terms

"chemical dependency" and "disease" interchangeably and inaccurately. Calix tends to stick with the more nebulous term "illness."

14. Not to be confused with Rabbi and psychiatrist Abraham J.Twersky, another national name in the addictions field.

15. The information in my files states this fact but makes no attempt to explain it. It is possible that, since many Jews are professionals and many of those are in the medical field, they may have more readily available sources of drugs than others do. That, of course, is only a hypothesis.

16. A reference to A.A., N.A., Alanon, and similar traditionalprograms based on the 12-step construct.

17. Kirkpatrick, J. Single-page flyer from MFS, undated and with no identifying numbers thereon. (The MFS motto is suggestive of the Rational-Emotive Therapy approach devised by Dr. Albert Ellis.)

18. Most of the publications in MFS (and WFS) are not identified in any way, other than by year of origin, in this case 1976.

19. The Traditions of A.A. are, in effect, laws, and are interpreted as such by its members. A.A. would, of course, refuse to address this statement by declaring it an "outside issue" or subject of controversy. A simple explanation would be helpful to all concerned, but A.A., it seems, prefers allegations to explanations.

20. The 90/90 exercise is often talked about in A.A., sometimes tried, and rarely accomplished. Only those with the doggedness of a pit bull should even attempt it.

21. In the introduction to *SOS Sobriety: The Proven Alternative to 12-Step Programs,* Christopher accuses Rational Recovery of commercialism and of waffling on the abstinence issue (p.11). The significance of Christopher's charge is not so much the accusation itself (simply not true), but its indication of a competitive spirit that seems to be slowly developing among the independents. RR, MFS, MM, WFS, and SOS hold some grim views about A.A., however mildly expressed, but none of them, up to this point, has attacked any of the others, except in this instance. RR, on the other hand, has never criticized SOS, and on several occasions has mentioned it favorably in published form. We in RR are puzzled by this expression of apparent antagonism on the part of SOS. It is possible that Christopher's remarks may damage RR to some degree, but it is certain that continued attacks of this nature will serve only to diminish the stature and credibility of Jim Christopher and his fine organization.

22. *Free Inquiry,* June 1985.

23. *How to Stay Sober,* p. 51.

24. Abstinence is one major area of common ground among the eight self-help support groups. The ninth group, Moderation Management, is concerned with problem drinking, as distinct from what is generally understood as "alcoholism." It focuses on the prevention of problems associated with alcohol consumption, and the rectification of any existing problems so as to allow a return to responsible social drinking. (See Chapter 14)

25. In *Unhooked,* Christopher references Albert Ellis and David Burns on the one hand, *and* James Milam and Katherine Ketcham on the other. Strange bedfellows.

26. It would be nice to be able to remark on A.A.'s relationship to SOS but, as

usual, A.A. "has no opinions," and no spokesperson. It is difficult to see how A.A.— deeply involved in a support program for alcoholics—can consider SOS, RR, MFS, et al., all involved in an essentially common cause, as "outside issues."

27. Note, however, that A.A.'s view of "disease" is that it has "physical, emotional, and spiritual" components. The A.A. concept is too often construed only in its physiological aspect. The adjectives which A.A. applies could probably, in keeping with their apparent significance to A.A., be reordered as "spiritual, physical, and emotional."

28. Physicians often prescribe disulfiram privately and in institutional settings, regardless of A.A.'s proscription against the use of this valuable drug. They do so wisely, not to "cure" the problem, but to allow the body to heal itself—to prevent further damage to it—thus enabling the patient to deal with his or her problem. The A.A. notion is that "a drug is a drug is a drug." One wonders if those who believe this recognize the benefits of an occasional aspirin tablet.

29. Male dominance continues in the addictions field, even at the level of research. This is a cultural expression of a still-maturing society. At Christmas, we still give toy guns to boys and Barbie dolls to girls. It's a young country and Jean Kirkpatrick is impatient. Who can blame her?

30. Positivity is a better word than "positiveness," and is not to be confused with August Comte's *positivism,* a philosophy basing knowledge solely on data from the senses or experience.

31. From a pamphlet by the same name, 1976 and 1987.

32. A practical and smart idea. I remember an A.A. meeting with 55 people in attendance; there was no semblance of a group dynamic nor any possibility of one.

33. This practice has been widely criticized, but it has some merit. A neophyte *needs* support during this critical period of vulnerability. For the beginner, however, this is also a time of great susceptibility, during which time indoctrination can take place, unhampered by resistance or logical inquiry.

34. She seems to approach pantheistic concepts here, in the manner of the original Americans who saw the sacred in all things, animate and inanimate.

35. In *Alcohol, Health, and Research World,* Summer 1992.

36. *Metaphysical* is a word that is often misunderstood. It is a technical term in philosophy. *Metaphysics* is that branch of philosophy which deals with first principles and seeks to explain the nature of being or reality and the origin and structure of the world. It is closely associated with the study of the nature of knowledge (epistemology). Nothing esoteric or kooky about it.

9

Rational Recovery Systems Network

This chapter is dedicated to Dr. Albert Ellis, on the occasion of his eightieth birthday. Ellis has no need to stand on the shoulders of giants such as Freud, Adler, and Jung in order to see further and more clearly. He had better vision to start with.

"People are disturbed not by things, but by the view they take of them."
—Epictetus, 1st century B.C.E.

Rational Recovery Systems Network (RRSN, RR for short) is a free, self-help support organization, designed primarily but not exclusively for the benefit of for those with chemical dependency problems. It is a total abstinence program. Essentially, RR is an educational and mental health program, an application of the constructs of Rational-Emotive Therapy, a psychological problem-solving tool kit devised in the 1950s by Albert Ellis, an internationally respected author, researcher, and psychotherapist. RR is a 501-C-3 non-profit organization based in Lotus, California. It has chapters in over 700 cities throughout the United States, Canada, and six other countries. RR also operates a residential program near Sacramento, California.

RR was founded by Jack Trimpey, who is a dirty, rotten, no-good (dry, for the last 12 years) alcoholic—according to many traditionalists who perceive him as an adversary, a dangerous man, or, worse yet, a creative thinker. That's what everyone (except his tireless and talented wife Lois—co-founder of RR) thought until about 12 years ago when Jack decided to quit drinking and establish (four years later) Rational Recovery. Now people say that Jack Trimpey is an original thinker, a courageous pioneer, an organizational and computer genius, a man of conviction and persuasiveness, and in general, a fine fellow. That's right; he is, and I am privileged to count him and Lois as friends. I work for RR as a full-time volunteer and will not pretend that this chapter is totally detached from healthy emotion or personal conviction. But neither is it a mindless promotion of RR, devoid of analysis or criticism.

When Jack and Lois started RR in 1986 they met heavy resistance from the A.A.-orientated treatment establishment. RR was well received, however, by addicts, especially by those who had tried A.A. and N.A. programs and found them unsuited to their needs. Since 1986, RR has added about 70 to 100 chapters each year, and the rate of expansion continues at an ever-increasing pace. Lois recently remarked, "Our only big problem is how to manage accelerated growth." The media responded enthusiastically to the birth of RR. Articles appeared in *Newsweek, Lear's, The New York Times, The Washington Post,* and about 150 other publications. Jack appeared on Good Morning America and four other national talk shows.

During RR's first few years, Jack and Lois were inundated with thousands of "Joe six-pack" calls—and they still come in by the thousands—but since about 1990 there has been an increasing number of calls of a different nature. About 40% of their calls now come from professionals such as therapists and social workers, and from organizations such as universities, mental health centers, the Federal Aviation Administration, the Unitarian-Universalist Church,[1] hospitals, treatment centers, and the Veterans Administration.

The phenomenal acceptance of RR reflects the growing awareness that prevailing principles and practices in the addictions field have not worked. The reason? There are several, but the primary reason is that the prevailing addiction care system is out of sync with fundamental conceptual and social shifts taking place today. For example, there is a move toward individualism and away from conformity; a move toward self-empowerment and away from institutional control; and a move within the self-help movement to adapt and design its programs to meet the needs of its users. RR's program reflects these three trends.

RR recognizes and appreciates the power of the human mind. It knows that people can and do change. It offers a cognitive-behavioral (knowing-doing) program of change based on the Rational-Emotive Therapy[2] constructs of Albert Ellis, one of the world's most respected mental health practitioners. The Trimpeys adapted the thinking of RR board of directors member Ellis to a specific problem area, that of chemical/psychological dependence. The basic reason that RR is successful—and will continue to be so—is that it addresses a fundamental human need, the need to survive and be happy, regardless of the number or intensity of problems encountered in life.

In RR, personal problems are recognized as a normal part of living. Some of these problems can be prevented, others managed, all endured. By themselves, problems do not and cannot prevent us from achieving the near-universal human goal of happiness; however, the *mismanagement* of problems can defeat us at every turn.[3] In RR, mismanagement can be equated with maladaptation—maladaptation to problems, for example, that concern anger, boredom, frustration, habit, and so on. Problems get out of hand because we lack either effective coping skills or employ ineffective ones—such as drinking or drugging.

The *management* of problems, on the other hand, can be understood as the body of techniques with which a person effectively solves problems. An effective problem-solving tool kit contains only three things: information, skill, and self-discipline. Self-discipline is the highest skill; Scott Peck writes, "Discipline [is] a system of techniques of dealing constructively with the pain of problem-solving . . ."[4] In Rational Recovery, effective management is characterized as rational and reasonable. Those two words—rational and reasonable—are often used interchangeably in RR and elsewhere, and although similar in meaning, are distinct from one another. From Webster:

> *Rational,* adj.–of, based, or derived from reasoning [rational powers], not foolish, but sensible. From the Latin, to reckon, plan, or think. The ability to draw conclusions from judgments; sound thought or judgment, good sense.

> *Reasonable,* adj.—Reasonable is a less technical term and suggests the use of practical reason in making decisions, choices, and so on.

Rational and *reasonable* are the key words. RR is neither a philosophy nor a set of tenets to be accepted and believed. RR is a philosophy to be examined and accepted or rejected, but it is also a method, a project-oriented, thought-full approach to problem solving. Maxie Maultsby and Albert Ellis list five basic principles against which an idea [or a program incorporating a set of ideas] can be judged as rational or irrational, reasonable or unreasonable.[5] Here is the formula:

1. If I believe this thought to be true, will it help me remain sober, safe, and alive?
2. Is this thought *objectively* true, and upon what evidence can I form this opinion?
3. Is this thought producing feelings I want to have?
4. Is this thought helping me reach a chosen goal?
5. Is this thought likely to minimize conflict with others?

In RR it's OK (and expected) to utilize *and* analyze. It's OK to think and ask questions—and there are no dumb questions. You can never be too smart or too dumb to make it in RR; just use the brains and common sense you have. Take the cotton out of your ears and throw it away. Speak up, agree, disagree, ask questions. Crosstalk is OK in RR. Here's a little exercise in clear thinking that we recently discussed at a local RR meeting.

Glancing at her husband's motorcycle, a woman says, "The difference between men and boys is the size of their toys." Her neighbor nods agreement. But consider what was really said. The statement is prejudiced and irrational. It puts the man down and declares him a boy. The "boy" may be a great husband and father, community leader, and a company manager. The boy-charge leveled against him ignores the fact that people have a right to choose their own forms of recreation. They may view biking as a money-saver, and bikes do, in fact, get more miles per gallon than anything else on the road. They may find bikes enjoyable and convenient for short trips. Bikers enjoy moments of solitude and a special kind of freedom. There are millions of bikers on the roads, men and women, adults who simply enjoy bikes for reasons of their own, not subject to your approval or mine. Now, try these, if you like:

• Women are so alike. They're so emotional!
• There are no atheists in foxholes.
• Men are all alike. They've got only one thing on their minds!
• If there were no God, we would have to invent Him.

That which is rational and reasonable is the *essence* of Rational Recovery, a program based on the acquisition of information, the power of the human mind, and our ability to act sensibly. This *power*

—the force of the human mind—is not only Rational Recovery's "higher power," but humankind's highest natural power. In RR, we hold that to be rational is the only civilized way to live.

But RR is sometimes labeled "intellectual," or even "elitist." That's nonsense; it isn't, any more than common sense is. Rational Recovery's program is a tribute to the human mind, not an affront to it. Jack Trimpey has written, "Whatever amount of intelligence you have will be sufficient, provided you use it." Common sense and intelligence are much the same thing, but like a hammer and a saw gathering dust on a shop bench, they are useless until they are put to use.

In RR we sometimes tend to overemphasize the power of the human mind, and we must, at times, remind ourselves that we are rational-*emotive* beings, and that without healthy emotions a human being can degenerate into a thinking machine. (In RR I have hugged and cuddled more than one grown man or woman crying like a child in despair.)

Rational Recovery can also be described as a pro-choice program; it acknowledges your power of choice (volition, decision making) as self-evident. To addicts, it all boils down to this: you either are or are not responsible for your life. Can you—are you able to—make a decision as to whether you will or will not take a drink? *If you decide to read the next paragraph, you can decide to drink or not to drink.* Decisions are decisions.

The Purpose of Rational Recovery

RR's purpose is to help addicted people quit drinking or using drugs. What members do with their lives after that is up to them. We of RR are not concerned with imposing a philosophy, religious or other, upon members. We are concerned with the achievement of mental health and a rational-emotive approach to living. We are also concerned with eating disorders, and Lois Trimpey, co-founder of RR, has written a book on the subject, *Fatness: The Small Book.*

To sum up, RR is a program devoted to substance-dependent people who want to survive and be happy. RR provides them with information and problem-solving techniques with which they can get the job done. It's that simple.

With Emmett Velten, Albert Ellis recently published *When AA Doesn't Work For You: Rational Steps to Quitting Alcohol.*[6] The authors point out that there are five *irrational* beliefs that many of us hold and that we can learn to unlearn them. The notorious five are:

A. *Musterbation* (shoulding, demandingness). (I *must* succeed and obtain approval.)
B. *Awfulizing.* (I lapsed two weeks ago. Isn't that just awful?) [No.]
C. *Low Frustration Tolerance.* (I can't quit smoking; it would be too hard for me.) [Cancer is even harder.]
D. *Rating and Blaming.* (I'm worthless because I made a mistake, or, The world's a rotten place to live.) [Know a better one?]
E. *Overgeneralizing* (Always or Never Attitudes). (A.A. is good for everybody: it worked for me; or, A.A. is a lousy outfit: I tried it and it didn't work for me.)

Conclusions that can ruin your life flow from these mental distortions. The authors list common irrationalities, and then trash each of them with common sense thinking and practical examples. Here are the ten offenders, compliments of Ellis and Velten:

a) All-or-nothing thinking
b) Perfectionism
c) Jumping to false conclusions
d) Catastrophizing and focusing on the negative
e) Always-or-never thinking
f) Disqualifying the positive
g) Labeling
h) Emotional reasoning
i) Personalizing
j) Phonyism

Personal Worth

Rational Recovery is convinced that every person—without exception—has intrinsic worth. The recognition of this fact results in acceptance of oneself as valuable and unique. In RR we stop drinking *because* of this inherent quality, not in order to achieve it. In *The Small Book*, Trimpey writes, "We do not remain sober in order to think well of ourselves; it is because we like or *value* (emphasis added) ourselves that we do not drink." Our personal worth is a given, a constant, an inherent quality. Trimpey comments:

The idea that you'll have more intrinsic worth sober than drunk is a wrongheaded view. . . . The opposite and rational idea is that individual human worth is self-defined . . . and is the lowest common denominator of mental health. Without an unswerving sense of personal worth we become dependent on others for approval, and we subject ourselves to variations of mood that put sobriety at risk.[7]

The meaning of self-worth is that, and something more. Survival is the universal primary value, and a conviction of self-worth can be considered an affirmation of that value. A perception of "non-worth," exhibited in the form of self-destructive drinking, denies the ultimate survival "instinct," or value, and thereby invites death—the ultimate self put-down.

Some people seem to think that their personal worth is a variable, somehow determined and measured by others. A critique of the *doctrine of variable worth* is a key construct in the Rational-Emotive Therapy of Ellis, and has become a vital part of Trimpey's Rational Recovery. Ellis, Velten, Trimpey, Tate, and thousands of others recognize the doctrine of variable worth as a construct that highlights the pernicious—that is to say, rotten—idea that "in order to be a good, decent person, one must rate oneself according to certain rules"[8] The basic rule is that you must accept the judgment of others about your worth.

Thus, at 10:00 a.m. your boss says that you are a terrific performer, and you feel great. At lunch, someone says that you messed up on a job, and you feel terrible. At 2:00 p.m. an old friend tells you what a fine person you are, and you feel great again; but at 4:00 p.m. the receptionist makes a snide remark about your dress, and you feel awful about that. (Maybe the receptionist lacks good taste?)

Human worth is independent of outside opinion and is not subject to anyone's approval or disapproval. It's appropriate to accept compliments and to listen to criticism from others, but it's inappropriate to determine personal worth on the basis of either. The fact is that *they*, whoever they are, don't walk in your shoes, don't live inside your head, and don't have all the facts on which to make sound judgments, even if they were in a position to judge. Your essential worth as a human being is a constant, not a variable, and certainly independent of what "they" may think. Believe it; better yet, think about it.

Rational Recovery recognizes human fallibility, the fact that we all make mistakes—according to scripture, seven of them (sins) each day. In RR we choose self-forgiveness over guilt and shame. We feel regrets, remorse, or sadness—all normal reactions to certain situations—but we need not condemn ourselves. We also think that a decision to (or not to) rectify the effects of past mistakes is a matter of individual judgment. RR does not dictate ethics. In his list of the "Central Beliefs of Alcoholism," Trimpey writes:

> "The rational idea is that doing is more important than doing well, trying is the first step toward succeeding, and accepting myself as fallible, yet inestimably worthwhile as a human being, is entirely possible. Succeeding does not make me into a success, and failing doesn't make me into a failure.

Behavior, Responsibility & Disease

In normal human beings, behavior implies action with intent, that is, a willful act which a person can either do or not do. Thus, an epileptic seizure is not a willful act, but taking a drink or drug is. Personal responsibility is inevitably linked to behavior, other than in cases involving brain damage, insanity, or simple lack of ability to perform in a purposeful manner; a baby crying at 3:00 a.m. is not responsible for awakening its parent(s). Choice is the key issue. If your cat kills a bird, it is not responsible for doing so, and there's no reason to become angry about it. That's what cats do; they eat, sleep, play, and kill birds, because their instincts drive them to do these things. They have no choice in the matter. But you are not a cat or a dog; you are an intelligent and capable human being—essentially different from all other forms of life because you can think, and because you can think of alternative solutions to a problem, you can choose among them. Unless, of course, you're sick, diseased, powerless, dependent, hopeless, helpless, etc.—all the things you were told and came to believe.

Are you diseased? Contagious, maybe? Would I dare shake hands with you or hug you? Did your family "get" the disease from you, or did you "get it" from them? A common argument for the disease notion is this: "Of course alcoholism is a disease! The AMA says so." Scholars classify that position as the logical fallacy they call "the argument from authority." In this busy world we tend to take shortcuts, but sometimes it's better to gather the facts, do your own thinking, and reach your own conclusions—especially in areas that concern human behavior and matters of life and death. Those who still think of the AMA as a benevolent and infallible organization are inclined to accept its pronouncements without question. The AMA, however, is not infallible; it has changed its position on many issues many times, and has for decades demonstrated a marked tendency to serve its own interests under the guise of serving the public interest. It has fought every piece of legislation—including Medicare and Medicaid—intended to make health services available and affordable. It votes diseases in and out of existence. In the case of alcoholism, it seem seems that its position on the disease issue is based more on matters of money (insurability) than of fact.[9] An example: it has now decreed that if you refuse to be labeled an "alcoholic" (denial), *you therefore are an alcoholic!* That's insane. (Using the "denial" criterion, if you admit you're an alcoholic you're an alcoholic; if you deny you're an alcoholic, you're an alcoholic.) In hospitals and treatment centers everybody gets "cured," that is to say, "discharged," at the end of 14 or 28 days.[10] That's when the insurance runs out.

Has your physician shown you the lab test that confirmed this so-called disease? No, and for good reason: there is no lab test for alcoholism. And do we even know what a disease is? In an article in *USA Today* we find this:

> The persuading of the public that alcoholism is a disease (79% in a 1982 Gallup poll)—well-defined, identifiable, and rendering its victims out of control—has been so successful that even those who should least accept it often do so. . . . [example: Mothers Against Drunk Driving]
>
> *Although the public may not feel confused about alcoholism, the medical community certainly does.* [emphasis added] There is even a debate in medicine as to what "disease" means. . . . The public usually conceptualizes disease in a simple, straightforward way as meaning a biologically unhealthy condition with a clear medical cause, such as infections. However, the "disease" of alcoholism is diagnosed mostly by criteria of behavior. . . . If the medical community is divided on what constitutes disease, they are in near anarchy[11] as to what alcoholism is. The well-received 1987 work, *The Medical Basis of Psychiatry*, argues that research on "alcoholism" [is] hopelessly confused by conceptual inconsistency: [Studies are] bedeviled by the uncertainties of what to measure and how to measure it. . . . Most researchers agree that the behaviors we call alcoholism are a result of a complex combination of innate influences, simple learned behavior, and freedom of choice.[12]

Perhaps the best way to solve the disease question is to turn to some other field such as semantics, logic, or economics. It is certain that excessive drinking of anything, including water, alcohol, and fruit juice, can produce diagnosable physical effects. In a small percentage of cases, the excessive and prolonged consumption of alcohol does cause cardiovascular complications, cirrhosis, gastro-intestinal problems and so on, but the *drinking* is not the disease; its *effects* are. Drinking remains a volitional act, a behavior, regardless of the influences that are exerted on that behavior. Even disease advocates such as J. Milam, K. Ketcham, and M. Gold say that you have to "trigger" the alleged disease by *deciding* to take that first drink. Once you do so, they say, the disease kicks in and you lose control. But if you decide *not* to take that first drink, the so-called "disease" *can't* "kick in" any more than a gun can fire without someone pulling the trigger. It's a simple decision—an act under your control—whether or not to pull that "trigger." (The "loss of control" myth was exploded by Jeffrey Schaler in a superb article in *Society*.[13] Dozens of controlled studies have refuted that absurd—and dangerous—piece of fiction.)[14]

The general perception remains, however, that if you have the "disease" of alcoholism, then you are not responsible for your actions. That's nonsense, as we have seen. Neither traditionalists nor nontraditionalists teach that. And if you actually believe—that is, accept on "authority"—that you are diseased and that once you take that first drink you'll be unable to stop, then you still have to explain that first drink.[15]

That first drink is not an isolated decision; it is only the last of a series of decisions. Thus, you may drink, but must first decide to buy a shot, quart, fifth, six-pack, or case. You decide on beer, vodka, wine, or distilled spirits. You decide to go with Bud Light or Colt 45. You decide to go to a liquor store or Joe's Place. You decide to sit at the bar or in a booth, and if you buy a fifth from a liquor store, you then decide to put it either in the trunk or on the car seat. Having made all those decisions, you make one more: I will drink. Drinking doesn't just happen; it's planned and made to happen.

Actually the disease question is irrelevant. In his *Small Book*, Trimpey said that if you believe that alcoholism is a disease, you can drink and become sick. On the other hand, if you think that alcoholism is not a disease, you can drink and become sick. The "cure" for alcoholism is also clear: if you believe that alcoholism is a disease, don't drink; if you think that alcoholism is not a disease, don't drink. Abstinence is the word, total and permanent. In *The Small Book*, Trimpey gets right to the point; he advises, "Just knock it off!" So it hurts for awhile. So what? *Not* knocking it off hurts even more. Your body, and the police, courts, probation officers, em-ployers, and jail keepers see to that.

Trimpey's insight puts the disease issue in the same category as the question posed by medieval theologians: "How many angels can dance on the head of a pin?" The best answer to a question like that is "who gives a damn?" As they say, let's get real. In *The Small Book* we find:

> But many people *do* care if alcoholism is a disease because their jobs depend on alcoholism being defined as a disease. Others make "I am an alcoholic" their personal identity, and this admission the password to their recovery clubs. Still others can forgive themselves for their drunken behavior only if they believe the disease was responsible. Many accept the disease idea as an article of faith, and in normal conversation feel compelled to join the word "alcoholism" with "the disease of" . . . some others use the disease idea as a gun to their heads, imagining catastrophic results if they have just a sip of alcohol, ever.[16] Still others seek leniency in court by focusing on the powerlessness that is said to accompany the disease of alcoholism.[17]

Professors John and Phyllis Craig disposed of the disease issue simply by applying logic.[18] They said that because heavy drinking is not a disease, it can't be "cured," but because it is a behavior, it can be changed. They point out that "alcoholism" is a descriptive rather than a diagnostic term, since the words *alcoholic* and *alcoholism* describe an observable form of behavior.[19] The Craigs carry their logic a step further: swimming, eating, flying, drinking, and working are activities, behaviors, things we do. They are not "conditions," defined as states of health, as in "What's the patient's condition today?" Or, as in "He has a heart condition." The word *condition* clearly pertains to a state of health or illness. The Craigs reason that "If it's (swimming, drinking, eating) *not* a condition, no one can *have* it; and, since no one can have it, we cannot cure them of it."

The Social Aspects of Rational Recovery

Rational Recovery knows that although recovery is essentially a personal issue, it involves more than enlightened self-interest; it includes a concern for the happiness of others. This relates to RR's social aspect, its awareness of the way in which heavy drinking adversely affects the lives of others. In RR the statement, "When I drink I'm only hurting myself," is considered a prime example of irrational thinking. Stanton Peele, Archie Brodsky, and Mary Arnold in *The Truth About Addiction and Recovery* also stress the social aspects of addiction in their "Life Process Program." They take the view that "a person needs to replace an addiction with deeper satisfactions and better ways of coping. These include marital and family therapy, social skills training, job skills, and stress management."[20]

A.A. recognizes the impact of heavy drinking on the lives of others, and it has Alanon for friends and relatives of heavy drinkers. Rational Recovery, as yet, has nothing comparable to Alanon. RR invites concerned parties to participate *directly* in the recovery process at regular RR meetings. I'm not sure which is the better approach.

Dependence and Independence

Rational Recovery is a program of independence, not dependence. It takes issue with the traditional view that "because I am an alcoholic, I need something or someone stronger or greater than myself upon which to rely." (Central Beliefs of Alcoholism, #12) RR insists that *dependency* is the problem, and that it's important for alcoholics to learn to think and act *independently*. (Hence, there are no sponsors in RR.) The logic carries through to the higher power/God issue. It's reasonable to think that if a person has a problem with nail-biting, shyness, drinking, or over eating, that such behaviors should be classified as mental health problems and handled as such. But A.A. advocates the idea that divine assistance is *required* in the case of heavy drinking. Rational Recovery does not agree, but concedes that those who believe that God can help them overcome a drinking problem would be well advised to avail themselves of that assistance.

Rational Recovery does not promote spirituality or religion, which is *not* to say that it is opposed to any or all of these things. RR is neither theistic nor atheistic, but simply nontheistic. We are convinced that anyone can change a behavior pattern related to smoking, drinking, drugging, or eating without the supernatural intervention of a God or higher power, real or imagined. It is said that "God helps them who help themselves." People with spiritual and/or religious orientations are welcome in RR and usually do well if they separate their personal beliefs and convictions from RR's cognitive (learning) approach to understanding and dealing with problems. In RR we understand the subjective nature of spiritual concepts. We understand religion as a formal and institutionalized relationship to God, and we consider that relationship a personal issue separate from but not alien to the recovery process. We of RR recognize that religious and spiritual values can be and often are compatible with the principles of mental health. Many members of Rational Recovery consider themselves spiritual or religious beings, or both. And this, from Jack Trimpey:

> Rational Recovery, for all its agnosticism and irreverence, is obviously a friend of traditional religions in that we separate health care from religion and strongly suggest that people go to the church of their choice or consult with clergy on matters of a spiritual or theological nature. RR gladly renders to the churches what is theirs. Incidentally, there is no consensus on the definition of either spirituality or religion, from theological, sociological, or legal perspectives.[21]

Matching

Rational Recovery champions the idea that the most effective self-help group is the one that matches and meets the needs of its members. It does not see itself as "the one and only." Those who come to RR and for any reason find it unsuited to their needs are actively assisted in finding an alternative, such as A.A., WFS, or SOS. (As mentioned earlier, RR published a list of all of the self-help support groups for alcoholics in its 1991 quarterly journal.) We are convinced, however, that as a program that emphasizes the value of information and clear thinking, RR can be an asset to members of any group, including groups with strong traditional inclinations.

Professional Advisors

Professional advisors are highly regarded in RR, as they are in WFS and MFS. Advisors are volunteer professionals—therapists, psychologists, social workers, educators, mental health practitioners, and occasionally nurses, physicians, or psychiatrists. Their primary function is an advisory one, but in emergency situations, such as those involving psychotic behavior or signs of possible suicide, they take appropriate action. At many meetings, professionals are called upon for comments regarding group progress, changes observed, and group dynamics. An RR coordinator may solicit the advice of the attending professional at any time. RR has long enjoyed a respect for and warm relationship with the professional community.

Certainly, no one accuses RR of being anti-professional or anti-intellectual. Advisors never solicit clients, but RR members are free to seek them out for private consultation.[22]

One Day or One Life at a Time?

One *day* at a time? In RR we feel that a 24-hour short-range plan is little more than crisis management. A drinking problem is not all that overwhelming. Days can be endured, but long-range objectives can be accomplished. In RR, when we talk about total and permanent abstinence, we aren't talking about one day; we're talking about all of them. It's the difference between changing a behavior and restraining a disease. In RR, we plan ahead—for life.

Addictive Voice Recognition Training (AVRT)

We talk to ourselves, sometimes audibly, always quietly. It's called self-talk, the perpetual silent internal conversation that goes on within all of us. You're probably aware of this phenomenon, but if not, try this: stop reading for a moment and listen—to yourself. You will hear yourself talking to yourself. Your mind is in perpetual motion and you can't stop it (at least without training and practice in meditation). Try. It goes on anyway, often with sound effects and color. What an astounding capability! Trimpey suggests that "our voices express our perceptions of reality, our ideas and beliefs about life and ourselves, and our evaluations of experience and circumstance."[23]

Credit Jack Trimpey with Addictive Voice Recognition Training (AVRT), the development and application of this self-talk phenomenon in the addictions field. AVRT is a consciousness-raising tool with which an addict can tune into the workings of his own mind. The key concept is *awareness*, the awareness of silent conversations within us debating the pros and cons of drinking or drugging.

We need to be especially on guard against one of these voices, the voice of irrationality, the self-destructive, immature part of our minds. Bill Knaus, well known through his books dealing with procrastination, comments on the voice of irrationality:

The founder of psychoanalysis, Sigmund Freud, called it the "id." Gestalt therapist Fritz Perls called it the "Wheedler." The father of Recovery Inc., Abraham Low, called it "comfort things." Jack Trimpey calls it the *addictive voice*. What does the *it* in these different systems have in common? The *it* stands for strong, shortsighted urges for immediate gratification, and the avoidance of exposure to normal discomfort. You may think of the *it* as an alien part of yourself, but— *you own this voice.* Trimpey explains that all of us entertain ideas that are rational and serve our best interests, *and* ideas that are irrational and self-defeating. In non-addicts, the voice of reason is [usually] dominant; in addicts, the voice of non-reason (irrationality) is dominant. With the addictive mindset in control (during "blackouts" [temporary amnesia] the "it" is in total control), alcoholics are at a severe disadvantage in protecting themselves from the predictably harmful results of overindulgence. In this way, a self-generated "alcoholic philosophy" is generated [as] a subset of the person's over-all philosophy, so that one may function quite sanely and rationally in many significant ways and yet have firm convictions regarding alcohol that seem to deny human intelligence.[24]

Trimpey has dubbed the "it" of Freud, Perls, and Low with another name: The Beast. Happily, as Trimpey explains, there is no such thing as The Beast; it's an image as far removed from reality as it is from demonology. It is merely a consciousness-raising device that helps us become aware of that irrational part of ourselves that prompts us to drink or drug. Trimpey's Beast is actually an acronym, as explained in *The Small Book.*

B–stands for the **Boozing opportunity**, any circumstance or thought about drinking or using.

E–stands for **Enemy voice recognition**, any idea that supports and encourages you to drink or use. Here you think about your thinking, and recognize it for what it is, the irrational voice prodding you toward self-destruction.

A–stands for **Accuse the voice of malice**, by "actively and assertively [responding] to the coaxing of the Beast. Anger, sarcasm, and wit are effective tools of confrontation. So is imagery. Bill Knaus suggests that one can generate the image of a "feeble mouse, wearing a mask of a ferocious lion." So– strip off the mask, step on the mouse, and toss it into the garbage!

S–stands for **Self-control and self-worth reminders,**
remembering always, as Trimpey points out, that "We do not
remain sober in order to think well of ourselves; it is because
we like or value ourselves that we do not drink," and a little
later, this beautiful phrase, "to drink would be poisoning a
friend, oneself."[25]

T–stands for **Treasure your sobriety** by "taking an overview
and reaffirming the intrinsic value of sobriety, focusing on
how life's pleasures are possible only in a consistently
[continuous] sober state.[26]

The Beast has no power other than that which we grant it. And
it's not really a beast at all; it's a kitten posing as a lion. To drink,
or not to drink; that is the question; and "ambivalent" is the word
that best describes the self-contained discussion that swings between
excuses for drinking and reasons for not doing so. You say No. It
says Yes. You and *it* argue, but you have a distinct advantage; you,
compared to *it*, are smart, very smart. You can gather facts, organize
them, analyze them and act in a self-preserving and life-enhancing
way. Given ten problems, you can come up with several possible
solutions to each. You can evaluate, judge, and decide issues, and
you can do so with your legitimate self-interest in mind.

The Beast, on the other hand, is not so gifted; it has the IQ of a
moron. Although it is not intelligent, it is clever, devious, persuasive,
malicious, dangerous, and selfish. Given ten different problems, it
comes up with the same answer to each: "Drink! Drug!" How
unimaginative. It says, "One for the road; we can make it home all
right." It says, "The only way I can relax after a hard day's work is to
drink." It says, "I feel frustrated and down, so I'll drink." That's how
The Beast thinks, in spite of the fact that the last 20 times you drank
your frustration did *not* decrease, but increased.

The Beast has no memory of the past, or sense of the future. Bill
Knaus says, "It has no sense of time, other than *now*."[27] The Beast is
your enemy, a teasing, wheedling, whining, spoiled brat. It's heart-
less too; it would gleefully bury you alive, given a chance to do so.

And so it is, that within that sacred space between your ears,
within the mind itself, reside your best friend and your worst enemy,
engaged in endless combat. Your best friend is you, the voice of
reason; your worst enemy is "it"—the voice of irrationality. When
Trimpey named that *other* voice—the voice of irrationality—The Beast,
he provided us with a useful image for identifying the voice of that
non-reasoning animal that lurks within each of us.

"The Beast," is, of course, a figment of our imagination, but naming it and visualizing it is a convenient way to confront it and destroy it. Trimpey says that although it may be cowed into submission, it never really dies, but lies patiently in the bush, one eye open, waiting to pounce. In *The Small Book* he writes:

> The central task in the rational mode of recovery is to help the rational voice of survival and personal gain to grow in strength so that it may dominate the ruthless, commanding, and sometimes seductive, addictive voice that argues endlessly for intoxication. Instead of beseeching the addict to surrender to a Higher Power, RR helps unleash the awesome power of the human intellect upon an inferior mentality—the addictive voice that many participants refer to as "the beast" . . . a key insight is that it is not humanly possible to have a drink or consume drugs without devoting a significant amount of *conscious* thought to it . . . Addictive voice recognition training (AVRT) is simple: "Any thinking that supports any use of drugs or alcohol in any amount, in any form–ever." AVRT plays the same vital role in RR as the HP [Higher Power] does in AA.[28]

RR advisor Judith Rae, whose book *Daily Rational Reflections* will be published in the winter of 1993, has devised a "hot thought" (e.g., anger)/"cool thought" format for externalizing the internal "irrational/rational" self-talk that often precedes drinking or drugging (inspired by David Burns in his *Feeling Good*). Example: Jeff, three months sober and accused of drinking, entertains a "hot thought"—"Damn! Three months sober, and she accuses me of drinking. May as well do it then." The "hot" thought is then overshadowed by a "cool" one: "Yeah, I can believe it after all the times she's come home and found me drunk. She has good reason to wonder about it. It must be hard for others to believe that this time I've really changed."

The internal conversation goes on—the self-defeating, irrational statement first, followed by a self-preserving, rational counterstatement. Rae recommends that these mini-exercises be written out in column form, Hot Thoughts vs. Cool Thoughts, or pro-drink vs. no-drink. The writing makes a difference. We've followed her format at many RR meetings, and it works like a charm.

A Few Specifics about RR

1). Anonymity: a personal choice, always respected. A surprising number of people in RR are not concerned about this issue, but others, worried about the social or occupational effects of disclosure, are more circumspect. We live in a prejudiced and judgmental society, and some degree of discretion may be advisable.

2). Confidentiality: we assume it and insist on it. We are courteous and civilized people. Virtually all self-help support programs promote this principle.

3). "Drunkalogs," often termed "war stories," are 20-minute speeches ("leads") given at traditional meetings. RR does not indulge; we consider A.A.-type tell-it-all, gut-wrenching confessions imprudent and therapeutically inadvisable. Those concerned with confidentiality would do well to consider the risks involved in the full-confession drunkalog. Some things are better said to close friends or professionals, and the trauma of genuine emotional catharsis is certainly better managed by a professional than by a group of well-meaning amateurs, some of whom are one-time visitors still committed to heavy drinking and/or drugging. In traditional circles the assumption is made that emotional catharsis (even in a lay setting, and usually before strangers and acquaintances), is somehow inherently therapeutic. RR and most professionals would not agree. In RR, we delve into the past lightly and with discretion. Our emphasis is on how to manage the present, and plan for the future.

4). In RR we explore and solve problems in a variety of ways. We share insights and information. We study the works of rational and cognitive therapists and researchers, such as those by Ellis, Trimpey, Schaler, Bufe, Dorsman, Peele, Brodsky, Arnold, Room, Miller, Ragge, Kirkpatrick, Hester, Barrett, Burns, Maultsby, Fingarette, Engs, Marlatt, Andrews, and many others. Our meeting format includes outside speakers (on nutrition, biofeedback, transactional analysis, etc.), discussions with crosstalk, *Small Book* discussions, problem-solving and stress management techniques, and so on.[29]

5). We never say, "I'm _____ and I'm an alcoholic." (By which definition?) But we might say, "I'm _____, and I'm here to solve a problem related to alcohol or cocaine." We don't put ourselves or others down by using meaningless labels.

6). There are no tokens, chips, or "birthday parties" in RR. Symbolic victories may be gratifying, but in RR we concentrate on learning, changing, and *graduating*—free and recover*ed*—not recover*ing*.

7). Crosstalk: In RR we encourage people to think, question and to offer helpful suggestions to others. We learn from our own experience and that of others. Advice and insights are well received in RR meetings. We guide but do not dictate. We train our coordinators to keep things flowing and orderly.

8). About professionals: We welcome them (see previous entry on professional advisors) as advisors or as visitors. RR is neither anti-professional nor anti-intellectual. We are, however, faced with the fact that many professionals seem wary of a mental health approach to addiction problems. How strange! Many of them still cling to traditional ideas about powerlessness, the need for dependence, and the disease myth. Some of them, when asked their opinion of Rational Recovery, respond by saying, "Never heard of it." That response is not only unacceptable, it is unconscionable. A mark of a true professional is to stay current with developments in her or his field. Those who know nothing of RR or, worse yet, pretend ignorance of it, are less than professional and must face the ethical issue of committing a disservice to their clients by withholding information from them.

9). Friends and relatives of heavy drinkers are welcome at RR meetings, as are those who are seriously interested in the field of chemical dependency.

10). There are three guidelines in RR: attend meetings, gather information, and use it. Because Rational Recovery is an educational program, we expect participants to read, study, and freely discuss the major issues in the addictions field. For starters, we encourage them to read *both* the Big Book and *The Small Book*.

11). Money: We pass the hat. We encourage members to contribute something, even if it's only a nickel or a dime. Grants and private or corporate donations are welcome. (Poverty, it seems to me, is more than an inconvenience; it is an impediment to the development of any organization.)

12). Court-mandated persons are welcome in RR, and are gradually appearing in greater numbers. Coordinators sign attendance slips. We are fully aware that some people mandated to RR are not "alcoholics" by any definition of the word, but we also know that most of them can learn much from RR's mental health approach to managing life's problems. RR willingly participates in the mandate program, but, like A.A., does not participate in case supervision or reporting.

13). Attendance: We suggest that people attend four to six meetings before deciding to join the group or leave it. For those who stay, we suggest regular attendance as a matter of common sense. We encourage people to be clean and sober when they arrive, but do not demand it. We reserve the right, however, to eject from the group anyone who is drunk or high, and whose behavior is, or may become, harmful to the group. We tell new members this: We're in a win/win situation. Attend regularly for your sake and for that of others. We're friendly but serious too, so don't waste your time or ours. We're here to get a job done and get on with life. Please do your part. You are responsible for your conduct and your life.

14). We cater to those who have found the traditional 12-step approach unsuited to their needs. Most of us have had the experience. We understand.

15). We help with setup and cleanup because it's the right thing to do. And we don't smoke at meetings because it's not the right thing to do. It's also impolite. (Before, during the break, or after—outside the meeting room—is just fine, however.)

16). THE BIG PLAN in RR: RR does not advocate a one-day-at-a-time approach to problem solving. We do not see dragons on our doorsteps every morning. Nor do we see a habit-problem as something we must live with forever. Drinking is a way of life; so is non-drinking. Frankly, the changeover is not that big a job, and there are better things to do in life than devote it to recovery and endless meetings. Getting the job done, however, requires more than information and common sense; it requires willpower and action.

Willpower is an old-fashioned word, one that like other old-fashioned words—loyalty and dedication for example—still rings true. Albert Ellis and Emmett Velten wrote a beautiful commentary on willpower in their *Rational Steps*:

Realize that the power in your "willpower" is not merely your decision and determination to change. It is your steady, persistent *action* to implement your decision. Willpower equals your clear-cut decision and determination to change, *plus* your acceptance of the pain of changing, *plus* your action to implement change. Without discomfort and action, you may have a strong *will*, but no real *power*.[30]

But is there a power greater than willpower? Yes. It's called inertia—doing nothing—and some famous author (H.G. Wells, or some other guy by the same name) said that it is the greatest power on earth. It can keep you drunk or high and in a rut forever. To use or not to use: that is the question, to which you, of course, already know the answer.

17). Graduation from RR: It usually takes years to acquire an addictive habit, but only six to eighteen months in RR to get rid of one. We're not in the business of collecting warm bodies and sentencing them to sit in stuffy, smoke-filled rooms for life.[31] Recovery is change; it has a beginning and an end. Trimpey writes, "This practice (graduation) is consistent with RR's thinking." Exactly. When you've solved the problem that brought you to Rational Recovery, it's time to leave and get on with life. When to graduate? One certain sign is that moment when you finally recognize that the world does not revolve around you, but that you are an important and vital part of it. Another sign is a consistent feeling of happiness, based on the realization—with full credit to yourself (and a little to RR)—that you did a good job. As Trimpey points out, RR never saved anybody, but it has provided the means whereby individuals can save themselves. RR is more like a holding tank with an inlet and an outlet than a bottomless pit.

18). No one in RR bothers with the more than 225 slogans of the traditionalists. I can remember asking a few questions during my years in A.A., and being answered with slogans such as "Keep coming back," "You'll understand in time," and "Let go and let God." I am neither the brightest nor the dumbest guy on the block, but when I ask a question I expect an answer and have a right to it. Slogans are not answers. Admittedly, however, we have a few slogans in RR:

1) Bring the mind, the body will follow.
2) Learn and think or drink and sink.
3) We're concerned with thriving, not just surviving.
4) We don't give up alcohol and illicit drugs. We get rid of them.
5) You act as you feel and you feel as you think.
6) Just say "know!"
7) Think about your thinking.

19). Good intentions and willpower alone won't get the job done; you've got to know *how* to tackle the problem. In that psychological tool kit provided by Albert Ellis there is a special tool marked A-B-C. It's designed to break the intoxication cycle, and when used with a little common sense, it does just that. It is, as Ellis and Velten point out, a method that "enables people to get a handle on their own self-defeating thinking, emotional reactions, and behavior."[32] The authors suggest that we start with an objective, something practical, like staying alive and being happy.

After reading the section that follows, use a single sheet of paper and write out your own A-B-C. We assume a *goal*, which is to stop drinking or drugging (or both) in order to survive and be happy. The following is an abbreviation of the format presented by Ellis and Velten in *When A.A. Doesn't Work for You:*

A) **Activating Event**: any event or events, including thoughts and memories, that precede drinking.

B) **Beliefs**: what you tell yourself about A, the Activating Event. What you believe will either help you to achieve your goal or prevent you from doing so.

C) **Consequences**: your feelings/actions that stem from A & B.

Here are two examples. In each case A, the Activating Event, is the same. Only the Bs, the Beliefs, and the Cs, the Consequences, differ:

Activating Event: In heavy, home-bound traffic, a car suddenly cuts in front of Mr. Able. Able swerves sharply and manages to avoid a serious accident.

Beliefs (pro-goal): I wonder what happened to that guy? Dodging a chuckhole maybe, or got sideswiped, or just a jerk? I'd love to have a couple of drinks about now, but that wouldn't help. I've been down that road before. I'd enjoy it all right, for a while, but then there's always the morning after, not to mention my job and marriage. Maybe even a DUI. I'm not a child and I've had my share—and more. I can handle this.

Consequences (pro-goal): Mr. Able calmed down and went home.

Activating Event: Same as above

Beliefs (anti-goal): What an idiot! He shouldn't have cut in like that. Why do these things always happen to *me*? Better stop and have a few to relax. I'm stressed out and really need to do it. It'll calm my nerves. And to hell with tomorrow; that will take care of itself!

Consequences (anti-goal): Able felt rotten and had a hangover the next morning. He overslept and was late for work. He felt bad about himself and lost some self-confidence. And that little piece of "relaxation" cost him $35 he couldn't afford.

That's the ABC of it. Trimpey covers the subject in detail in his *Small Book*, and adds a D and an E.[33] His D stands for Dispute—the rational voice engaging the irrational voice (The Beast). Mr. Able confronted and overpowered The Beast with his powers of reason (with his pro-goal beliefs). It was not that hard a fight; Able, a heavyweight, found himself in the ring with a bantamweight. The Beast shut up, backed off, and slithered away. After several engagements, The Beast lost energy and stamina. In time, Able learned to cut the thing off at will. Able defended himself by attacking, and he won.

Trimpey's E stands for Effects, the fruits of that victory. In the first scenario, Mr. Able felt great, proud of himself. He had confirmed his fundamental worth by treating his friend, himself, intelligently and with respect. He achieved his goal—to self-preserve and be happy.

RR's Effectiveness

RR works, but how well does it work in comparison to A.A.? The question is at least somewhat beside the point—which is to save lives; A.A. works for some, and RR works for others. The January/ February 1993, Vol. 5, Issue No. 3 of the *Journal of Rational Recovery* (JRR) discusses a Harvard University study (summarized here) at length. Rational Recovery had been compiling statistics since 1989 and was delighted when Harvard University Medical School offered to take over its research project. Rational Recovery readily accepted the offer, and Harvard later concluded, on the basis of the ongoing, scientifically conducted longitudinal study (at last report, 29 months) of 133 respondents who had attended RR, that *91% of them were currently sober.*

In August 1992, Jack Trimpey presented the results of the Harvard Study at the RRSN annual conference. Cean Willis, Ph.D., the Harvard researcher who conducted the study, presented the results in November 1992 to The American Association of Behavior Therapists. Both presentations evoked a collective sigh of relief to the effect that "Now, finally, the addictions field is on the road to sanity!"

The effects of those reports? RR's acceptance increased dramatically, and its growth exponentially. RR's phones rang off the hook and staff was added to handle the overload.

As mentioned above, the Harvard Study is a longitudinal project, and it will continue for years to come. RR, in stark contrast to A.A., is eager to be *objectively* evaluated, and is delighted that Harvard University is conducting this study.

New York University Medical School is also conducting a major project measuring the effectiveness of RR. Among the RR members it studied, it found a fascinating progression: after one month in RR, 35% of the membership was sober; after two months the percentage increased to 50%, and after three months—75% (figures rounded out). The New York University Medical School study is still in progress, and the results are very encouraging. Jack Trimpey comments on the RR members involved in this study: "Their success . . . is more a tribute to human competency than proof that Rational Recovery saves lives." What a decent thing to say, and in keeping with RR's tenet that "We don't save lives; we help people to do that for themselves." A full report on the NYU study will be published in a forthcoming issue of JAMA, the *Journal of the American Medical Association.*

Additional Information

• RR has a 20-person Board of Directors and a five-person Executive Committee.

• Primary text used in RR is *The Small Book: A Revolutionary Alternative for Overcoming Alcohol and Drug Dependence,* by Jack Trimpey, LCSW. It's published by Delacorte Press, Bantam Doubleday Dell, 1992 (4th ed. since 1989), Library call number: 362.292. Plus everything by Albert Ellis and works published by the Institute for Rational-Emotive Therapy. (See Bibliography and Sources of Help, Chapter 13.)

• **Main Office: Rational Recovery Systems**
Jack Trimpey, Executive Director
Lois Trimpey, Associate Director
Box 800, Lotus CA 95651-0800
Phones: 916-621-4374 and 916-621-4374
Fax: 916-621-2667 [call first to activate]

Summary and Review

RR is a cognitive/behavioral program, an application of Rational-Emotive Therapy (RET) applied to problems related to the use of alcohol and illicit drugs, and to eating disorders. It is an educational program with an emphasis on total abstinence and mental health, and it views addictions as learned behaviors subject to change. RR recognizes the legitimacy of all self-help support programs in the addictions field. We of RR respect those who are concerned with spiritual and religious matters, but hold that such issues are personal, and that dependency, upon either a natural or supernatural being, is not a requisite to behavioral change. We recognize the power of the human mind and the ability of any person to make decisions and assume personal responsibility for her or his life. RR is a time-limited, project-oriented program from which members graduate when they judge themselves ready to do so. We learn to live as self-respecting, happy, fully mature, and civilized human beings.

1. The Unitarian-Universalists comprise the only organized religion that has consistently offered support to Rational Recovery. In 1991 Jack Trimpey was invited to address its General Assembly in Hollywood, Florida, and was very well received by its national delegates. The principles of the Unitarian-Universalists and those of Rational Recovery are a near-reflection of one another.

2. Note the hyphenated word, *rational-emotive.* Rational-emotive therapy promotes a healthy balance between clear thinking and appropriate emotional expression.

3. In *The Road Less Traveled,* Scott Peck advises that problems are not only inevitable but can be welcomed, since they are opportunities for personal growth and development.

4. Peck, S. (1978). *The Road Less Traveled: A New Psychology of Love, Traditional Values and Spiritual Growth,* p.4. New York: Simon and Schuster. Note: Peck defines discipline as a set of four basic techniques: delaying gratification, assumption of responsibility, dedication to the truth or reality, and balancing (pp. 44-78).

5. Maultsby, M.C., Jr. & Ellis, A. (1974). *Techniques for Using Rational-Emotive Imagery.* New York: Institute for Rational-Emotive Therapy.

6. Fort Lee, NJ: Barricade Books, 1992.

7. *The Small Book,* p. 32.

8. Ibid., p. 182.

9. For an inside view of the AMA, I suggest *Ceremonial Chemistry: The Ritual Persecution of Drugs, Addicts, and Pushers,* (revised ed., 1985) by Thomas Szasz, published by Learning Publications, Inc., Holmes Beach, Fl. Index headings: American Medical Association, addiction, disease.

10. The word *arrested* rather than *cured* is used in such places, the word choice reinforcing the notion that heavy drinking is a an incurable disease that can be only restrained and endured, but never eliminated from a person's life.

11. An unfortunate word choice. What the writers really mean is "chaos." The word "anarchy" (at least in the sense used by anarchist theoreticians) implies order based on mutual aid and voluntary association, that is, order achieved without organized violence and coercion. –Editor

12. Vatz, R.E. and Weinbert, L.S. *USA Today.* (September, 1989). (pp.68-70).

13. Schaler, J. In *Society,* Vol. 28, No. 6, pp.42-49.

14. See Herbert Fingarette *Heavy Drinking* for references to many such studies.

15. In the Big Book, Bill Wilson stated that there are times when there is no defense against even that first drink–other than that provided by God. (His artful dodge, "Higher Power," has been explained elsewhere in this book, and by Ernest Kurtz in his book, *Not-God.*)

16. I've been sober about ten or eleven years, and every year I go on a private silent retreat at St. Meinrad's Abbey and monastery in St. Meinrad, IN. I was once a Catholic, and when on retreat, attend daily Mass. Sometimes I receive Communion under the forms of consecrated bread and wine. I do this for several reasons, all of them personal. The quantity of wine is, perhaps a teaspoonful. There is, of course, no "chemical trigger," and no desire to return to my former pattern of heavy drinking. I have participated in this central act of the Catholic Mass many times and will, upon completion of this manuscript, do so again. (I am now a Unitarian-

Universalist, with theistic inclinations.)

17. *The Small Book*, p. 4.

18. John Craig is a nationally known speaker, trainer, educator, and author, with some 20 years experience in substance abuse and chemical dependency in the areas of criminal justice, treatment, education, research, consultation, and administration. He is a professor at Indiana University. Phyllis Craig is a psychologist and administrator, with extensive experience in test development, measurement methods and assessment techniques. She is Director of Special Services for a large special education co-operative and has taught undergraduate and graduate courses in psychology at Indiana University. Elsewhere in this book, I refer to John's "Compass," an alcohol-diagnostic instrument of the highest caliber.

19. Physicians who sign off on patients departing a treatment center or hospital write *alcohol dependence*, a functional and descriptive phrase, on the exit form; this, in keeping with the guidelines provided in the *Diagnostic Statistical Manual* (DSM-III-Rev.), compiled by the American Psychiatric Association. Also, insurance companies won't pay for a diagnosis of "alcoholism."

20. pp. 169-170, 277-302.

21. A statement to this effect was submitted to RR as a proposed position statement on the issue of religion and spirituality. It was published in the *Journal of Rational Recovery*, Jan./Feb. 1993, Vol. 5, Issue No. 3, with a request for evaluation and comment. As of this writing, it is not an official RR statement, but an unofficial interpretation of RR's position on this subject.

22. Those who view themselves as adversaries of RR often allege that RR advisors charge for their services and solicit clients at meetings. They also suggest that RR advises moderated drinking. Both charges are false, and are usually made out of ignorance, and, sometimes, malice.

23. P. 57.

24. From pages 18 and 59-60 of a booklet (a primer) which he designed as an introduction to Rational Recovery. (Available through RR)

25. P. 69.

26. Pp. 64-70. An interesting variation on this concept may be found in *Alcohol, How to Give It Up and Be Glad You Did: A Sensible Approach*, by Philip Tate (referenced elsewhere, see bibliography). Chapter 5, pp. 27-34.

27. Knaus, P. 19.

28. P. 63.

29. See Appendix under "Educational Format."

30. Pp. 170-172

31. Rational Recovery, Women For Sobriety, and Men For Sobriety agree on this point. It is often asserted that it is the "God stuff" in A.A. that turns so many away from it. Possibly, but I think that there are more significant reasons: 1) novices reject the idea of powerlessness as demeaning, even insulting, and often view it as a debasement of their personal integrity; 2) they intuitively know that their problems are behavioral, rather than disease-based; and 3) they abhor the dictum that in order to maintain sobriety they will have to attend meetings for the rest of

their lives. After that, the "God stuff." It would seem that the religious component of A.A. is compatible with the ethos of a country which is thoroughly religious, and primarily Christian. The shocking inability of A.A. to retain members ("Comments" document, P. 12, Fig. C-1—reproduced on page 66 of this book) would suggest that all of the above-mentioned factors may be at work, possibly in the order listed.

32. *Rational Steps*, p. 3.

33. P. 136.

10

Traditional Recovery Management

This chapter addresses traditional forms of institutional recovery management. Although I am critical of the principles, practices, and effectiveness of the traditional approach, I am generally noncritical of the people, lay or professional, who have devoted their lives to it. I have found such people to be conscientious and dedicated, and it is to them that I dedicate this chapter.

The word "management" suggests a source of control outside the individual. That is, in part, what this chapter is about—the treatment for alcoholism provided in free-standing and hospital-based institutions. A person can, however, self-manage, as with a household budget or work schedule. Self-management for substance abusers[1] can be facilitated by seeing a private therapist, by joining a self-help support group, by individually solving a problem with the help of information from friends, books, or other sources, or—as in the large majority of cases—by simply "maturing out" of addictive behavior patterns.[2] Now, let's take a look at traditional forms of institutional recovery management.

The word "recovery" has strong medical overtones that suggest a physical problem or disease. The presumption that alcoholism is a disease, distinct from diseases that can be produced by chronic and heavy drinking, is usually the only reason offered for the existence of inpatient treatment facilities (other than the occasional legitimate need for supervised detoxification). To justify their existence, therefore, treatment centers and hospitals must first demonstrate that the *act* of heavy drinking is *not* a behavior, but a disease, and they must further demonstrate that they effectively address that problem by producing the desired effect—total abstinence. They *assert* that alcoholism is a disease that cannot be cured, but only arrested—held in permanent abeyance. And how to arrest the disease? Quit drinking.

That's a good but expensive bit of advice, which in no way relates to legitimate medical treatment. Even if the advice is taken, nothing happens until an individual makes a personal decision to quit drinking. Thus, traditional "treatment" is little more than encouragement to *self-treat*, and there's nothing wrong with that. But who can afford that kind of encouragement at hospital rates? And that kind of "treatment" is available at no cost at A.A., RR, WFS, SOS, MFS, and other self-help support groups. If institutional advice were more effective than free advice, that would be another matter. But that's not the case.

The research team at *Time* concluded that after inpatient care "only 12% to 25% (an average of 17.5%) of patients manage to stay on the wagon for three years."[3] That's very short-term "permanent abstinence." And the majority of researchers in this field would consider the *Time* estimate optimistic.

For example, in a 1986 article F.S. Tennant, Jr. reviewed the studies done on institutional "success" rates:

> [A] review of other studies of continuous abstinence from alcohol following treatment shows that various types of treatment do not influence continuous abstinence rates, particularly when the subjects are assessed at 12 months after treatment.[4]

Consistent with Tennant's conclusions, Herbert Fingarette states the following in *Heavy Drinking:*

> After an extensive review of the literature, the authors of the report, sponsored by the U.S. Congress, Office of Technology Assessment, were willing to affirm only that "The conclusions of many of these reviews is that treatment *seems* (emphasis added) better than no treatment." Even this cautiously qualified statement appears overly confident compared to the report issued by [George] Vaillant after a highly ambitious and elaborate eight-year clinical experiment (CASPAR). Vaillant candidly concluded that "there is compelling evidence that the results of our treatment were no better than the natural history of the disease."[5] . . . Pessimistic, too, was his analysis of the results of ten long-term follow up studies covering a wide variety of treatment methods. Two years after treatment, Vaillant

explains, about 20% of the drinkers were abstinent, 15% continued drinking but showed improvement, and 65% were still abusing alcohol. Because these proportions were the same for a comparable population of drinkers who did not enter any treatment program, the best that can be said, Vaillant concluded, is that these programs didn't make matters worse.[6] [!]

One result of this general pattern of failure—and the concomitant reluctance of insurers to pay for such "treatment"—is that many treatment centers and hospital addiction wards are in financial trouble. They all feel the pinch of a shrinking market. Some merge in an effort to survive, and others have filed for bankruptcy. The treatment center advertising hype on TV is a clue; even the AMA has criticized it as tasteless and inappropriate. The unrelenting search for patients is almost pathetic, but the search goes on.

There is a solution to the problem. It may be found in this little (true) parable: The original Henry Ford had a corner on the automobile market. Customer demand increased beyond his wildest dreams as thousands of black, Model-T, two-door automobiles rolled off his assembly lines. One day, a certain Mr. Jones asked, "Henry, could you make me a *red*, two-door Ford?" Henry said, "No, we make only *black* two-door Fords. Take it or leave it." So the customer took it because he had no choice. Then Henry died and new management took over. A new car company began to manufacture a car called the Xmobile in a plant just down the block from the Ford plant. The Xmobile was available in two colors, black *and* red, and the next time Mr. Jones bought a car he chose a red Xmobile. Before long the Ford plant was making cars in black, red, *and* blue.

The vast majority of hospitals and treatment centers still sell a 12-step version of a black, two-door Ford. (There are two exceptions, covered in the next chapter.) The business, marketing, and public relations people who work for such places are in a tough position. Back in their college days they took GB-101, General Principles of Business Management and Marketing. They learned about satisfying the needs of the customer, the need for product diversification, and the need to change with the times.

Then a certain Mr. Brown, diploma in hand, landed a job as marketing manager at Easy Does It Treatment Center. He was told that he had one product to sell and that all other products were unacceptable. Down the road and across the country every marketing manager was told the same thing. Each of them discovered that although they could fiddle with the bells and whistles, handle the advertising, give the speeches, and encourage the field reps to get out there and sell the product, they could not tamper with the product itself, the traditional 12-step program. When marketing managers asked about the marketability of that program they were told, "Competition is tough, but it's the best product on the market, and has been for over 50 years. We've always done it that way. Don't change a thing."

The people—customers and potential customers—know that the 8,000 or so hospitals and treatment centers across the country[7] are little more than carbon copies of each other. Each offers the same thing.[8] No options. The bells and whistles differ in tone, timbre and size, but the programs remain the same. That doesn't cut it. The competition have a few bells and whistles too, so the marketing managers ask themselves, "What do we do now?" Any middle manager at Chrysler could field that one; the answer is diversification, coupled with product quality (the two-track Vestibule Inpatient Program, VIP, for short). But for now, let's continue to analyze traditional institutional treatment (which I've called "Institutional A.A."), and the reasons for its general ineffectiveness.

Though the reasons are known, they are strangely ignored by those who would most profit by understanding them. They were provided on June 16, 1988 by Bill Miller, a professor at the University of New Mexico, in testimony to the U.S. Senate Committee on Governmental Affairs. The document he presented to that Committee was a summary of findings from 175 controlled clinical studies of the effectiveness of the treatment modalities used in recovery management. He grouped them in three categories:

A. TREATMENT METHODS SHOWN TO BE EFFECTIVE IN FEDERALLY FUNDED AND OTHER RESEARCH

1. Brief Advice/Feedback Intervention
2. Community Reinforcement Approach
3. Covert Sensitization
4. Disulfiram (Antabuse) – monitored, including implants
5. Marital Therapy (Behavioral)
6. Self-Control Training
7. Stress Management Training
8. Social Skills Training

B. TREATMENT COMPONENTS COMMONLY USED (U.S.)

1. Alcoholics Anonymous
2. Confrontational Counseling
3. Counseling (General)
4. Disulfiram (Antabuse) – not monitored
5. Educational Lectures/Films
6. Group Psychotherapy
7. Individual Psychotherapy (Insight)

C. OTHER TREATMENT MODALITIES

1. Acupuncture
2. Aversion Therapy (Nausea Induction)
3. Aversion Therapy (Electric Shock)
4. Cognitive Therapy/Relapse Presentation
5. Hypnosis
6. Marital Therapy (Nonbehavioral)
7. Psychotropic Medication
    a. Anti-Anxiety
    b. Antidepressants
    c. Antipsychotic
    d. Lithium
    e. Psychedelic
8. Videotape Self-Confrontation

The Miller study revealed some big winners—and losers:

A. Of the 69 studies listed in Category A, 79% produced positive results versus 21% which produced negative results.
B. Of the 40 studies listed in Category B, a 10% positive result was recorded against 90% negative.
C. Of the 66 studies listed in Category C, a 37% positive result was recorded against a 63% negative.

Miller comments:

An examination of Table 1 [above, in simplified form] suggests that there is a substantial gap between available research knowledge (much of which was produced from federally funded studies) and current practice. *The treatment modalities listed as "shown to be effective" by current research are, on the whole, rarely used in current U.S. practice.* (Emphasis Miller)

Four modalities (over 28 studies) rated 100% positive results: 1) Brief Advice/Feedback Intervention; 2) Community Reinforcement Approach; 3) Marital Therapy; and 4) Social Skills Training. Six modalities (over 23 studies) rated 0% (zero percent) positive results: 1) Antipsychotic Drugs; 2) Videotape Confrontation; 3) Alcoholics Anonymous; 4) General Counseling; 5) Individual Psychotherapy; and 6) Confrontational Counseling.

The lesson to be learned is clear: private therapists would do very well indeed to employ counseling methods such as Rational-Emotive Therapy, Reality Therapy,[9] Transactional Analysis, and Psychodrama, all encompassing major elements of the four winners listed above. Professional therapists are usually quite competent, but most of them are still locked into the traditional recovery approach in the addictions field and their reputations have suffered as a result.

Miller makes other significant observations:

1) Family interventions do not employ empirically tested behavioral methods and are largely based on strategies of unknown effectiveness.
2) Self-control training, rarely used in the United States, is a common practice in other countries.
3) . . . *traditional U.S. alcoholism programs are based on treatment methods that are largely unsupported by current research evidence. In contrast, treatment modalities that appear promising from current scientific evidence are mostly unknown or unused outside of federal V.A. or research-supported programs."* (Emphasis Miller) [Miller's research was completed in 1987.]

Miller asks "Is alcoholism treatment best conducted in a *hospital* (emphasis added) setting?" He found that of 20 studies, 19 found "no overall advantage for residential over non-residential treatment, or for longer versus shorter residential stays [all in traditional settings, of course]."

It would seem, as Miller points out, that the World Health Organization (Expert Committee on Alcoholism) was right when, back in 1951, it concluded that "the treatment of alcoholism would seldom necessitate hospitalization."

Which treatment is best for alcoholism? A better question would be "What kinds of people respond to what kinds of treatment?" (Or, as Sir William Osler [1849–1919] put it, "Ask not what kind of a disease the person has, ask what kind of person has the disease.") These are *answerable* questions. When we quit ignoring the findings of current research, we will make real progress.

So what does happen in treatment centers and hospitals? I have conducted dozens of interviews with individuals who have undergone "treatment" in such institutions. Less than a week ago, a man just out of a local treatment center summed up what so many have said: "It was the most expensive 28-day A.A. meeting I ever attended." In Chapter 6 I addressed the question of the effectiveness of Communal A.A. and concluded that it does work—but not very well. Since Institutional A.A. is a mirror reflection of Communal A.A., one can expect, and find, a similar result. Institutional A.A. also works, but again, not very well.

What goes on in treatment centers and hospital addiction wards is about as medical as a videotaped Father Martin chalk talk, or group discussions on gratitude or spirituality—which institutions call "treatment" and bill at hospital rates. There are Big Book readings and speaker meetings at which group members give "leads" (short talks, "war stories"). Placards listing the A.A. Steps and Traditions adorn the walls, and literature racks bulge with A.A. pamphlets and brochures. There are the opening and closing prayers at meetings, and the Lord's Prayer is reverently recited. There is a physician on staff—often as an administrator—or on call, and sometimes, but not usually, a psychiatrist, who spends an average of five to ten minutes a day with each patient.

The bulk of the program is handled by "paraprofessionals." The *para* in that word is taken from the Greek and means *assistant to*. They probably comprise about 60% of a typical treatment staff,[10] but information about their numbers, or numbers as a proportion of staff, is almost impossible to obtain—both for individual institutions and for the treatment industry as a whole.[11] The primary qualification of paraprofessionals is membership in A.A. and a minimum of two or three years of sobriety. They, of course, do not represent A.A. *officially* (no one does), but do so unofficially, actively, and openly. The rationalization is that only an alcoholic can understand another alcoholic. That is a logical absurdity, and a slap in the face to legitimate professionals such as social workers, nurses, and mental health specialists who hold two or more hard-earned university degrees. Aside from the issue of academic and professional qualification, paraprofessionals are among the most conscientious and dedicated people in the addictions field.

One legitimate medical aspect of institutional care is detoxification, a three-to-five-day procedure that is required for about 10% to 15% of new patients. (Patients, however, are generally expected to enter a center or hospital completely sober.) The only other legitimate medical procedures performed by treatment centers are very basic—drawing blood, taking urine samples, taking blood pressure readings, etc.

The medics also "sign off," i.e., sign forms that ensure payment of insurance claims at the time of customer departure. Legal liability, that is, the protection of the corporation, its property, and its staff, is also a factor in the sign-in-sign-off process. The document known as "The Patient's Bill of Rights" is unknown or ignored by virtually all institutions in this field.

"Treatment" is big business, but unavailable to many because it is so expensive. A 1987 *Time* magazine article[12] reported that there were "more than 8,000 treatment programs [in the United States], a 65% increase in the last six years alone."[13] In the Midwest, a typical 28-day stay at a treatment center was recently quoted to me at "between $12,000 and $15,000." Who can afford that? The ones *least* in need—the ones with a job, a home, security, and insurance. Who could benefit most from institutional care? The ones *most* in need —those without a job, a home, security, and insurance. It comes down to discrimination based on socioeconomic status and the dictates of the private commercialized medical industry. (The major treatment providers in this system are listed on the American and New York stock exchanges.)

In Chapter 5 we discussed the strange relationship between Communal A.A. and Institutional A.A., the first being anti-medical, anti-intellectual, and anti-commercial, and the second being tightly organized, thoroughly commercial, and a multi-billion dollar industry.[14] This peculiar relationship is easier to understand when one realizes that about a third of A.A.'s general membership is funneled into it by institutions which promote the A.A. program and buy A.A.'s books and literature by the ton (1989 "A.A. Survey" data). Only 7% of individual physicians refer their patients to A.A. (A referral is not necessarily a recommendation. Oftentimes, physicians can do little more. Their training includes knowledge of the physical effects of addiction, but almost nothing about addictive behaviors. As a result, they deal with alcoholic patients either by prescribing disulfiram or passing them on to A.A., about which they often know nothing beyond hearsay.)

In summary, it may be said that the prevailing treatment center and hospital approach to recovery from addiction is ill-conceived and ineffective, judged by any standard. (There is, in fact, *no* standard.) Judge for yourself whether it's a scam—or just a near-total waste of time and money.

Treatment, as we know it today, is on its way out.

———————————————————

1. There is a problem with lack of consistent terminology in this field, as in the case of substance *abuse* and *abusers*. The word *abuse* has a judgmental ring about it. Eventually we may all agree on less emotion-loaded terminology and learn to communicate with one another more effectively.

2. "Maturing out" is not an age-specific term; it can happen at any time between 16 and 86 years of age. This phenomenon is one of the best kept secrets in the addictions world and will be treated later in this book.

3. *Time,* May 2, 1988.

4. Tennant, F.S., Jr. (1986). "Disulfiram Will Reduce Medical Complications but Not Cure Alcoholism." *Journal of the American Medical Association,* 256:1489.

5. The studies quoted are: a) Saxe, Leonard; Dougherty, Denise; Esty, Katherine; and Fine, Michelle (1983). "The Effectiveness and Costs of Alcoholism Treatment." Health Technology Case Study 22. Washington, D.C.; Office of Technology Assessment. b) Vaillant, George E. (1983). *The Natural History of Alcoholism.* Cambridge, MA: Harvard University Press.

6. Fingarette, page 77. A new report by the OTA will be released in the fall of 1993. It is already in the hands of the NCADD, and preliminary reports indicate that the treatment industry is in serious trouble.

7. About 10 years ago there were 15,000 treatment facilities (hospitals and treatment centers); since then 7,000 of them have closed, amalgamated, or reorganized. Check with a professional broker or financial advisor before investing in one of these. I think that an investment in a company manufacturing high-button shoes or buggy whips would be a better investment. (Exceptions: Hampstead Hospital and Forest Hospital.)

8. Some variation of the Minnesota Model, whatever that is. There seems to be no written explanations of it, nor is it mentioned in the index of books in my private library. It is not in the database of the mainframe computer of the Indianapolis, Indiana system. It has something to do with Hazelden, out of Center City, Minnesota. I wrote to them; they sent advertising brochures only. I phoned the head of the Minnesota State Addictions Department who did not return my call. My best guess is that the so-called "Minnesota Model" is little more than an advertising gimmick that no one seems to want to talk about—including Hazelden.

9. Cory, G. (1982) *Theory and Practice of Counseling and Psychotherapy,* 2nd ed. Monterey, CA: Books/Cole. Cory explains that Reality Therapy is used a lot by school counselors and rehabilitation workers, but has been neglected in the addictions field. Glasser's approach, he says, focuses on present behavior, and the therapist functions as a teacher and a model who confronts clients in ways that help them face reality and fulfill basic needs without harming themselves or others. At the heart of Reality Therapy is the acceptance of personal responsibility, which Glasser equates with mental health. Reality therapists concentrate on what clients are able and willing to do in the present to change their behavior, and on the

means of doing so. These include a commitment to change, the development of a plan of action, and a consistent effort to follow through with that commitment. This modality, Cory says, "is active, directive, didactic, and cognitive." Thus, behavior is the focus, not attitudes, insight, one's past, or unconscious motivation. The author concludes that Reality Therapy is actually a form of behavior modification, and in institutional settings is essentially a type of non-rigorous operant conditioning. It is, in the view of this writer, highly compatible with Rational-Emotive Therapy and Transactional Analysis.

10. Hospitals and treatment centers are loath to publish information concerning the percentage of staff which may be designated "paraprofessional." The public usually doesn't know the difference between a true professional and a paraprofessional, and are certainly not advised about this by hospital and treatment center administrators. The qualifications of paraprofessionals are certainly not comparable to those of true professionals. Insurance companies have become aware of this situation and are increasingly reluctant to pay for paraprofessional "treatment." Hampstead Hospital in New Hampshire, and Forest Hospital in Illinois are notable exceptions to the rule; they employ *only* professionals. The day of the paraprofessional in alcoholism treatment is either over or soon will be.

11. One of the reasons may be economic. I talked with a paraprofessional who had recently been fired from the staff of a local institution because he had dared ask for a raise—anything above $15,000 a year. For the work they do, and they do most of it, paraprofessionals are badly underpaid.

12. November 30, 1987.

13. There is an apparent, but not real, contradiction with the previously stated fact that 7,000 addiction facilities have closed within the last 10 years. (Chains take over, small ones disappear, amalgamation of facilities takes place, and Chapter 11 bankruptcies are filed.)

14. A *Consumers' Research* article of December 1985 discussed some of the major corporate enterprises in the addictions field. There is Comprehensive Care Corporation, known in the trade as CompCare, which in 1985 controlled 27.3 % of alcoholism and drug treatment in the private sector, according to Ken Estes, CompCare spokesman. It has 110 treatment center contract service programs in community hospitals in the United States, plus 17 free-standing hospitals owned outright and used solely for the treatment of alcoholism. And there is Recovery Centers of America Inc., a wholly owned subsidiary of National Medical Enterprises Inc. of Los Angeles. (Under the name New Beginnings.) And so on.

11

Nontraditional Recovery Management

If the prevailing system described in Chapter 10 can be called one-track—in the sense of having a singleness of structure and purpose—its replacement can be called two-track. Guy Lamunyon provided an explanation of the two-track approach in the July/ August 1990 issue of the *Journal of Rational Recovery*.[1]

Lamunyon said that for treatment providers, the most important single fact is that the general population is about equally divided into two major groups: those that are "thinking oriented" and those that are "feeling oriented," what I've termed Types 1 and 2 respectively. Type 1s delight in facts, analysis, and orderly thinking, but Type 2s are more comfortable with intuition, insight, sensing, and feeling. Type 1s *think* and feel; Type 2s *feel* and think. Type 1s analyze, Type 2s intuit. No one is, or can be, all Type 1 or Type 2; individuals incorporate both orientations, but in different proportions. Obviously, we all have intelligence and emotions. Neither type is good or bad, right or wrong; nor are they "smart" or "dumb." They are exactly what they are, and they like it that way. They wouldn't want to change even if they could.

While all of this seems—and in fact is—overly simplified, it does have important practical implications. The most persuasive and persistent treatment center can't change fundamental personal inclinations, and it is therefore incumbent upon treatment providers to recognize those inclinations and adapt their programs accordingly. On the assumption that these two orientations—thinking and feeling—also characterize the chemically addicted segment of our population, it becomes obvious that the prevailing treatment modality (the 12-step program), based on Platonic notions of faith and feeling, is as appropriate for some members of one segment (Type 2s) as it is inappropriate for all members of the other segment (Type 1s). Those for whom the 12-step program is appropriate would likely be theistically inclined Type 2s who feel comfortable with the prospect of a lifetime of meetings in smoke-filled rooms as well as with declaring themselves perpetually diseased and dependent—that is, personally powerless and dependent on a rescuing Higher Power.

I say "some members of one segment," because A.A. is also obviously inappropriate for most Type 2s. If they make up half the population, as Lamunyon indicates, and if A.A. were truly appropriate for them, A.A.'s success rate would almost certainly be much higher than the 5% success rate suggested by A.A.'s "Comments" document. (A.A.'s true success rate is almost certainly even lower than 5%, as the 5% figure in the "Comments" document refers to A.A.'s retention rate of new members over a one-year period.)

Nevertheless, Lamunyon has exploded the inane notion that "one size fits all." It obviously doesn't, because people are different and therefore have different needs. Those differences are rarely recognized in traditional institutional settings, other than in a cursory or procedural way.

Lamunyon contends that staff personnel at typical treatment centers find it almost impossible to connect with Type 1 clients at the rational level, because they—both professionals and para-professionals—are oriented in the opposite Type 2 direction. There's nothing wrong with either orientation, but they don't mix well. Sometimes the leopard *cannot* change his spots, no matter how much pressure is put on him. In a typical traditional institutional setting, however, the pressure on Type 1 "nonbelievers"—perhaps "nonaccepters" is a better term—can be quite severe.

The reaction to that pressure is usually perceived as an unwillingness to "work the program"—and that's exactly right, as far as it goes. The client's resistance, however, to that which has been pre-judged as therapeutically desirable by the staff, is actually a sign of his or her *inability* to change from one fundamental orientation (Type 1) to another (Type 2). That inability (probably an impossibility) to reverse an elemental orientation is poorly understood in traditional settings. It is, instead, resented, and labeled *resistance*, *intellectualism,* and *denial.*

Resistance—whether active or passive—is often a declaration by a client that he will not tolerate an attack on his identity. It is a loud and clear proclamation that "I have a right to be myself and I will not give you, doctor, nurse, or therapist, permission to push me over the line that distinguishes me from others."

Lamunyon sums it up by suggesting that treatment center accusations of client "resistance" have less to do with refusal to accept A.A.'s program than with the maintenance of personal integrity, including the right to self-determination. Lamunyon declares that treatment centers consistently violate that right. I agree.

And to be *accused* of intellectualism? Note that the accusation is not against rationalization—the process of excusing one's behavior with false reasoning—but against *thinking* itself, which is a distinct cut above passive belief. It's a little scary; envision, if you will, its logical extension: the nightmarish world of George Orwell or a theocracy dominated by members of a powerful, punitive, and righteous religious right. *Intellectualism* is a loaded word that suggests eggheads, bookworms, and ivory towers isolated from the "real" world. It is also a word which is wielded like a bludgeon in many institutional settings.

For whatever reason, some people have a greater tendency to think than to feel, to question than to believe. They have every right to do so, and we have no license to tamper with their rights.

Denial is the third charge hurled against those "intellectuals" who have shown "resistance" to treatment. Gail Milgram, a quintessential promoter of the denial/disease position, blandly states, "Alcoholism can be called the disease of denial and self-delusion."[2] (Know of any other "disease" for which "denial" is a symptom?) Denial could just as well be called standing up for one's rights. If you've got a problem, and show up at a hospital, treatment center, or self-help support meeting, you've admitted the problem, not denied it. Few of us brag about our shortcomings or draw attention to them; instead, we try to hide them, minimize them, and, on occasion, actually deny them. But it is still said (as ASAM and the NCADD recently pontificated) that "denial" is a symptom of the "disease." Bullshit. Red spots on the skin are a symptoms of a disease called measles; "denial," especially in institutional settings, is often a courageous act, a statement that proclaims, "Here's where I stand. Don't even try to force me into a mold into which I don't fit. You said you'd tailor the program to my needs. Do it. I'm different, and I'm a customer."[3]

Denial is also disagreement; "I am *not* powerless and I can lick this problem. Furthermore, I am *not* diseased and I will make my own religious and spiritual decisions, thank you!" Many therapists realize that denial is sometimes also a thoughtful rejection of stereotypical notions of alcoholics as skid-row bums or irresponsible and morally weak persons.

How, then, are resistance, intellectualism, and denial handled in a typical treatment center? Mainly through organizational pressure and confrontation.

The pressure comes from the staff, all of one mind, all in positions of authority and control, most of them with close ties to A.A. Lamunyon calls it "groupthink mentality," a mindset that is perpetuated by a systematic bias in personnel selection. Free speech and thought are not encouraged, and objections to the program are squashed by peer pressure and staff pressure. Conformity is expected and exacted. The more stalwart objectors refuse to become wards of such places (thus, institutional populations are limited and self-selected) or have left them in disgust, a.m.a. (against medical advice) after refusing to say the medically prescribed Lord's Prayer, for example. The many empty beds in hospitals and treatment centers reflect the absence of such people.

But the confrontation goes on. The thought-inclined person asks questions and is told not to think! Slogans are thrown at him or her like smoke bombs: "Utilize, don't analyze," "Your best thinking got you here (so shut up and listen)," and "You're a prisoner of the intellect." It is better, perhaps, to be a prisoner of the intellect than a refugee from it. It's also more appropriate, and far more respectful, to respond to questions with answers rather than with slogans. As Lamunyon points out, "No evidence exists to support an inverse relationship between intelligence and abstinence from alcohol or drugs." (Even many emotion-oriented people feel that their individual perceptions are neither respected nor considered important in A.A.)

There has to be a better way, and there is. With permission from Rational Recovery Systems Network, I have included in this chapter an exposition of the two-track (A.A./RR) Vestibule Inpatient Program (VIP). It was co-authored by Jack Trimpey, LCSW, President of Rational Recovery (and past president of the American Hospital Association Society of Hospital Social Work Directors, Northern California Chapter) and Forrest Martin, M.D., who at that time was the Medical Director of Rational Recovery Systems.[4] The document quoted below suggests an institutional paradigm shift from the prevailing "Let's do it *my* way" to "Let's do it *your* way, and together we can solve the problem." Here (slightly edited) is their program:

The Vestibule Inpatient Program

Recognizing the individual differences in philosophical orientation of patients in a general population, hospital-based CD [Chemical Dependency] units "match" patients to highly contrasted therapeutic approaches ("tracks") based on differential diagnosis between subsets of alcohol dependence (DSM-III-R). Administrative rationale for the two-track Vestibule Inpatient Program (VIP) is provided along with clinical guidelines for running cognitive-behavioral therapy groups. The VIP is incorporated into a community-based two-track system with outpatient follow-up provided in both A.A. and RR meetings for the first year following discharge.

At present, practically all American inpatient addiction care is based on the 12-step program of A.A. Statistics have shown that the majority of patients continue their addictions during the year following discharge. Client receptivity to the central concepts of the 12-step program is predictive of treatment outcome. Ideally, patients with a secular or humanistic orientation would select institutions where non-spiritual and non-religious methods are employed, either as a matter of personal preference or on the advice of a referring professional, but these services are not presently available (other than through RR Residential, and Hampstead and Forest Hospitals). VIP is a means for any 12-step inpatient program to immediately diversify its theoretical basis for addiction care and to clinically accommodate those patients who give early indicators that the 12-step approach will not lead to a satisfactory outcome.

Transition to the two-track VIP system is accomplished through systematic staff development with administrative support and encouragement. On-site consultation with qualified RRS consultants is highly recommended in order to benefit from in-service training in clinical methods. The material presented here includes:

1) Conceptual Backdrop
2) Guidelines for Differential Diagnosis
3) Demographic Considerations
4) Competitive Conditions
5) The Solution
6) Operations
7) Common Problems in VIP
8) Clinical Protocol
9) Conducting the Daily RR Group Sessions

10) The Role of the Family in VIP
11) Suggestions for Rational Milieu Therapy
12) A.A./RR VIP Outpatient Follow-up

The required readings in the VIP are *Rational Recovery from Alcoholism: The Small Book,* by Jack Trimpey, LCSW, and *Rational-Emotive Therapy with Alcoholics and other Substance Abusers* by Albert Ellis, Ph.D., John F. McInerney, Ph.D., Raymond DiGuiseppi, Ph.D. and Raymond Yeager, Ph.D., of the Institute for Rational-Emotive Therapy, New York. It is assumed that therapists are already familiar with Bill Wilson's "Big Book" (*Alcoholics Anonymous*) and the program of Alcoholics Anonymous.

Conceptual Backdrop for VIP: A philosophical dichotomy has been present throughout history, and its division continues today in our pluralistic American society. Aristotelians (rationalists) and Platonists (supernaturalists)[5] hold fundamentally different premises, and therefore require different psycho-emotional management. Addicts themselves represent a cross section of the general population, as reflected in their viewpoints on matters such as politics, religion, philosophy, psychology, education, economics, and chemical dependency. Indeed, values and perceptions concerning all of the above vary widely from country to country and from culture to culture. Although the physiology of addiction may be fairly uniform between social and ethnic groups, the philosophical underpinnings are not. Therefore, we have defined two subsets of Alcohol Dependence (DSM-III-R) that must be differentiated as part of the diagnostic protocol. It's called Differential Diagnosis, the purpose of which is to identify traits of personality and philosophy that will promote, for any given person or group of persons, a high degree of success in one program as distinct from a high probability of failure in another.[6]

Subtype 1: Aristotelian, without theistic beliefs: RR
Subtype 2. Platonic, with theistic beliefs: A.A.

Guidelines for Differential Diagnosis: Proper treatment reflects a proper differential diagnosis. For a program to be successful, it must be relevant to the client. The diagnosis of addiction itself is sometimes a challenging, multi-faceted task. We obtain the client's subjective complaints, observe his or her behavior, take a relevant history, sometimes obtain the observations of friends and family, and from this database can determine the appropriate diagnostic category for any person. Those who are alcohol dependent, Type 1 or Type 2, may be differentiated on the basis of values assessment. Differential diagnosis, in this context, is the quest for additional information that will help in the selection of the treatment of choice. Just as age, or other concurrent diagnoses, allergies, cultural and ethnic considerations, client motivations, history of previous treatment outcomes, chronicity, and lethality issues bear on treatment, so do religious and philosophical orientations. [The Myers-Briggs Type Indicator may be especially helpful in this determination.][7]

[In *The Small Book,* Trimpey notes that professionals often assume that their clients hold a fixed belief about the existence of God. They further assume that in cases of uncertainty, ambivalence, or non-belief, clients are both willing and able to construct a positive theistic belief in order to build a better life. He points out that these are not valid assumptions, and when put into practice can often be harmful to clients. These assumptions may also be construed as a projection of the personal values of the therapist, imposed on the client.

The typical institutional therapist seems to feel that the purpose of differential diagnosis is to identify traits that suggest success or failure in the 12-step spiritual healing program, whereas Martin and Trimpey would argue that the purpose of differential diagnosis is to identify those personality traits that would produce a greater probability of success in either a traditional or a nontraditional program. Thus, two sets of traits, two programs. It would be well to remember that some clients will strongly prefer the orientation of one program over the other, but will not necessarily reject all of the tenets of the other program. The two programs are indeed antithetical, but not necessarily antagonistic to one another, and there is some common ground. To continue now with Trimpey and Martin:]

There are two ways to tell if a chemically dependent person is a candidate for a given therapeutic approach: 1) a history of recidivism in that approach; and 2) the client's answers to our questions. There is no reason why we should not ask a patient if he or she believes in God, especially when this element represents one of the major differences between A.A. and RR.

It is vital and proper to inform the client of the treatment proposed before asking him or her to consent to it [especially since informed consent is a legal right]. A copy of the 12 steps of Alcoholics Anonymous may be presented to the client, and he may be frankly asked, "What do you think of this way of handling your problems with alcohol?" Is there anything about it that you find hard to understand or difficult to accept? If the client expresses no objections, but has had previous unsuccessful experiences with A.A., it is fair to ask, "Why did you leave A.A. the last time? Was there something you didn't like? Were you able to use the Higher Power concept?" To these questions, many addicts will confess their faith in God and assert their willingness to pursue a spiritual awakening as a way of remaining sober. But others will say that they don't want to seek spiritual goals, that they do not even know or want to know what the word *spiritual* means, and that the idea of a rescuing deity for alcoholics seems absurd to them. Some may say they have no belief in God, others may say they believe in some kind of a cosmic being, but choose not to bring that belief into the recovery process. Still others may say that all that "God stuff" in A.A. bothers them.

It has long been common to interpret these kinds of statements as resistance to treatment, as a sign of poor motivation, of passive aggression, or an expression of a desire to continue drinking. Disbelief in a higher power and refusal or failure to work a program of moral betterment are still regarded by many in the field as part of the illness of alcoholism. Thus, nontheistic treatment plans are often viewed as not only incompatible with standard recovery concepts, but pathogenic, in the sense of being a cause or a contributing factor to the disease of alcoholism.

In the VIP, however, the client is regarded as a Very Important Person with very important opinions. Assertions of doubt and skepticism are the basic strengths upon which RR builds a sober life. Rather than suggest that the client had better "come around" to the theistic A.A. viewpoint, VIP treatment staff commend 12-step-resistant clients for exercising critical judgment, and advise them that they are well-suited for RR, wherein they will be encouraged to turn that critical energy inward to eliminate the ideas and beliefs that have caused and maintained their state of chemical dependency.

Demographic Considerations: Because of the diversity of clients who come to a typical hospital chemical dependency unit, it will be impossible, for reasons of time and money, to have programs catering to each cultural and ethnic group, for example, separate programs for Catholics, Protestants, Black Americans, Hispanics, and Jews.[8] A.A. has already shown that one program fills—with serious limitations—the needs of a segment of a population of Type 2 (emotionally oriented) clients; however, A.A. does not help those who find the 12 steps unsuited to their needs. Many clients who have fixed humanistic values (Type 1s, and some Type 2s) will have specific objections to 12-step requirements such as those pertaining to the Higher Power, group dependency, personal confession, moral inventories, and lifelong recovery. Other people may offer no serious objections to the spiritual and religious approach, but by virtue of their recidivism demonstrate the need for a different approach to the problem.

As the market for inpatient services becomes saturated, and as insurers become more disposed toward outpatient rather than inpatient service, some new programs based on humanistic values are targeting persons resistant to A.A.'s 12-step program. There is a very clear trend toward diversification of treatment. It is supported by humanistic organizations and by the media. The market for recovery programs of a non-spiritual nature is expanding.

Competitive Conditions: Until recently, bed occupancy supported continued growth of inpatient care for addictions. But in addition to an overall tightening of health care dollars in recent years, new outcome studies have contributed to current occupancy problems by raising questions about the cost-effectiveness of inpatient versus outpatient programming. (Hence insurers have become increasingly reluctant to pay for inpatient treatment.) Doomsayers predict the collapse of the hospital-based inpatient concept, while the hospital industry continues with traditional marketing approaches in which the spiritual healing model is the *sine qua non* of hospital-based practice. Market saturation and the decrease of third-party (insurance) dollars seem to explain low occupancy.

But administrators face a dilemma when they contemplate breaking away from traditional patterns. They have reason to fear that they will lose credibility with referral sources because of established loyalties to the 12-step program. The more orthodox A.A. believers hold that anything other than the 12-step approach is not only inferior, but harmful. In a few cases, key people feel that if they were to recognize a recovery plan that was not based on spiritual principles, they would then fall from grace with their own personal deities and lose the resolve to remain sober themselves. Such is the totalistic quality of 12-step recovery (among some of the "recovering") that the Higher Power itself seems to argue for strict adherence to traditional programming.

Still, there are many recidivists who come to the attention of local mental health and law enforcement officials, and many of them are prime candidates for alternative programs. Convincing these relapsers and recidivists to endure yet another round of 12-step therapy, however, is all too often impossible.

The Solution: The vast majority of these refuseniks and recidivists will be good candidates for Rational Recovery, an application of the system of self-help and psychotherapy devised in the 1950s by eminent psychologist Albert Ellis. The system is called Rational-Emotive Therapy (RET), and it is taught to the helping professions in most universities. Based on the scientific method, it is ideal for those with inquiring, skeptical attitudes, and it has been shown to provide potent guidance for persons seeking personal change.

For decades, experts in the field of chemical dependency have recognized the high degree of relevance of RET to addiction care, so that today many 12-step recovery programs already offer RET or one of its cognitive-behavioral variants as an adjunct to their spiritually oriented programs. RRS, in its Vestibule Program, presents RET as a comprehensive alternative to traditional programming. Between A.A. and RR, both comprehensive plans for the achievement and maintenance of sobriety, we make a workable program available to perhaps 99% of those in need.

Rational Recovery Systems, started in 1986, is a coalition of qualified professionals who advocate for individuals with fixed humanistic values and who are, therefore, poor candidates for traditional services that include spiritual and religious components.

Local RR groups have professional advisors who, by virtue of being professionals, are qualified to handle special problems that pertain to psychotic states, mood disorders, suicide risks, etc., and who can make referrals to medical and other resources when indicated. Among RR's many advisors are Albert Ellis, Ph.D., Forrest Martin, M.D., Emmett Velten, Ph.D., Raymond Yeager, Ph.D., and Joseph Gerstein, M.D., all of whom are active in the movement advancing the two-track service system.

The VIP program offers an innovative market approach that requires negligible capital outlay to reach a large, ready clientele. In addition to an inventory of *The Small Book*, the only other expense (recommended) may be monies apportioned for an on-site RRS consultant, full time or part time. Demographically, the market for recovery programs that depart from the traditional recovery model will expand during a time when existing markets are diminishing.

Market share will be based more on a regional presence than on gaining a larger share of a local market. Working, well-fed alcoholics, who have been refractory to previous 12-step programs, will travel many miles to avail themselves of a program that appears relevant to them. Identifying and targeting Type 1 substance abusers will provide new statistical support for an industry based on the waning concept of inpatient care for substance abuse.

Operations: As a way to explore multi-modal inpatient care, RRS encourages direct communication among managers and administrators who are contemplating the A.A./RR Vestibule two-track system. This document would make a good agenda item for any meeting of managers or administrators, whether or not an RRS representative is present. When the discussion begins, you will probably find a common concern for the many clients who go away with complaints about the 12-step program and then proceed with their addicted way of life. Most managers have an inner sense that there are many possible ways to fill an inpatient treatment day, and they realize that A.A. is only one of them. By talking with your peers you may get a clearer sense that there is plenty of leeway for innovation in the two-track Vestibule arrangement. In fact, you may come away hoping to be among the first to address a vast, untapped market of agnostics, humanists, atheists, freethinkers, Buddhists, Jews, and liberal and nominal Christians who have been avoiding traditional 12-step recovery programs.

Getting started in RRS:VIP will require an initial survey of the clinical staff to determine the degree of readiness for and commitment to organizational change. The perceptions of your clinical staff are critical to the success of VIP, but experience has shown that uniform or unanimous support among the staff is not necessary. To the contrary, you will be looking for the predictable spectrum of opinions from "liberal" (pro-RR) to "conservative" (anti-RR), and then assigning responsibility for RR to those who show an inclination to work outside of the traditional 12-step paradigm.

Some administrators may view multi-modal inpatient care as a way to preempt perceptions that their institutions skirt or even violate equal opportunity employment practices. Traditional hiring practices, whether by default or design, favor applicants who show evidence of accepting the steps and traditions of A.A., many of which have theological content. Some agencies have designed application forms with specific questions about the 12 steps, for example, "What do you think about the Higher Power idea?" Other pre-employment inquiries have to do with the extent of participation in A.A. meetings and organizational involvement.

The VIP will provide ample evidence that any treatment center employing it is not violating equal employment opportunity provisions relating to religious preference.

Common Problems in VIP: We may anticipate some early difficulties in transition from homogeneous 12-step programming just as we would in any major program change or development. Some problems may center on how A.A. and RR interface ideologically and socially. The following issues may surface among staff or within the patient population. They are perceptions that are natural, understandable, and ultimately desirable in the process of program development. Although most mature organizations will have the depth of supervision to manage the probable transitional problems listed below, a skilled RRS practitioner may well serve as an invaluable adjunct to staff.

Issue No. One: A.A. is the only thing that works. It is timeless and proven, but RR is new, unproven, and troublesome.
Within the fellowship of A.A. there is consensus that there are many paths to recovery, and many who are loyal to A.A. admit that their own recoveries were atypical, that they bent the meaning of the 12 steps to suit their own fixed values. If A.A. is to work through attraction rather than coercion, then the presence of an alternative program would not seem to pose a problem.

Because of the virtual monopoly of the 12-step program in hospital settings, it has become the standard of the industry. Therefore, research statistics largely reflect outcomes of the 12-step approach. Even though there has been little against which to compare 12-step recovery statistics, it is widely assumed that statistics prove the effectiveness of that approach when applied to the general population. For example, if a report shows that 24% of those discharged after completing a 28-day program are sober after one year, we tend to think of that program as successful. But how can a program be considered successful if it has a 76% rate of non-sobriety? If 24% constitutes "success," then a 76% relapse rate must be considered acceptable.

But if we interpret the hypothetical but not unrealistic figures above to simply mean that only 24% of the patients were receptive enough to the 12 steps to achieve one-year's sobriety, then we are left with an unknown percentage who may have been candidates for

RR. If Vaillant is correct in observing that "Some treatment is better than no treatment," then we may easily extrapolate that "Treatment perceived as relevant by the patient is better than treatment perceived as irrelevant." To use a loose analogy to the hospital CD unit, think of a blood bank. If type A.A. blood is the only type given to all patients, and 24% of them survive, how many more could be treated successfully by adding type RR blood to the inventory? If either blood type helps more patients than the other, can we then say that one kind of blood is better than the other? If so, for whom?

Issue No. Two: Ideological contempt.

It is true that the differences between A.A. and RR *outnumber* the similarities, but the similarities *outweigh* the differences. As the differences become apparent, it may be helpful for the clinical director to emphasize the following viewpoints that are common to both A.A. and RR:

> *First,* the goal of treatment is to enable a patient to become reasonably happy and successful in life without psychoactive intoxicants;[9]
> *Second,* group meetings centering around the goal of abstinence are ideally suited to helping individuals free themselves of alcohol dependence; and
> *Third,* the only qualification for participation in the program is a sincere desire to stop drinking and remain sober.

Occasionally tension can develop between staff members with divergent clinical orientations. Focusing on management priorities, rather than on differences of opinion, will give a broader format for the resolution of problems of this kind. By consistently supporting both parties, escalating conflict with an eventual loser can be avoided. Some staff may defensively note that *The Small Book* presents an aggressive critique of the 12 steps and also portrays A.A. as having overstepped its role in addiction care to the point of being detrimental to some recovering alcoholics. Staff may become alarmed that RR seems to undermine the very faith that is required in 12-step recovery, that RR directs one toward self-centered sobriety, and that RR views the issue of "control" in a clearly opposite way to that of A.A. Staff members may perceive RR as a program that, in effect, strengthens character defects rather than treats them.

At this juncture, you or your clinical director may suggest that they review Chapter 4 of the Big Book and put themselves in the place of a humanist who values his disbelief just as highly as others may love God. If they will do this, they will find there is mutual antagonism between the Big Book and *The Small Book.* Moreover, you may remind your dissenting staff that whatever conflict exists between theistic and humanistic alcoholics was started by Bill Wilson and Bob Smith in 1935, and that this is one institution that will no longer exclude those who sincerely want to stop drinking but have little use for the 12 theological steps of A.A.

Both A.A. and RR vigorously and unashamedly argue for their respective viewpoints in things philosophical, but neither would intentionally place the importance of its own ideology above the individual lives that are at stake in addiction recovery. When proponents of each approach recognize the value of the other to those who choose that route to recovery, we will have placed a transcendent value on the principle of self-determination.

The VIP is an advanced concept in addiction care, in that management is aspiring to a higher principle than that contained in any clinical methodology. The unifying concept is the value placed on helping clients abstain from drinking alcohol or using drugs and then growing in society.

Issue No. 3: Failure to accept a higher power is part of the illness of alcoholism.

There are two common versions of this view: first, that disbelief in mystical beings or higher authority is a symptomatic character defect of drunkenness; and second, that this character defect is part of the cause of alcoholism. It is well known that acceptance of a Higher Power is traditionally viewed as intrinsically therapeutic, and inculcation of it is therefore a necessary therapeutic task.

While this may be true for many who aspire to sobriety, others with fixed human-centered values will find a thoroughly secular, cognitive-behavioral approach more palatable and effective. When humanists, agnostics, atheists, Buddhists, and other disbelievers are told that their central values are symptoms of a terminal illness, their chances of remaining in treatment and of benefiting from it are seriously reduced.

Some authors make a convincing argument that devout belief in supernatural entities is a form of mental illness; indeed, a number of such books—well-written ones at that—do exist. But this is an extreme point of view, and one that can incite conflict between believers and disbelievers. No one likes to be diagnosed as "sick" because of what he or she believes.

Clinical Protocol: The purpose of the Vestibule is: 1) to give each patient an exposure to both programs as a way of ensuring informed consent to care; and 2) to enhance commitment to recovery through participation in treatment planning. "Vestibule" refers to a status that is assigned to each patient at the time of admission. While the patient is "in the vestibule," s/he is unassigned (and uncommitted) to either recovery track, but he or she is free to make a program selection as early as the second day, and no later than the third day. The patient will be provided reading material from both programs, including pamphlets, short articles, and the two books, the Big Book of AA and *The Small Book* of RR. The patient can be advised to attend meetings of A.A. and RR during this preliminary and exploratory period.

Concerning the books, some guidance is desirable and practical. For example, the Big Book is indeed big (575 pages), but only because more than two-thirds of it consists of personal narratives. The actual text consists of only 146 pages. In *The Small Book* (275 pages of text) the patient could be advised to concentrate on the first 200 pages, including the introduction (by Albert Ellis) and the preface.

Having done this reading, the patient then experiences the Orientation Interview, the object of which is to select a recovery program: track one, RR, or track two, A.A. The importance of this interview is obvious. The interviewer can be a department head or a highly experienced caseworker, but must always be a professional. It is extremely important that the patient make the final decision regarding her or his participation in the recovery program. Nothing is rigid, and there will always be a number of borderline cases in which professional guidance is needed.

Conducting the Daily RR Group Sessions: The therapist shall have a working knowledge of Rational-Emotive Therapy, gained from university training in cognitive-behavioral methods, or through the Institute for Rational-Emotive Therapy, or through RRS-sponsored consultation or in-service training. An RET therapist may of course be recruited from the community on a full- or part-time basis. Paraprofessionals may assist in RET sessions under the supervision of a fully qualified professional. Group sessions will be held twice daily, a 60-minute morning session and a 90-minute afternoon session. The morning session will be devoted to information about RET presented by a therapist. This session, although essentially didactic in content, will provide opportunities for patient participation. For example, questions may be asked, illustrations made, and specific exercises employed.

The afternoon session will be less structured and more spontaneous, and the therapist will interject lines of rational thought as he or she directs the group therapeutic process. An RR therapist will meet with each patient individually at least once during the course of a hospital stay, and more often if clinical judgment indicates the need.

The Role of the Family in VIP: In contrast with traditional approaches, family members are not viewed as afflicted with an illness or adjustment disorder stemming from having a chemically dependent family member. Because they may have purposely or unwittingly enabled the addict to use or drink prior to hospitalization, family counseling sessions would seem to be in order so as to address these issues. Accordingly, they are helped through direct one-to-one RET counseling to start thinking, emoting, and acting more independently of their alcoholic spouses or relatives.

Suggestions for Rational Milieu Therapy: *Rational-Emotive Therapy With Alcoholics and Other Substance Abusers*, by Albert Ellis, Raymond Yeager, et al., includes a chapter on RET in the therapeutic community. This chapter provides some excellent examples of the RET "ABCs" in structured residential programs. Generally, the hospital milieu is regarded as consisting of many consecutive activating events, emotional consequences, and behavioral consequences. These consequences become the grist for endless therapeutic interventions by alert staff members who can help the patient identify the specific irrational beliefs that are causing dysfunctional emotions and behavior. The staff can learn to help the patient to dispute the irrational beliefs that are causing emotions such as anger, guilt, and depression.

A.A./RR VIP Outpatient Follow-up: Your community may already have an active RR chapter. If so, arranging for this kind of patient follow-up will be as simple as the familiar referral to an A.A. group. Because RR was established less than ten years ago, some communities do not yet have an RR chapter. In such cases it then becomes very desirable to start an RR chapter as a project that will be a part of your VIP program development. Little effort is required, and RR will help by identifying professionals who will participate, even as staff members from the hospital may choose to do.

RR meetings are usually held twice a week, often in the early evening hours and on weekends. They are always free of charge, and they last 90 minutes. These meetings are actually a continuation of the sessions begun in the VIP program, and they will, of course, be open to new members who seek them out or are referred to them from community agencies. Any hospital would do well to promote such meetings, not only as an extension of its VIP program, but as a matter of public relations. Certainly, when inpatient care is needed, the legitimate self-interest of the hospital is also served.

Administrators and professional therapists will immediately see the logic and workability of Trimpey's VIP program. Just as important is the quality of its underlying concern, its humanity and its compassion. I have paraphrased and quoted Trimpey's and Martin's article on the VIP program at length and with little comment because I could not have expressed it any better, or even as well. If the VIP program is not the wave of the future, there is no future. We can no longer continue to do things because "they have always been done that way." That didn't work; the VIP program will work, and in fact, is already working.

It's working well in Hampstead Hospital, in Hampstead, New Hampshire, which is an outstanding example of an institution that has installed the two-track system. The effort was spearheaded by Alan Karney, Director of Chemical Dependency Treatment, and it has worked like the proverbial charm. Initially there was some of the anxiety that change—any change—always brings. The staff of Hampstead, however, are totally professional (as distinct from "para-professional") and were familiar with both the traditional recovery approach and the cognitive/behavioral concepts of Albert Ellis, Maxie Maultsby, William Glasser, Eric Berne, and others. Although most of the Hampstead staff had been immersed in the traditional system since graduate school, they were immediately appreciative of the merits of the two-track system and adapted to it with little difficulty.

It is highly significant that the patients of Hampstead Hospital have enthusiastically accepted the new system.[10] While in the "Vestibule," they listen to lectures about each track (A.A. and RR) and, with help from the staff always available to them, choose the program most suited to their needs and compatible with their basic life values. Problems have not appeared; they've disappeared.

I've talked with Alan Karney about the spirituality issue. Again, no problem. "What patients really want," Karney said, "is a tool kit, a 'how-to' approach to problem solving." Some patients, it seems, resent the theological component of A.A., or are turned off by the drunkalogs ("war stories") presented at meetings, or resent being told that they are powerless over their addictions. But others welcome the life-long support program of Alcoholics Anonymous. They find that A.A. enhances their spiritual and religious convictions, and they freely accept the traditional tenet that the "disease" of alcoholism can be constrained, but only in cooperation with a Power greater than themselves. (It seems that a few patients in both tracks retain belief in the disease concept as an ace in the hole, a built-in excuse for a possible future drinking bout.) Incidents of A.A./RR criticism among patients are minimal; members of both groups respect the decisions made by their peers.

The overriding feature of the Hampstead approach is patient participation in a program which they themselves have selected as applicable to their needs. Others talk about "fitting the program to the client," but Hampstead Hospital does it, and in doing so, has made history. For further information write to:

Hampstead Hospital
East Road
Hampstead, New Hampshire 03841
Phone: 603-329-5311 (day/night)

The two-track system is also working (as of April, 1993) at the 175-bed, non-profit Forest Hospital (an affiliate of Forest Health Systems) located in a northwest suburb of Chicago, Illinois.[11] Susan C. Sardo, Director of Public Relations, provided me with a packet of information descriptive of the amazing range of services (36 programs) offered at Forest Hospital. The packet included a brochure titled "THE AGE OF REASON Has Come to Addiction Care." It announces the inclusion of Rational Recovery (on a parity basis with Alcoholics Anonymous), among its services.

I spoke with Margo Reiner, Director of Addiction Services, who answered my every question fully and without hesitation. I sensed that at Forest there is no pro/anti positioning of staff (and, as at Hampstead, the staff is 100% professional) or patients relative to A.A./RR, and that Forest's only concern is the welfare of the patients. And again, patients *participate* in decision-making. Here the works of Albert Ellis and the Trimpeys are appreciated and integrated into a program that includes the mental, emotional, and physical aspects of total health. (Patients in the addictions program are presented with free copies of *Feeling Good* by David Burns and *The Small Book* by Jack Trimpey.) For further information write or call:

Forest Health Systems, Inc.
555 Wilson Lane
Des Plaines, Illinois 60016-4794
Phones: 24-hours: 708-635-4100
and 1-800-866-9699 (Ask for Addictions Dept.)

Finally, Rational Recovery itself operates a small 10-bed residential (non-medical) program near Sacramento, California. It caters exclusively to people with problems associated with a variety of substances, especially alcohol. Again, like Hampstead and Forest, it offers a program based on Ellis/Trimpey mental health constructs. For further information, write or call:

Rational Recovery
Box 800
Lotus, California 95651-0800
Phones: 916-621-2667 and 916-621-4374

---

1. G. Lamunyon, "Anti-intellectual Foundations of Spiritual Healing."

2. Milgram, G. (1990). *The Facts About Drinking: Coping with Alcohol Use, Abuse, and Alcoholism.* New York: Consumers Union (p. 59).

3. Most people understand the word *patient* to mean someone who is physically sick, and they think of drugs as things that sick people take as prescriptions to get well. Words such as *patient, client,* and *student,* mean the same thing: customer.

4. Professor Joe Gerstein, M.D. is now Medical Director and President of RRSN's Board of Directors. Tom Horvath, Ph.D. is Vice-president of the Board.

5. The terms "Platonic" and "Platonist" are normally used in a different sense than that used in this monograph. They normally refer to philosophical idealism rather than supernaturalism as such. —Editor

6. Here, I combined certain documents from Trimpey for the sake of brevity, and although the quoted material is gently reworded in part, it reflects his meaning in the context in which it was originally presented.

7. For full information write to Consulting Psychologists Press, Inc. 577 College Avenue, Palo Alto, CA 94306. The Myers-Briggs is not a "personality test," but a powerful Type Indicator, concerned with the differences in people that result from

the way they like to *perceive* and the way they like to *judge*. The types are identified by letters (INTJ, for example), and each letter is significant. For example, if you are an "INTJ" (as I am):

> I–You focus on the inner world of thoughts,
> feelings, or impressions.
>
> N–You focus on possibilities and relationships and
> look toward the future.
>
> T–You base your judgments on logic and objective
> analysis; tend to be more task oriented.
>
> J–You like a planned, organized approach to life;
> tend to want things settled and decided.

All in all, the Myers-Briggs Personality Indicator is a superlative tool, tested and validated, and perfectly adapted to the Vestibule system as devised by Martin and Trimpey.

8. In time the two-track approach suggested by Trimpey and Martin could be expanded, within limits, into a true pluralistic approach, catering to a multiplicity of special groups such as black Americans, homosexuals, the Hispanic community, and others. The VIP program may be just the beginning of an entire movement to "actually fit programs to the needs (including cultural, religious, and sexual orientations) of clients. For the moment, we have more lip service than practice devoted to this concept. The next chapter touches on this subject briefly. Trimpey's two-track approach will probably, in time, be considered only the first step toward a truly pluralistic system.

9. Originally, there were four items on this list, the first of which addressed the disease issue as related to other documents published by RR. With no equivocation, however, RR is convinced that beyond any reasonable doubt heavy drinking is a behavior, subject to but not caused by external influences.

10. Matthew MacDonald, CRRT (Certified Rational Recovery Therapist) at Hampstead Hospital, confirms this in an article in the March/April 1993 issue of the JRR (p. 20) in which he affirms that "Hampstead patients are whole-heartedly satisfied with the program, as surveys have shown."

11. In the Winter 1992 quarterly publication *Branching Out*, Forest Hospital describes itself and its services: The Forest Hospital Foundation is a not-for-profit affiliate of Forest Health Systems, which includes Forest Hospital, Des Plaines [Illinois], a fully accredited, 175-bed private psychiatric hospital offering treatment programs for children, adolescents, and adults suffering from mental or emotional disorders. The hospital also offers comprehensive programs for eating disorders, dual diagnosis and substance abuse, as well as a range of outpatient programs.

12

Non-Institutional Recovery

This chapter concerns *self-directed*, as distinct from *other-directed*, recovery from addiction. As we have seen, traditional institutional programs insist that one size fits all. (Given that circumstance, the traditional approach may be characterized as aggressive/passive; that is, aggressively imposed by the institution and passively assimilated by the client.) We have also seen that nontraditional programs offer choices, options tailored to the individual.

There is a third kind of recovery, that of the "take charge, do-it-yourself" type. Its existence is one of the best-kept secrets in the addictions field, but it happens every day. It takes four forms:

1) Recovery expedited through a private therapist
2) Recovery with the help of a self-help support group
3) Recovery as a bottomed-out, instant decision
4) Recovery through the natural process of "maturing out"

Recovery expedited through a private therapist: Working with a private therapist is a good way to solve personal problems—including addiction problems. In Professor Miller's study of the effectiveness of treatment modalities, he noted that the three studies done on the effectiveness of confrontational counseling had produced 0% positive results. Three studies on general counseling produced the same (0%) result, as did the seven studies on individual psycho-therapy (insight). One might be tempted to strike personal counseling off the list of ways to solve drinking problems, but that would be unwarranted. It would, perhaps, be more reasonable to recognize that therapists provide an invaluable (and sometimes affordable) service but that, for some reason, they have been shown to be ineffective in *one* area. Why? And what can be done about it?

When a client has a drinking problem, the typical therapist usually refers that client to A.A. The average therapist learned about alcoholism in a traditional setting and absorbed the popular notion that A.A. is the only road to recovery, and that its program is highly effective. But most therapists *know* very little about A.A. and have neither read its Big Book nor attended a single A.A. meeting.

Clients usually follow the advice of their therapists, and thereby become the victims of conflicting ideologies. On the one hand, A.A. tells the client that he or she is *powerless*, that heavy drinking is an incurable disease, and that "once an alcoholic, always an alcoholic." (But the Big Book on page 64 also says, "Our liquor was but a symptom. So we had to get down to causes and conditions."[1]) The novice is further told to acquire greater humility, and that dependence on God is a prerequisite to the achievement and maintenance of sobriety.

The therapist agrees with Wilson that heavy drinking is but a symptom of the problem, and tries to *empower* the client so as to solve the underlying problem. The client is advised that substantive change is not only possible but achievable, and that he or she will benefit by becoming less dependent and more personally autonomous. How can a client be other than confused? Perhaps that explains the 0% effectiveness rating assigned to counseling.

Therapists are concerned with helping their clients achieve mental health. It would therefore seem appropriate to refer a client to a self-help support program that promotes a mental health approach to recovery. Rational-Emotive Therapy, Transactional Analysis, and Reality Therapy, among others, are cognitive/behavioral approaches oriented toward the achievement of mental health and personal autonomy. The self-help programs of Rational Recovery, Moderation Management, Women for Sobriety, and Men for Sobriety all follow cognitive/behavioral principles. (There are, of course, other mental health approaches, though to the best of my knowledge no national self-help support programs utilize them.)

How many therapists have checked the efficacy of the A.A. program, or are even aware that there are eight other self-help programs available to their clients? How many have read *The Small Book* (or the Big Book), or know that it is on the shelves of most bookstores and libraries? Therapists must realize that when they are not up to date, they are out of date.

The therapeutic tools provided by cognitive-behavioral therapy (Ellis's RET, Glasser's Reality, and Berne's TA, for example) have long been available to clinicians and much used by them—except in the area of addictions. Trimpey's contribution was specificity; he adapted, implemented, and applied RET to the area of addiction.

We now have yet another tool available to clinicians and their clients. It is *Problem Drinkers: Guided Self-Change Treatment*, by Mark B. and Linda C. Sobell of the Addiction Research Foundation in Toronto, Canada.[2] It was my good fortune to review pre-publication selections from this book, the new title announcement page of which reads:

> Epidemiological studies from the last two decades have shown that *problem drinkers*, rather than alcoholics, constitute the majority of persons with alcohol problems, despite the greater amount of attention given to alcoholics. This book describes—in detail sufficient enough for clinicians to put into practice—a tested, motivationally based treatment specifically designed for *problem drinkers* . . . The treatment is brief and highly cost-effective, and the procedures are practical and easily implemented by counselors and professionals.

This book is a marvelous tool with which clinicians can help any problem drinker, and with which any problem drinker can help him or herself. Anyone with a reasonable degree of intelligence can benefit from reading it, and, when used in coordination with a professional counselor, the book can work wonders.

Recovery with the help of a self-help support group: There is much confusion concerning the designations "self-help" and "support." Throughout this book, however, I have used the combinational designation "self-help support" in an effort to highlight the common ground shared by the two approaches.

Credit Stan Katz and Aimee Liu who, in their *Codependency Conspiracy*, differentiate between support and self-help programs.[3] Obviously the terms "self-help" and "support" are not mutually exclusive, since each self-help or support program contains elements of the other approach, but differ from one another in emphasis and orientation. Using Katz' and Liu's criteria, but not their terminology, one can make the following distinctions:

Self-help groups encourage their members to view their problems as just that—problems—and not to build their identities around them. They encourage their members to work toward complete recovery. Support groups, on the other hand, often encourage their members to identify themselves with their problems ("I'm Joe, and I'm an alcoholic") and to believe that they can never be rid of those problems. Hence, members of support groups are always recover*ing* and never recover.

Self-help groups encourage members to attend for a limited period of time to deal with specific problems. Support groups encourage members to attend meetings for life, because they preach that problems can never be fully overcome, only arrested—with the ongoing help of the support group.

Self-help groups are often supervised or assisted by professionals. Support groups are normally led by nonprofessionals, and may prohibit participation by professionals.

Self-help groups normally allow "crosstalk," the sharing of advice and experiences, but do not attempt to prescribe behavior in areas unrelated to the specific problems being dealt with. Support groups, however, normally prohibit "crosstalk," but may attempt to dictate beliefs and behaviors to their members.

To illustrate the differences between the two kinds of groups, consider a group designed for those who have lost a child. As a *self-help* group, it provides information, coping techniques, and the compassionate understanding helpful in enduring a tragedy of such magnitude. Members, however, do recover and leave the group after learning how to handle the soul-shaking trauma of such a loss.

In contrast, A.A. and N.A. are mutual *support* groups [programs] because perpetual support is considered necessary for those who consider themselves diseased and in need of support, whether it emanates from a group, a sponsor, or a Power greater than themselves. In this instance, the permanent support group is consistent with the notion of a permanent (but arrestable) disease, as in the case of alcoholism as perceived by A.A., the NCADD, the AMA, et al. The underlying belief is that "I can't do it alone," now or ever. Thus, the recover*ing* alcoholic and the need to attend meetings for life.

Obviously, such programs, whether self-help, mutual support, or both, serve a vital need, and we tend to assume that most recoveries take place within them. But read what Jack Trimpey, founder of Rational Recovery, has to say:

> It is well understood within the RR group that more people recover from chemical dependency in the privacy of their own homes than get better in recovery programs . . . local RR meetings may accelerate the learning process."[4]

That's right, of course, but how refreshing for the leader of a self-help program to make such a statement. For many people, however, the prospect of recovering in about a year, with help (from RR), rather than doing it on their own (often over a much longer period), is very inviting. True, most people do "mature out," but why not mature out a little earlier? Recovery doesn't have to run some predetermined course. The primary purpose of a self-help support group, RR, A.A., or any other, should be to expedite and accelerate the normal, healthy process of recovery and survival.

Recovery as a bottomed-out, instant decision (self-control): This is well explained by Jack Trimpey in Chapter 3 of his book. It took him just two pages to say what the whole world knew but needed to hear. With permission, I have included his remarks here. Please give the last three lines of this quotation your special attention:

> This chapter will be the shortest and bluntest in *The Small Book*. It will come swiftly and directly to the point. Unless you stop drinking or using drugs, the rest of *The Small Book* will be of little help. You see, persistent use of intoxicants impairs your ability to think in the abstract, and even though you are intelligent and seem to understand much of what you read, you may fail to gain self-awareness of your own addictive thinking. Remember now, addiction is a philosophy, not your self-drugging behavior. As long as you continue to drink or use, you are practicing the *philosophy* you want to change. Because drinking and using feel good, it is very difficult to even criticize, let alone change, the irrational philosophy that produces such gratification. As you will see in the chapter "Voices," there is a lot of mental activity taking place each time you drink or use. In order to hear your mental voices that lead you to drink, you must stop drinking and at least *intend* to stay stopped.
>
> You are in control of your drinking or drugging every day. You have been in control all along. You may like to think you can handle it and stop at any time you want, but deep down you cling to the idea that addicted or "alcoholic" people can't control their behavior. It gives you a perfect "out": Who can blame someone who is "out of control"?
>
> When the pain and losses caused by your habit exceed the pleasure you get from it you will be ready to quit. If you want to stop drinking, you can quit right now and you know it. When you have suffered enough, you will finally quit. There is nothing to stop you from doing so. Quitting alcohol or drugs is simply a matter of making a decision and then sticking to it by stubbornly refusing to indulge. There may be some initial discomfort, but that is just a physical craving, and it will fade within seventy-two hours. After that, physically speaking, you are in the clear. You will never again have a physical craving for alcohol, unless, of course, you resume drinking.

For most of us, quitting alcohol, heroin, or cocaine is no worse than a mild or moderate case of flu. It's no biggie. About one in four or five of us, though, may experience DTs (delirium tremens), with mental confusion, agitation, great restlessness—not just the usual "shakes"—and even weird visions. Those persons are generally over forty, or have been drunk a long time. About one-fourth of the persons who have DTs die, so if you suspect, based on your experiences, that you will become ill this way by going cold turkey, then get to a medical doctor any way you can and explain your desire to withdraw from alcohol.

If you believe that you must "taper off," though it is statistically doubtful that you will be better off in doing so, then *do it*, for one day only, consuming only *one* beer (12 ounces) during the entire day. If you drink more than that, you are merely sustaining your addiction, and you will "forget" that you are trying to save your life by quitting. If your problem is other drugs that have withdrawal syndromes, such as Valium or barbiturates, go to a drug clinic for professional supervision. So, pick a time—like NOW, or tomorrow morning—and KNOCK IT OFF! I'm sure that none of the above comes as news to you.

Be honest now; is there any part of that you didn't, couldn't, or refused to understand? Anything about "Knock it off!" that is not clear? Oscar Levant was never so witty as when he said, "I envy people who drink; at least they know what to blame everything on." You and I both know that drinking problems have nothing to do with the drink, and everything to do with the drinker.

The next time you feel sorry for yourself, read Viktor Frankl's little masterpiece, *Man's Search for Meaning: An Introduction to Logotherapy*, in which he recalls the ineffable horrors that he experienced in a Nazi concentration camp:

> There were always choices to make. Every day, every hour, offered the opportunity to make a decision, a decision which determined whether you would or would not submit to those powers which threatened to rob you of your very self, your inner freedom, which determined whether or not you would become the plaything of circumstance, renouncing freedom and dignity to become molded . . . Fundamentally, therefore, any man can, even under such circumstances, decide what shall become of him—mentally and spiritually.[5]

Recovery via "maturing out": It has nothing to do with age or hospitals and treatment centers. It involves a gradual diminishment of addictive habits over a period of time. Seventeen-year-old men "mature out" every day and some 40-year-old boys never get around to it.

The phrase "maturing out" suggests to some people that if they do nothing at all, somehow the addiction will just go away. But addictions never just go away; they have to be thrown away.

The fact that so many people mature out of addictive behaviors may be the "best-kept secret in the addictions world"—possibly because this form of recovery is free. In March 1990, *American Health* magazine published an article by J. Gurion, which confirmed what has long been known to addiction experts. According to a scientific Gallup Poll, "people are about ten times as likely to change on their own as with the help of doctors [physicians], therapists, or self-help groups." The survey found:

> Professional help had surprisingly little to do with important life changes, even health-related ones. Doctors helped people change only 3% of the time—while psychologists and psychiatrists, self-help groups and religious counselors got the credit even less often. Support was much more likely to come from friends (14%), parents, children, or siblings (21%), or a spouse, boyfriend or girlfriend (29%). And 30% of the time, people simply did what they had to do on their own, often with striking success.[6]

It is known, for example, that most heroin addicts mature out in their twenties and thirties. Stanton Peele and Archie Brodsky comment on the maturing out process in their *The Diseasing of America:*

> [It's] the best-kept secret in the addiction treatment industry—that many more people give up addictions *on their own* than through treatment. [Everyone can] benefit from knowing that the great majority of people with addictive habits—particularly young people— can outgrow them without entering a hospital program or following a 12-step regimen. As most people mature and assume responsible, satisfying roles, life-disturbing habits become less appealing to them. These natural developments in people's lives can be encouraged by therapies that focus on real skills in coping and self-management.[7]

Peele and Brodsky recommend The Life Process Program, which is not a form of therapy but a change-oriented program based on personal strength and self-empowerment. It's a tool kit which will enable you to:

A. Assess where you stand in life and what a particular habit means to you, what it does for as well as to you.
B. Set realistic goals for change, based on your personal resources and values.
C. Strengthen your life as you strive to change your habit, and create environments for yourself and others that make addiction both unnecessary and undesirable.

This change-oriented program recognizes that addictive behaviors not only reflect many false beliefs (e.g., genetic inheritance), but are consistent with a chosen lifestyle. Example: you're a member of the Knights of Columbus, and you and your buddies meet at the club to do what? Pray? On occasion perhaps, but a certain amount of time is also devoted to drinking and gambling. So, tear up your membership card and extricate yourself from an environment that reinforces your old recreational habits.

Before trying The Life Process Program, you might do well to read a few of the nontraditional books on addictions mentioned in this book (and in its bibliography). Also, you'd probably do well to attend a few RR meetings, or those of any organization oriented toward mental health. Sometimes combinations of approaches work better than a single approach.[8]

You are now privy to the best-kept secret in the addictions world: the four non-institutional paths to recovery. You can tailor any or all of them to your personal needs just by using your common sense and a little imagination. There is and always will be a place for recovery under institutional auspices, but it isn't the *only* way. You have other options.

Straight talk to addicts: People who maintain their addictive habits tend to be selfish and are often unaware that their lifestyles have a truly rotten effect on their spouses, friends, employers, employees, and families. Addictions damage your best friend—you—and they *always* harm others. They are, in addition, often illegal and dangerous. And something else—in the old days heavy drinkers were *universally* considered weak and spineless. That was a simplification, of course, but the fact is that there are still a few of those people around, and you may—or may not—be one of them. We've all known people who were so weak, lazy, and irresponsible that they didn't even try to quit, so they continued to screw up their own lives and those of others.

You've just read about several ways out of the mess you're in. Pick the one that suits you—and knock it off.

---

1. Wilson's remark is essentially negative. The *symptom* he refers to reflects the absence of a spiritual connection which has produced a disease, the remedy to which is the establishment of a relationship to a Higher Power (God). (Therapists usually use the word *symptom* in the sense of an observable behavior that reflects the root problem.)

2. Sobell, Mark B. and Linda C. (1993). *Problem Drinkers; Guided Self-Change Treatment.* New York: Guilford Publications, Inc.

3. Katz, S. and Liu, A.(1991). *The Codependency Conspiracy: How to Break the Recovery Habit and Take Charge of Your Life.* New York: Warner Books.

4. From *The Small Book*, Chapter 8.

5. Frankl, V. (1959). *Man's Search for Meaning: An Introduction to Logotherapy.* (A newly revised and enlarged edition of *From Death-Camp to Existentialism;* translated by Ilse Lasch, with preface by Gordon Allport). Boston: Beacon Press, (pp. 65-66).

Note: Frankl, a survivor of Nazi death-camps, departs from Freud in interpreting neuroses. Freud was concerned with conflict and unconscious motives, and what might be termed "the pleasure principle." Frankl, in the "Third School of Viennese Psychiatry," understood neuroses as the failure of the sufferer to find meaning and a sense of responsibility in his existence. Freud is dead, literally and figuratively, and the school of existentialism which Frankl devised has enjoyed only limited acceptance, more so in Europe than in the United States. If you read his little book, you may find it not only difficult but impossible to feel sorry for yourself any longer, regardless of the circumstances of your life.

6. Gurion, J. (March 1990). "Remaking Our Lives." *American Health,* (pp. 50-52).

7. The authors also review this subject in *The Truth About Addiction and Recovery.*

8. In *The Truth About Addiction and Recovery* (pages 277-302) the authors list necessary life skills and provide an in-depth discussion of each. The skills listed are: 1) Problem-solving; 2) Communication; 3) Relaxation; 4) Being alone; 5) Intimate relationships; 6) Job skills; 7) Refusal skills; 8) Breaking the flow; and 9) Self-efficacy.

There is obviously a certain amount of overlap (as in problem-solving) between the Rational Recovery and the Life Process programs. That, however, would seem to indicate the complementary nature of the two approaches.

13

Short Topics

Some subjects did not fit snugly into the plan of this book, but were important enough to warrant inclusion in this special section. Here are 11 of them:

- Adult Children of Alcoholics
- American Medical Association
- Antabuse (disulfiram)
- Bashing (RR, A.A., etc.)
- Bottoms, High and Low
- Children's Books
- Codependency
- Cult: A.A. As and As Not
- Denial
- Detoxification
- Employee Assistance Programs

Adult Children of Alcoholics

An article titled "Study Challenges Tradition of Adult Children of Alcoholics" appeared in the *Milwaukee Sentinel* on September 12, 1990. Jack Trimpey reviewed it in the *Journal of Rational Recovery*:

It is unfortunate that bogus trends in health care cannot be prevented before they sweep into the media with sensational claims, but at least the scientific community is occasionally able to come to the rescue. At the University of Wisconsin at River Falls, two professors, Richard Seefeldt and Mark Lyon, conducted a most interesting study of the hypothesis—now taken as fact by most professionals and by the public at large—that adult offspring of problem drinkers are a unique population deserving specialized treatment of their emotional problems.

Using the thirteen characteristics described in Janet Woilitz's 1983 best-selling book, *Adult Children of Alcoholics*, Seefeldt and Lyon designed a study of 147 students (54 ACAs and 93 non-ACAs) to determine if there were any differences between the two groups. Each group was tested for each of Woiltiz's 13 characteristics using a battery of personality tests and questionnaires about the partici-pants' substance abuse and that of their parents. Significantly, all subjects were told that the study was about the characteristics of college students in general, as a way of minimizing bias.

Seefeldt and Lyon reported, "We found that there were absolutely no differences between the ACAs [ACOAs] and the non-ACAs. In comparing the characteristics of the two groups, Seefeldt and Lyon used a technique that enabled them to use the Woilitz characteristics to predict which students belonged to each group. They found that only 39% of all subjects could be correctly classified. Lyon com-mented "That is a very huge margin of error."[1]

Seefeldt remarked to *Sentinel* reporter Donna Sanders, "I thought Woilitz's characteristics of ACOAs were very general and could apply to almost anybody," and "the current attitude toward ACOAs . . . is really dangerous. It may even alter the course of a person's life." The two professors also pointed out that ACOAs need assurance that just because their parents may have drunk too much doesn't mean that they will experience problems themselves.

The message is clear: if you are an ACOA (a rather deprecating term), and are having problems which you perceive as directly related to the drinking habits of your parents, then ACOA may be for you. I suspect, however, that the everyday problems of life for most young adults are not causally related to the lifestyles of their parents. Mental health professionals continue to accept the broad ACOA thesis on faith. It's time to check it out.

The ACOA phenomenon presents the perennial question in the addictions field: Who's in charge here? Am I a victim of the past? Have I been shaped like wet clay by people and circumstances in the past, and am I therefore not responsible for what I am, do, and think? Good question, and the answer to it is No. You are responsible, and you are not an "adult child" and can't be because the words form an oxymoron—they're mutually exclusive. You are an adult, and therefore responsible.[2]

The whole issue was summed up nicely in an article by D. Sifford that appeared on page 5-C of the January 2, 1989 *Philadelphia*

Inquirer. The title is "A Psychiatrist Discusses Creative Writers and Alcohol." Sifford comments on and quotes the work of Don Goodwin, Professor and Chair of the Department of Psychiatry at the University of Kansas Medical Center, and the first researcher (in the 1970s) to establish a link between heredity and alcoholism.[3] Sifford says:

> Goodwin said that "all the stuff" that has been written in recent years about adult children of alcoholics has been, in his judgment, something akin to a hoax. Adult children of alcoholics are about like adult children of everybody else with a problem, he said, and it's hard to build a reasonable case for giving them extraordinary attention.

Again and again the issue of personal responsibility comes to the fore. To members of ACOA, please consider this: if you had a rotten childhood, Mom and Dad undoubtedly played a large part in that. And though your past can influence, it does not determine, your behavior. Your parents probably did as well as they could, but you'll never really know because you'll never have all the facts.

At one time I hated my parents, then judged them, and finally just accepted them. At that point I became a full adult, and responsible for my life—as you are for yours.

American Medical Association

This association—which makes the Teamsters look like a bunch of boy scouts—has been consistently inconsistent in its views on addiction. We reviewed (in Chapter 2) its position on the disease question, with emphasis on its formal joint opinion (expressed as a resolution) with the NCADD. This opinion is weasel-worded and much less enlightened than the position of the American Psychiatric Association, as expressed in DSM-III-R. Compare the AMA's recent "official" views with this once (1921) "official" AMA position on addiction:

> Public opinion regarding the vice of drug addiction has been deliberately and consistently corrupted through propaganda in both the medical and lay press . . . The shallow pretense that drug addiction is a "disease". . . has been asserted in volumes of "literature" by self-styled specialists.[4] [Thanks to Thomas Szasz, Professor of psychiatry at New York Upstate Medical Center for that quotation.][5]

In contrast, today's AMA/NCADD position reverses this statement and endorses the "disease" concept, as discussed in Chapter 2. One strongly suspects that the reason for the AMA's flip-flop on this issue has to do with the handsome financial rewards for treating the "disease" of alcoholism. [Ten years ago this would have been a shocking statement; today, many prominent figures in the addictions field would agree with it. —Ed.]

A true story: The Indiana State Medical Association published an article by Kete Cockrell, M.D. in the November 1991 issue of *Indiana Medicine.* The article, "The Wounded Healer," was an unabashed promotion of A.A., complete with multiple references to "Power," spirituality, God, shame, dry drunk, guilt, etc. I wrote to the editor and suggested that an article on detoxification procedures or the prescription of disulfiram (Antabuse) would be more appropriate in a scientific medical journal than an advocacy article concerning a spiritual and religious organization. I concluded the letter with:

> If the good doctor feels he really must write a promotional article in behalf of a self-declared "spiritual" program, he could, in the name of objectivity and fairness, at least mention that there are now seven [now eight] other self-help groups available to heavy drinkers (list attached) . . . Physicians and their patients have both a need and a right to know that alcoholics now have choices available to them in the area of self-help. It is, I think, unprofessional and unfair to deprive them of that knowledge. Dr. Cockrell is undoubtedly serious and dedicated, but would be well advised to stick with medicine when writing for a respected medical journal.
>
> If you would like an article concerning the emergence and orientation of the other seven self-help groups for alcoholics, I will, on request, write it.

The magistrates of the Indiana State Medical Association chose to ignore my letter, so after a long wait I followed up with a letter and a phone call. The response was less than enthusiastic; it was, in fact, antagonistic.

Significantly, a serious question of ethics is involved here pertaining to the *withholding* of vital information from both patients and physicians. My observation regarding the ethical issue was ignored by the Indiana State Medical Association. I hereby repeat my offer to the Association to write an article for its journal, and await a courteous response.

Antabuse

You can pay $70.00 or $16.72 for one hundred 250-milligram disulfiram tablets, depending on whether you buy them under the brand name Antabuse, or the generic name disulfiram. Just tell your physician to write the prescription as a generic. You'll save $53.28.

Disulfiram is *not* a crutch, and taking it is often a courageous act. Taking it buys time in which your body and mind can heal, thus enabling you to engage the Beast—the voice of irrationality—at a later time when you have full control of your faculties. Sooner or later, however, you must make the final decision to quit without benefit of chemical help. It's easier, however, to make that decision when you're in good mental and physical shape. I took disulfiram many years ago and it worked well. I recommend it. It's a smart move.

Jack Trimpey states that "you may resume drinking alcohol about five days after discontinuing Antabuse. . . ." The statement needs qualification. Depending on your weight, general physical health, and how long and heavily you drank before taking Antabuse, you can resume drinking anywhere from five to fifteen days after taking an Antabuse tablet. Talk with your pharmacist or doctor about it. It used to take me ten days to two weeks to get Antabuse out of my system and get back to heavy drinking.

Disulfiram, by itself, is not dangerous and produces virtually no side effects in the vast majority of those who take it, *but,* combined with even small amounts of alcohol it will produce sickness, vomiting, nausea, arrhythmia (irregular heart beat), and other effects which are terrifying and sometimes lethal. Follow your doctor's advice on this; and take disulfiram only when you are sure that *all* alcohol is out of your system. I used to abstain for three days before taking it, and even then started with one fourth of a tablet and increased my intake gradually. You can't be too cautious with this stuff. A patient information sheet comes with the prescription; usually, however, it is not "user friendly." It was written not to help you, but to inform your doctor and cover its manufacturer legally. If you don't understand the information sheet, tell your pharmacist that you want a "user friendly" sheet and then take a look at it. If it makes sense, buy the generic drug it comes with. If it doesn't make sense, go elsewhere. Solid information is available and pharmacists are very helpful, but drug manufacturers usually care more about your doctor than they do about you. Check the library too, under magazine articles. It's your life and your money.

To repeat, for the sake of emphasis: **Remember this: Once you take disulfiram, DON'T DRINK!** Not a spoonful, not a drop. Even a tiny amount of alcohol will make you sick,[6] and a larger quantity can kill you. If it doesn't, you'll wish it would.

Bashing (A.A., RR, etc.)

Like other four-letter words, *bash* is not nice. It comes from the Latin, *basca*, to strike, and it means to attack or strike with a violent blow, to smash. The word is often used as an objection, as in "A.A. bashing," to *any* criticism of Alcoholics Anonymous.

The curious notion that something—anything—is above criticism is patently absurd. God, popes, saints, the Bible, and the U.S. Constitution have all been subjected to critical evaluations. A.A.'s reaction, after even a softly whispered suggestion that it might be less than perfect, could well be termed a Sacred Cow Syndrome, "SCS" for short. Jack Trimpey is convinced that the term "AA-bashing" is *steptalk*, used to suppress any serious criticism of A.A. or the 12-step approach. Given the fact that according to its own figures (in the "Comments" document) A.A. has a dropout rate of 95% over the first year alone, it would seem that A.A. is not quite perfect. Hence, it should be subject to scrutiny, and—God forbid—even criticism.

Consider, if you will, this serious play on words: As a member of Rational Recovery, I have this to say about alcoholics who are spiritual and religious:

To one who feels he is spiritual or religious, the experience of rational living seems impossible, but to continue as he is means disaster, especially if he is an alcoholic of the hopeless variety. To be doomed to an alcoholic death or to live on the basis of rational thinking are not always easy alternatives to face.

This statement is rigid, narrow, and irrational. But what you have just read is merely a transposition of words from the second paragraph of Chapter 4, page 44, of the Big Book, which reads:

To one who feels he is an atheist or an agnostic such an [a spiritual] experience seems impossible, but to continue as he is means disaster, especially if he is an alcoholic of the hopeless variety. To be doomed to an alcoholic death or to live on a spiritual basis are not always easy alternatives to face.

Chapter 4 ("We Agnostics") of A.A's Big Book reeks of the righteous omniscience, condescension, and absolute certainty characteristic of fundamentalists. The Big Book is the first, and prime, example of bashing. It bashes those who tried and found A.A. unsatisfactory. An example, from page 58, Chapter 5 ("How it Works") of the Big Book: "Those who do not recover [in A.A.] are people who cannot or will not completely give themselves up to this simple program, usually men and women who are constitutionally incapable of being honest with themselves." Even Jimmy Swaggart would be ashamed of a remark like that. If A.A. doesn't fill your needs, you are "constitutionally" dishonest, whatever that means.

When offended or insulted, saints may choose to turn the other cheek; we sinners defend ourselves—by attacking when necessary. The ranks of RR are filled with former A.A. members who report that all "alternative" self-help organizations are either ignored by A.A. or are treated with contempt. To condemn and criticize these organizations, without even a cursory knowledge of them, is an expression of ignorance and arrogance, and to simply ignore RR and the other seven self-help support programs is an insult of the first magnitude.[7] Courtesy may not be a cardinal virtue, but it is a virtue. Let's practice it.

We of RR now formally request that the spiritually enlightened members of A.A. quit bashing RR. RR is the *counterpoint* to A.A. It's true that the differences between them, according to Jack Trimpey, "are *not* superficial, but specific and irreconcilable." Yet, though RR and A.A. may never be friends, we need not be enemies. Let the bashing stop. It started with A.A. Let it stop there.

Bottoms, High and Low

After describing a set of unfortunate events, a person at an RR meeting said, "It was right there that I hit my bottom" (an A.A. expression). The discussion soon turned to the question of what is a *high* bottom as distinct from a *low* bottom. (There is, I believe, no *middle* bottom.) And what in the world is a bottom, anyway? The anatomical reference is clear (falling on your butt), but how does that relate to the timing of a lifestyle change?

Generally, "hitting bottom" suggests a kind of inevitability, a stage in a drinking career that *must* be reached before things can get better. It's as though life must always get worse before recovery becomes a possibility. That's muddy thinking, and it's self-defeating.

An example: let's say that Theresa McEntire is Chief Executive Officer of Superbig Industries, Inc., and that there are 50 executive levels below her. She drinks a little, then a lot, and gets into trouble. She then finds herself six notches down the ladder, as the Vice President in charge of Overseas Operations. At that point she "hits her bottom" and quits drinking. What really happened?

She allowed her behavior to adversely affect her performance and her career. The situation then became intolerable to her. She, to use that slightly vulgar but popular phrase, "hit her bottom." What she probably did was to make a rational evaluation of the damaging effects of drinking on her life and career, and decided to quit. She became aware of the addictive voice within her, debated it, won the debate, and made a decision: I will quit drinking. (A snap, unthinking decision to quit was also possible, though less likely.)

Thus, "hitting bottom" for her was quite probably nothing more than a decision, a victory for her power of reason over The Beast, the voice of non-reason. Her bottom was, I suppose, what could be termed a "high" bottom. Had she been demoted to the level of shipping clerk, she would, presumably, have hit a "low" bottom—that is, made the same decision, somewhat delayed. What all of this has to do with buns and bottoms seems irrelevant. The high/low bottom notion is a fuzzy phrase, better scrapped than salvaged. But to criticize without offering something constructive is unproductive, so here is a workable definition of "hitting bottom":

> Hitting bottom is a reasoned decision to quit drinking, made by any person at any time, based on the recognition that the consequences of heavy drinking have become greater than its real or perceived benefits. It could be called a "MOD" that is a Moment Of Decision, as in "I finally reached my MOD and quit drinking." [No more "high" or "low" bottoms, and that should be the end of it.]

Children's Books

The children's section of your public library contains a number of books about addiction in general and alcoholism in particular. They are, to a large extent, carbon copies of one another and they almost exclusively promote traditional concepts. They explain, with the benefit of vivid pictures of scarred livers and dirty lungs, what happens to people who drink and smoke too much, and they explain how drugs adversely affect the body, as distinct from the body-mind. Some of these books are helpful, but most of them are, at best, merely harmless. Many authors of such books seem unsure of themselves and they evidence a lack information and clear perspective. Most of these books contain references to A.A., Alanon, Alateen, and Alatot, to the exclusion of all other sources of help. In one hour you can read six of them and may well conclude that there is an *enormous* need for authors who are better informed. The standard books generate fear, and are thus essentially negative in approach. I could not find one book written in a positive or nontraditional vein. The field is wide open.

Codependency

"Codependency" is a word that cannot be found, and probably never will be found, in any dictionary. New words have to exist for a while before they are accepted as legitimate additions to our language. The "codependency" notion probably won't last that long. It's a fad, promoted by several enthusiastic hucksters, and it will soon go the way of the hula-hoop and pet rocks. Unfamiliar with either or both? That's what I mean.

The "disease of codependency" is an affront to common decency and common sense. For example, the spouse of an alcoholic is often understanding, compassionate, helpful, self-sacrificing, patient, and forebearing, but often happens to lack information and coping skills. To label such a person sick is a gross injustice. S/he has adapted, perhaps not wisely, but as well as s/he could, to a miserable situation.

The spouse may have allowed her or himself to be *dependent* on the approval of the heavy drinker, but that's just a mistake of judgment, a mistake that is as human as it is correctable. Codependence, if it means anything, is a negative notion; it suggests a lack of positive and effective problem-solving techniques. Codependency is a straight jacket that some people choose to wear, unaware that they can discard it at any time.

Often, however, it is not discarded, and for one reason. The reason is a word—*disease*, as in "codependency is a disease." The word suggests some external force acting upon an individual, a force over which the person has no control. Stan Katz and Aimee Liu make this telling commentary in *The Codependency Conspiracy:*

According to codependence gurus such as John Bradshaw, Anne Wilson Schaef, and Melody Beattie, everyone is sick until proven healthy. This rule particularly applies to anyone who works in a medical or mental health profession. "Codependents are servers," writes Schaef. "They are volunteers, the people who hold society together, who set aside their own physical, emotional, and spiritual needs for the sake of others."[8] While some would give these individuals awards for their service, Schaef seems to feel that they should undergo radical treatment [by *other* codependents, no doubt] for their desire to help others. In fact, she implies, the desire to help others is a signal of ineptitude: "Most mental health professionals are untreated codependents who are actively practicing their disease in their work in a way that helps neither them nor their clients."[9]. . .

If codependence were a scientifically recognized disease, such a sweeping generalization would immediately be seized and dismissed by the scientific community, for it has no foundation either in fact or logic, but Schaef herself admits that codependence is no more than "a grass roots" idea. That is to say, people who admit to having the disease themselves . . . are developing theories about codependence, not professionals. . . . If Schaef's assessment of codependence is correct, the primary way helping professionals can stop "practicing the disease" is to stop caring for others . . .[10]

You may have seen the list of Beattie's some 254 "symptoms" ("characteristics") of codependency, as a "disease."[11] If we were to take that list seriously it would be very difficult for anyone *not* to classify him or herself as codependent. Here are some examples of the terrifying symptoms:

1) *Feel harried and pressured.* Comment: a rather common phenomenon in our fast-paced society. Given, say, a husband who has taken a second mortgage on the house, lost his job, and behaves like an unpleasant lout, it would seem that a spouse who feels harried and pressured is responding in a not unusual fashion to a miserable situation. She may be sick and tired of it; but she's not sick.

2) *Blame someone else for my present situation.* Well, if you're broke and your friends have avoided you because your husband drinks himself silly every night, who else is there to blame? You? No—that six-foot, 175-pound boy who is eating pizza, drinking beer, and watching TV in the other room, that's who. To blame him is to assign responsibility, and he qualifies.

3) *Wish something good would happen.* If you have this symptom, you're healthy and haven't given up hope. If you *don't* have this symptom— *then* you're sick.

Shall we proceed through the other 251 "symptoms" or simply dismiss these blanket allegations by a few hucksters, one of whom claims that *96%* of us are codependent, sick, and diseased? You don't need scientific studies to answer that one; your common sense will do nicely.

A more accurate view of the codependency notion is that it is an approval-seeking state of mind that precedes the recognition, as Lois Trimpey writes, that "my first responsibility [is] to take care of myself."[12] Put another way, caring too much for another person is the same as *not* caring enough for yourself. When that simple fact is accepted, the invented and expensive "disease of codependency" will disappear. Things that defy common sense and devalue human beings tend to pass like puffed-up clouds in a strong summer wind.

What does Rational Recovery think about "codependence"? Lois Trimpey states, "Rational Recovery does not diagnose or otherwise indict a recovering person's immediate family . . ." Friends and relatives of alcoholics are welcome at RR meetings, since they have been affected by the behaviors of the heavy drinker, and since they too need to learn and to adjust. That, however, has nothing to do with dependence, and everything to do with independence.

The National Institute on Alcohol Abuse and Alcoholism recently concluded that there is "no data at all" to support the theory that individuals can develop a "personality disorder solely on the basis of their family membership."[13] Enough said.

Cults

The following segment is essentially a defense of Alcoholics Anonymous, a task which A.A. itself seems either unwilling or unable to undertake. Some New Guard thinkers insist on labeling A.A. a cult, but that is neither fair nor accurate. Definitions of the term "cult" tend to be so broad as to be meaningless, as Charles Bufe points out in *Alcoholics Anonymous: Cult or Cure?*[14] Instead of attempting to redefine the cult concept, Bufe lists the specific characteristics of cults, then comments on each as it does or does not relate to A.A. I have followed a similar format, but recommend Bufe's work as the best available treatment of this subject. To resolve the issue, certain criteria can be applied to any organization to determine whether or not it is a cult. They are:

1) **Alienation**. In A.A., one experiences a degree of social isolation, but not in the form of alienation from or antagonism toward the larger society. Cults, like the French, tend to look down on everything but themselves. A.A. is self-centered, but friendly to the larger society of which it is a part. *Is A.A. a cult?* NO.

2) **Authoritarian Structure**. This is a characteristic of cults, especially those with a charismatic leader. This was never true of A.A., even at the pinnacle of Bill Wilson's career, nor is it true today. If anything, A.A. *lacks* sufficient structure. *Is A.A. a cult?* NO.

3) **Charismatic Leadership**. Bill Wilson is dead (1971) and A.A. no longer has a charismatic leader. Its General Service Board (board of directors) exerts great influence, but not directly, on groups and the individuals within them. The Board is real and quietly active, but maintains a low profile. *Is A.A. a cult?* NO.

4) **Deception**. A.A. is not deceptive in the least. Its literature is loaded with euphemisms, and it plays interminable word games, but it is not maliciously deceptive. *Is A.A. a cult?* NO.

5) **Diet, Change of**. Cults often regulate diets, but A.A. does not. Judging by the junk food offered at meetings, A.A. is anti-diet, anti-nutrition. A great place *not* to eat. *Is A.A. a cult?* NO.

6) **Elitism**. There is some of this in A.A. At a recent meeting I heard (for perhaps the 100th time): "We are God's chosen people." And A.A. tends to disdain (by ignoring) all other self-help support groups for heavy drinkers. Also, alcoholics in A.A. tend to look down on those who take "hard drugs" as people of a lower class than those who abuse licensed alcoholic beverages. But the term *elitist*, as such, cannot be applied to A.A. Brandsma's comments on A.A.'s membership, in his study of A.A.'s effectiveness, seem to suggest that A.A. is, perhaps, more plebeian than patrician. Is A.A. elitist? No. *Separatist* would be a better adjective. *Is A.A. a cult?* NO.

7) **Euphoria**. New members often experience this sensation after short periods of sobriety, but it wears off quickly. It's an emotional and physical high, a celebration of the body-mind that takes place

as a person's body and mind readjust to their natural states of being (health). Feeling normal is then perceived (in stark contrast to the previous state) as almost ecstatic—a natural high, like viewing the earth from a single-holer (a single cockpit aircraft) at 5,000 feet. In cults, a sense of euphoria is deliberately and systematically sustained over long periods. It is based on intimate and supportive personal relationships, the deliberate induction of hypnotic states (sometimes with the aid of chemicals), and induced transpersonal "experiences." *Is A.A. a cult?* NO.

8) **Exclusivity.** This is mildly characteristic of A.A., since its primary concern is alcoholics. Old timers have resisted the influx of those who are dually addicted. That resistance continues, despite the increasing number of members who are addicted to the abuse of both alcohol and illicit drugs. Many of those who are dually addicted are made to feel unwelcome in A.A., or referred to Narcotics Anonymous (which has a reciprocal prejudice toward A.A.'s members); but it's not a major problem. *Is A.A. a cult?* NO.

9) **Exploitation.** Economic exploitation of members almost always exists in cults, never in A.A. *Is A.A. a cult?* NO.

10) **Fatigue.** Cults cultivate this state of physical enervation in their members. A.A. does not. *Is A.A. a cult?* NO.

11) **Irrationality.** On page 83 of *AA: Cult or Cure?* Bufe comments, "cults discourage skepticism and rational thought." Several A.A. slogans reflect its pronounced anti-intellectual bias. True to its Pietist origins, A.A. emphasizes intuition, emotion, and "group-think" (referred to as the "group conscience"). "Evidence" intended to validate the A.A. program is offered in the form of personal anecdotes, unqualified allegations, and recounted experiences. Since A.A. is essentially a faith-based program based on spiritual and religious precepts, it may be said that it is more *non-rational* than irrational. Many of its tenets, however (e.g., "one drink, one drunk"), are irrational since they fly in the face of virtually all modern research. *Is A.A. a cult?* YES.

12) **Lack of privacy.** Strong in cults, absent in A.A. *Is A.A. a cult?* NO.

13) **Millennarianism**. From millennium, a thousand years. The sky is falling! The world is coming to an end! Possibly, I hadn't noticed. Cults such as the Jehovah's Witnesses preach such nonsense in order to produce a sense of immediacy and anxiety that, in turn, generates compliance with the dictates of their intellectually disadvantaged leaders. Millennarianism has no place in A.A. *Is A.A. a cult?* NO.

14) **Mind Control**. A.A.'s objective is to effect a substantive change in beliefs and personality through the process of mental and emotional indoctrination, and through social control via group pressure. Free and open speech is virtually prohibited. As long as a person remains in A.A., that person is subject to mind control that is as subtle as it is consistent. (Ken Ragge explains the A.A. indoctrination process with great insight in *More Revealed*.[15]) Attendance is voluntary in Communal A.A. (except in the cases of those 80,000 or so court-mandated persons), so people *can* always get up and walk out, but that's hard to do. As we have seen, however, in Institutional A.A. strong personal and organizational pressures are brought to bear on patients to conform to the 12-step program. The only difference here between A.A. and a typical cult is one of method. *Is A.A. a cult?* YES.

15) **Solicitation of Members**. It's done by many who do not "officially" represent A.A., which means, of course, that they do so *unofficially*. The source of promotional activity is irrelevant here, but its intent and results are the same, as in the case of institutional marketing programs, bumper stickers, public service announcements (tapes furnished by A.A.), visits to jails, prisons, treatment centers, health fairs, and so on.[16] A.A. was, at first, a program of "attraction, not promotion." Now it methodically and vigorously promotes itself. It has a right to do so, but it does not have the right to lie about it. And, although the courts force individuals into A.A., and although A.A. seems to resent this practice, it cooperates fully with it.[17] *Is A.A. a cult?* YES.

16) **Violence and Harassment**. Violence in A.A.? No, none. A.A. is not violent in the usual sense of that word, but it methodically and consistently does violence to the human mind. The 12-step program is presented as the unquestioned—and unquestionable—truth, a program to be accepted and believed, but not examined. The word "violence" suggests that which is physical, but violence goes far beyond that; mental and emotional abuse are more subtle but just

as damaging, and sometimes more so, than physical injury. This kind of violence often leaves scars that never heal.

In A.A. there are relentless pressures, both subtle and aggressive, to believe and to conform. Questions are met with the reproachful "Take the cotton out of your ears and put it in your mouth," or with a series of other slogans that discourage a thought-filled approach to the program.[18] (For an in-depth coverage of this subject I recommend Charles Bufe's *Alcoholics Anonymous: Cult or Cure?*[19]) *Is A.A. a cult?* YES.

17) **World View**. Cults want to change the world. The twelfth Step has a distinctly missionary flavor to it ("after a spiritual awakening . . . to practice these principles in all our affairs"). Yet, A.A. remains an in-group devoted to a specific issue. *Is A.A. a cult?* NO.

Conclusion: A.A. is not a cult, but it is, as Bufe points out, cult-like in a few ways (my tally: YES on four counts, NO on thirteen), especially in areas that concern thought and emotion. The evidence is clear, and for the most part A.A. is clean. Let the slurs on the good reputation of A.A. stop now. But let the truth remain.

Denial

Words of "denial" are often misunderstood, and the person speaking them accused or confronted, as in "You are in denial!" Denial, however, is essentially a position statement, a declaration that an idea or allegation presented is unacceptable, as in "I deny–I refuse to accept—the validity of the codependency idea."

"Denial" is occasionally employed as a simple defense mechanism, but in far more cases it is an expression of unwillingness by those who have a problem to do anything about it at a given time or under a given circumstance at the dictate of others. That is, denial is less often a description of a state of mind than it is a tool in the hands of manipulators, however well intentioned, to push people into traditional self-help support programs or the institutions which sponsor them.[20]

The true meaning of the word "deny" has been distorted. It means: 1) to declare a statement, idea, or position to be untrue or inapplicable; to contradict; 2) to refuse to accept as true or right; reject as unfounded; 3) to refuse to acknowledge *as one's own* (emphasis added); disown; repudiate

People aren't stupid; they don't usually deny the existence of a headache, a drinking problem, or a broken leg. They may not draw attention to these things, and they may resist attention focused on their problems, but they *know*. Definition one (above), as it pertains to a heavy drinker, may simply mean that the he or she does not accept the label "alcoholic." Definition two rejects the term "alcoholic," seen as an extreme, in favor of "a problem with alcohol." Definition three repudiates the charge of alcoholism. Example: a first-offense DUI defendant (a normally light drinker) is tested at .10% blood alcohol level after a Christmas office party and is sentenced to attendance at A.A., where he is told he is a diseased alcoholic. Of course he'll deny it. Who wouldn't?

The charge of denial is used in hospitals and treatment centers as a club to bludgeon vulnerable patients into passivity and conformity. Such places fail to recognize that the charge they levy is often an assault on the value systems of their customers. Yet, what Trimpey calls "denial hazing" goes on. Institutional mind managers deny this, of course. Perhaps *they* are in denial.

In Rational Recovery, we have little use for the term "denial." Our concern is with that silent internal conversation within each of us, the one in which the voice of self-defeating irrationality battles the voice of self-preserving rationality. "Denial," in Rational Recovery, is taken as an indication that the internal rational/irrational argument is still unresolved. Therefore, in RR we would never say "You're in denial!" We would say "I hear your Beast (voice of non-reason) talking. What is it up to now? What excuses is it offering you for drinking?" Thus, a person who is thinking about drinking, or who has had a lapse—or even a relapse—finds her or himself among understanding friends, not accusing inquisitors.

Detoxification

In *Addictive Drinking*, Clark Vaughan states that the purpose of a detoxification center, "whether it is located in a hospital, a recovery home, or an independent facility—is to sober up and to help an addict safely through withdrawal (detoxification) under controlled conditions." He is quick to add, though, that "the majority of people go through withdrawal (usually a three to four-day process) without going to any facility at all." [21]

Most people assume that detoxification is a complicated process that requires medical attention, and on rare occasions it is. Overlooked, however, is the fact that the major component of garden variety detoxification and withdrawal is *psychological* rather than physical.[22] Certainly, in perhaps a maximum of 15% of cases, a major physical threat is present in the form of delirium tremens (DTs), a withdrawal experience that can be life-threatening in about 25% of that 15% of cases, that is, in about four of every 100 persons with a history of heavy and prolonged drinking.

For the most part, ordinary detoxification is nothing more than *depriving* the body of toxins, thus allowing the body-mind to heal itself. Rest, good food, and plenty of liquids accelerate the natural healing process. Given an opportunity, the body tends to balance itself—to compensate for chemical imbalances caused by lack of food and rest, and the ingestion of chemicals foreign to it. Health is its natural state and your body is its own best healer.

During detoxification, the brain also heals and begins to function normally.[23] The use of tranquilizers during the course of ordinary mild detoxification is not always desirable because it prevent the addict from experiencing much of the pain and discomfort of withdrawal—a valuable experience well worth remembering.[24] A few days in jail is also a wonderful detoxifier, as is a parachute jump onto a deserted island. But as Fingarette notes in *Heavy Drinking:*

> . . . even for long-term heavy drinkers . . . this short-term medical aid only relieves the immediate distress of acute withdrawal; it is not in any way a treatment for alcoholism. Furthermore, professional medical attention is usually not necessary during detoxification. Even for diagnosed alcoholics, most often non-medical aid—a restful setting and emotional support—is sufficient . . . And hospitalization is necessary only if the detoxifying drinker exhibits [or may exhibit] gross physical and mental disorders (seizures, psychotic episodes, delirium tremens).[25 26]

As Jim Parker points out in a pamphlet on detoxification and recovery:

> The main battlefield the revolution is going to be played out on is in your mind. Your goal here is to understand and begin to reverse the mental processes that have contributed to your dependency.[27]

Detox, physical and mental, is the price you pay for the rewards you are to reap. For most people, it's about as uncomfortable as a case of the flu.[28] It's not a big deal, medical propaganda and TV dramatizations not withstanding.

Employee Assistance Programs

The development of Employee Assistance Programs (EAPs) since the 1970s has been phenomenal, and we can anticipate their accelerated expansion in the latter half of the 1990s. EAPs have a proud history and, given the impetus of the forces of change discussed in Chapter 7, they will continue to prosper.

The 1988 mission statement of the Employee Assistance Professional Association (EAPA) executive committee (formerly ALMCA, the Association of Labor-Management Consultants on Alcoholism) is candid and refreshing:

> An EAP shall be a worksite-based program designed to assist in the identification and resolution of productivity problems associated with employees impaired by personal concerns, including but not limited to: health, marriage, family and financial matters, alcohol abuse, the use of illicit drugs, legal issues, emotional upsets, stress, or other personal problems which may affect employee job performance.

It is clear that the primary purpose of EAPs is to help American businesses effectively compete in the world market. Practicality and compassion are not, however, mutually exclusive. The EAP professionals I know are not crass manipulators, but compassionate people who have become enablers (in the sense of empowerment) and expediters—with a talent for getting a two-for-one return on every dollar invested.

EAPs were born not of crisis, but of need. M. Holosko and M. Feit outline three generations of growth and development (in 23 years) in "Onward and Upward," an article which appeared on page 281 of the Vol. 3, 1988 *Employee Assistance Quarterly*. First came a front-runner movement which concentrated on "individuals with decidedly visible drinking problems which impaired their work performance."[29] Then came the "broad brush" generation, which addressed the full range of addictions, plus problems related to marriage, family, and a host of mental health issues. After that, the "new wave" EAPs, which encompassed all previous responsibilities but became more proactive, concerned with employee lifestyles and oriented toward prevention of problems through education. The fourth generation (since about 1990) is dedicated to "case management," the essence of which is the individualization of all services rendered.

All of the indicators are positive for EAPs. EAP representatives see themselves as team players who serve the interests of *both* employers and employees. They have produced a win/win arrangement, and—if they play their cards right—they will continue to win.

That's a rather big "if," however. A major concern of all EAPs is substance abuse, to which they devote about 40% of their efforts, but in the ten-inch stack of material which Boyd Sturdevant gave me to review, I found that 99% of all references to addictions (and advertising pertaining to them) reflect the traditional positions espoused by the AMA, A.A., N.A., and the NCADD.[30] EAPs are wedded to the old ways, and for the most part seem unaware of the research findings and the flood of new ideas produced in the last 15 years.[31] But a few EAPs are concerned with futuristic thinking and new ideas in the field of addictions.

For example, an article with a futuristic outlook and a realistic view of addictive behaviors, written by Dan Lanier, Jr., DSW, CEAP, was published in *EAP Digest* in 1991.[32] In it, Lanier demonstrates a full grasp of the big picture (including a probable future) and focuses on factors pertaining to increasing automation, changing family structures, ethnic compositions in the workplace, geopolitical factors, the graying of America, computerization, immigration policies, etc. Lanier's article is *must* reading for all EAP professionals. And if EAPs are to prosper in the coming years, they *must* adopt forward-looking positions on substance abuse problems.

Addendum: The greatest single step forward that any EAP professional can make is this: phone the Institute for Rational Emotive Therapy at 1-212-535-0822 and talk with Dominic DiMattea in Corporate Services. He will tell you about a 1-to-3-day workshop designed for EAP professionals. And, with appropriate modesty, I suggest that everyone in the EAP field would benefit by reading this book, especially Chapters 2 through 12.[33]

[Thanks to Boyd W. Sturdevant, Jr., M. Min., CEAP (Certified Employee Assistance Professional) and Director of Employee Counseling of Indiana,[34] who gave me a crash course on EAPs, a subject about which I knew little.]

---

1. Trimpey, J. (1990). *Journal of Rational Recovery.* (P. 23). Vol. 3, Issue 2, November/December.

2. See Katz and Liu, pp. 68-71 (*Codependency Conspiracy*) for a penetrating insight into yet another myth in the field of addictions. Note: in researching this field, it

becomes almost depressingly obvious that there is a gargantuan gap between what is *known* and what is *done*. Thus, the ACOA notion is pure myth, but it is still accepted, even by mental health practitioners, as fact.

3. Goodwin, *Is Alcoholism Hereditary?* (1976). New York: Ballantine Books.

4. Prentice, A. C., M.D. "The Problem of the Narcotic Drug Addict" in the *Journal of the American Medical Association,* 76:1551-1556 (June 4, 1921), p. 1553.

5. Szasz, T. (1985). *Ceremonial Chemistry,* p, 99-100. Holmes Beach Florida: Learning Publications, Inc. (On the AMA, see pages 77, 79, 125-129, 149, 164, 197, 199, and 200.)

6. There is no need to get paranoid about it. Mouthwash, some with as high as 22% alcohol content, is OK when rinsed, not swallowed. The alcohol in wine sauce evaporates in the preparation (heated) of that sauce. Common sense applies.

7. A bit of anecdotal evidence: I came across an acquaintance of mine recently, a member of A.A. I asked if he had heard of RR and he answered, "Yeah, I've heard they're a bunch of atheists that favor controlled drinking." I then asked if he thought his opinion was representative of that of his home group. He advised that although he couldn't speak for A.A. (no one does) he had attended several groups and they all thought the same thing. I advised him to the contrary, but he refused to believe me.

8. Schaef, A.W. *When Society Becomes an Addict.* (1987). New York: Harper and Row (p. 30).

9. Schaef, A.W. (1986). *Co-Dependence: Misunderstood–Mistreated* (P. 4). New York: Harper and Row.

10. Katz, S.J. and Liu, A.E. (1991). *The Codependency Conspiracy: How to Break the Recovery Habit and Take Charge of Your Life.* (P. 43). New York: Warner Books.

11. Beattie seems to use the words "characteristic" and "symptom" interchangeably.

12. Trimpey, L. (1989). "Sodependent No More," in the *Journal of Rational Recovery,* Vol.2, Issue 2. (p.10).

13. Reported in full by Beth Ann Krier in the article "Excess Baggage," which appeared in the *Los Angeles Times,* September 14, 1989: VI.

14. Bufe, C. (1991). *Alcoholics Anonymous: Cult or Cure?* (p. 82). San Francisco: See Sharp Press. <u>Note</u>: This is a thoroughly scholarly work in which the author states (p. 101), "Is Alcoholic Anonymous a cult? No, though it does have some dangerous, cult-like tendencies." The usual easy answer to Bufe's question is a simple yes or no, but the qualified answer, as in Bufe's case, is closer to the truth. See Marc Galanter on cults as well.

15. Ragge, K. (1991). *More Revealed: A Critical Analysis of Alcoholics Anonymous and the Twelve Steps.*(Pp. 101-140). Henderson, Nevada; Alert Publishing Co. Chapters are titled "Meetings," and "On the Broad Highway."

16. Ibid., pp. 191-201. The author details the manner in which A.A. is "spoken for" by many organizations, many of them with commercial interests in promoting the 12-step program. A.A. never resists these promotions, and has no need to raise its own voice when so many others are willing to speak for it—"unofficially," of course.

17. Most jails and prisons have an A.A. squad that visits inmates and presents the A.A. program to them. They presumably graduate, upon release, into Communal

A.A. See Ragge (two previous end notes) for a host of details on this subject.

18. For example: "Your best thinking got you here," "Utilize, don't analyze," "You're never too dumb to make it in A.A., but you can be too smart," and "KISS—Keep It Simple, Stupid." There are several other slogans that say much the same thing. Even Ernest Kurtz, a close friend of A.A., has recognized (in *Not-God*, pp. 186, 188-192, 213) the pronounced anti-intellectual component of the A.A. program.

19. Bufe, pp. 15, 89-90, 101.

20. The denial myth is promoted vigorously by A.A., the NCADD, ASAM, the AMA, the AAATP, and, of course, by the tradition-oriented treatment industry. Apparently the "symptom" of denial—declared by a committee to be unique to alcoholism—does not apply to diseases such as cystic fibrosis and muscular dystrophy. Denial, as a symptom, is patently absurd as it relates to any real or imagined "disease." ASAM and the NCADD did themselves and addicts a great disservice by including the hackneyed "in denial" phrase in their joint definition of alcoholism. The term was not invented by ASAM/NCADD, but borrowed directly from A.A. jargon.

21. Vaughan, C. (1982). *Addictive Drinking: The Road to Recovery for Problem Drinkers and Those Who Love Them.* (pp. 98-99.) New York: Penguin Books.

22. See the foreword (by Eric Berne) to Claude Steiner's *Games Alcoholics Play*, pp. X-Xi, in which Steiner refers to *withdrawal panic* as distinct from *withdrawal sickness*.

23. Severe and irreparable damage to the brain (brain cells) can be caused by *extremely* heavy drinking over long periods, but this phenomenon is quite rare. The threat of brain damage has been used as a deterrent to heavy drinking, and thus has served some purpose. However, the typical heavy drinker will, in high probability, never experience a tragedy of this magnitude. Having quit drinking, many people tend to explain ordinary acts of forgetfulness as being related to brain cell damage. In perhaps one case in 5,000 this could be true. The rest of us have nothing to worry about.

24. In *Addictive Drinking* (p. 98) Vaughan makes a cogent observation about drug-free withdrawal as a deterrent to further drinking. He suggests that withdrawal is at its best when it is *not* completely painless and masked by sedatives or other drugs. It then becomes something to remember, and to avoid.

25. Vaughan, p. 75.

26. See Shuckit, M. (1984). *Drug and Alcohol Abuse.* (p. 46)Miller   and   Hester (1986), p. 795.

27. Parker, J. (1986). *Everyday Detox: A Guide to Recovery from Almost Anything.* Pamphlet No. DIN 161. Phoenix, AZ: D.I.N.Publications—Do It Now.

28. Lewis Andrews agrees, in his *To Thine Own Self Be True*, pp. 146-147. *Detoxification*, again a big scary word, plays a significant part in the addiction game. The human body is eager to detox itself. The process usually does *not* require medical help because it is quite simple, although it can be uncomfortable. It is, however, rarely lethal.

29. Holosko and Feit, p. 282.

30. William J. Sonnernstuhl provides a beautiful example of the kind of thinking that can benefit all EAPs. He says, in *Inside an Emotional Health Program: A Field Study of Workplace Assistance for Troubled Employees,* published by ILR Press, New York State

School of Industrial and Labor Relation of Cornell University, 1986):

"Underlying all other phenomena that have contributed to the increasing number of emotional health programs is the general tendency of society to make a medical problem of troublesome behavior. . . . Interest groups such as AA and the National Mental Health Association [plus the AMA and NCADD], and physician activists pressured local, state, and federal legislatures to pass laws making such behaviors medical problems and to provide funds for their treatment by medical personnel."

31. For example, not one article or book reviewed mentioned the existence of the eight other (than A.A.) self-help support programs now available to substance abusers (Chapter 8). This fact, I think, does not necessarily reflect a prejudiced view; rather, it indicates a lack of information about developments in this area.

32. Lanier, D. (1991, May/June). "New Century, New Challenges, New Opportunities," *EAP Digest*, pp. 10, 41-47.

33. To seasoned EAP veterans: I worked as a sales engineer for 20 years in the field of industrial power transmission (conveyors, chain, vee-belts, etc.) and another 20 years in a large stained and beveled glass shop. The address of the Institute for Rational-Emotive Therapy is 45 E. 65th Street, New York, N.Y. 10021-6593. And here's an unsolicited piece of advice: your future may hang on your getting up to date in the addictions field.

34. Located at 205 North College Avenue, Suite 610, Bloomington, IN 47401. Phone (24-hour) 812-336-7814, and 1-800-822-4847.

14

More Short Topics

This chapter is a continuation of Chapter 13. It covers the following important topics:

- Ethics, Treatment Centers and the Law
- Genetic Predisposition
- Lapse and Relapse
- Moderate, Controlled, and Social Drinking
- National Council on Alcoholism and Drug Dependence
- Organized Religion and Addictions
- Privacy, Confidentiality, Computers, and Victims
- RR and Other Addictions
- THIQ (TIQ)
- Transactional Analysis
- Twelve Steps Re-Ordered

Ethics, Treatment Centers, and the Law

First, thanks are due to the authors of an article titled "Addictions Program Management."[1] The article outlines a major problem facing treatment centers today and supplies a practical answer to it (touched on later in this section); the problem is that when clients enter a typical treatment center, they are offered only one program and may soon discover that it's unsuited to their needs and incompatible with their values and philosophy of life. The treatment center then faces serious therapeutic, ethical, and legal problems.

The addictions field is the concern of many professions, each with an established code of behavior. Because they have not yet agreed on a universal code of ethics, professionals must often make subjective judgments on a case-by-case basis. The zealous, almost evangelistic, enthusiasm with which A.A.-oriented staff promote the 12-step program makes it difficult for them to recognize the limitations of that program, and it virtually precludes their referral of clients to other programs. They know that there are alternative programs, but they refuse to discuss them or even acknowledge their existence. They actually believe that "one size fits all." This position is unrealistic *and unethical* because it involves the withholding of available information from the client, who is then prevented from seeking therapy more appropriate to his or her needs. There are names for this kind of thing: manipulation and malpractice.

Jack Trimpey of Rational Recovery and Edwin Comber, J.D. (RR's legal counsel) note:

> Many people reach out for help with personal problems, expecting customary counseling approaches that are associated with professional training. If they go to a community mental health center, however, they may be referred to a chemical dependency treatment program. The problem, of course, may very well be that they are not candidates for spiritual healing in the first place and would do far better with a university-trained therapist at the mental health center that made the referral. When documented efforts to obtain conventional mental health services result in repeated referrals back to a program that prompts one to seek a spiritual remedy (God), it may be said that human services are being withheld from an eligible person, and that he or she may rightfully sue the mental health center, the referring person, or the county of residence for redress. . . . Many people return to expensive inpatient programs several times, only to be told that they are not "working the program" correctly. In the field of medicine, it is agreed that when one therapy doesn't benefit the patient, it should be re-evaluated so that alternative forms of therapy may be instituted. Informed consent, including information on risk factors and alternative treatment approaches, is also a standard element in competent medical care. It is well known that many people, probably a large majority, recover from chemical dependence outside of AA-oriented programs. . . . Patients in hospitals quite often express their wish for a rational alternative by stating clearly, "I don't understand anything about this [12-step] program," or " I don't have a Higher Power and I don't want one."

When these requests by patients for something more relevant to their needs is ignored, and results only in further exposure to 12-step therapy, it may be said that appropriate care is being withheld, and the patient may rightfully sue for redress. The defendant in such cases may be the attending physician, the health care institution, or both . . . [In the cases of federal entitlement programs (Medicare, Medicaid, Social Security, et al.)], when a patient is eligible for treatment . . . that is funded by state or federal third party programs, the choice between the spiritual and rational modes is also necessary to ensure relevant care. When no alternative to 12-step spiritual healing is offered, then a patient may initiate legal proceedings against the social welfare agency.[2]

Consider the ethical and legal implications of being forced to attend A.A. meetings in an institutional program. It is a clear violation of the establishment clause of the First Amendment to the U.S. Constitution, given the clear religious component in A.A. That's a very serious matter, especially when deceptive, unethical, or coercive practices occur under the auspices of publicly supported health care centers. These things often occur, let us remember, in situations involving patients who are vulnerable and often under the influence of various toxins.

It's encouraging that some institutions, such as Hampstead Hospital in Hampstead, Massachusetts, and Forest Hospital in Des Plaines, Illinois (detailed in Chapter 11), have already changed over to a two-track system, A.A. *and* RR. I predict that within 12 to 18 months Hampstead and Forest hospitals will have a waiting list of patients, even as other hospitals and treatment centers are scrounging for them. When the marketing managers of chain operations discover what's happening, they will change over, for reasons of profit (and, one hopes, for reasons of ethics and compassion as well), and a new phase of the revolution in addiction treatment will have begun.

Genetic Predisposition

Scientists have done a good job in this area, but the popular press and TV have not. The media have dramatized early studies and presented them in such a way as to imply a causal connection between genetic inheritance and behavior, despite the fact that research scientists have qualified their findings with many disclaimers. At present, we simply don't know whether there is a gene that is associated with, much less *causally* related to, alcoholism.

The so-called alcoholism (D_2) gene has become the focus of bitter controversy according to John Horgan, who wrote an article for *Scientific American* in which he explored this controversy. In a side bar he lists authorities in the field who take opposing positions on the subject—and there are many on both sides of the issue.[3] As well, reports published in JAMA (*Journal of American Medical Association*) contradict one another within a matter of months. The field of genetics is young, and more is unknown than is known; studies must be replicated and validated before any firm conclusions can be drawn.

Premature interpretations of early genetic studies have done more harm than good. Peele and Brodsky note:

> David Lester, a leading biological researcher at the Rutgers Center of Alcohol Studies, after reviewing several surveys of genetic research on alcoholism, concluded "that genetic involvement in the etiology [causation] of alcoholism, however structured, is weak at best."[4] [5]

Authors such as Ronald L. Rogers and Chandler Scott McMillin simply ignore the question of genetics in their *Under Your Own Power*.[6] And Alan J. Mooney, Arlene Eisenberg, and Howard Eisenberg cover the debate on genetics in one-half of one page of their 597-page *The Recovery Book*.[7] They state, "Researchers are searching for a possible gene for alcoholism/addiction, and it could be tracked down soon." (You might want to read that sentence twice; it's also possible that—if still alive—Nixon *could* be elected president in the year 2000.)

(In a highly significant sign of the times Mooney and friends discuss RR, SOS, and WFS[8] in their book, while Rogers and McMillin cover RR and SOS,[9] but omit WFS. My compliments to the authors for their openness. [Both books are thoroughly traditional in orientation.] To their credit, James Milam endorsed the Rogers/McMillin book in spite of its mention of self-help support programs other than A.A., and Stanley Gitlow and James West endorsed the Mooney/Eisenberg book. Very encouraging.)

The key word in the genetics debate is *predisposition*. If, say, Mary Brown is one day found to have a gene associated with the abuse of alcohol, she will then know that she is more vulnerable to the *effects* of alcohol consumption than, say, her friend, Henry. Knowing that, she can then decide to drink, and risk the possible consequences, or not to drink. Most proponents of the genetic hypothesis do not support the "one drink, one drunk" notion, the allegation that there is a chemical or genetic trigger that is actuated *after* that first drink, at which time all personal control is lost. Some day it may be shown that after a drink or two some people find themselves strongly inclined to consume more alcohol, or that it takes a greater quantity of alcohol to produce the desired effect. We simply don't know, and grasping at straws doesn't help.

Even if we did know, *predisposition* is not synonymous with causation. You may be inclined for many reasons to do this or that, but for this or that to happen, you must first *decide* to make it happen. Again, we're back to the issue of control and responsibility. Is your behavior *internally* controlled (decision-directed), or *externally* controlled (like that of a robot)—by a gene, a disease, a metabolic imbalance, or neurological aberration? All or none of these things may one day prove to be an *influence,* among dozens of other influences, on your behavior, but *an influence is not a cause. You* are the cause of your drinking or your abstinence; you always have been, and always will be. Richard L. Plagenhoef and Carol Adler said the same thing, but more softly, in *Why Am I Still Addicted?: A Holistic Approach to Recovery:*

> Again, we are trapped in the language of illusion. Tendencies are not causal explanations. They do not give us reasons for certain behavior. Like all addictions, alcoholism is a combination of energy imbalance and learned habitual responses to our human circumstance.[10]

The evidence for the genetic hypothesis is weak and contradictory. Scientists may someday actually discover an "alcoholism gene"—but I wouldn't bet on it.[11]

Lapse and Relapse

The words *lapse* and *relapse* come from the Latin *lapus, labi,* meaning a slip or a fall. When a person slips on a banana peel, that's an accident, but when a bottle of vodka is purchased, transported, opened, poured, and raised to the lips, that's a five-stage *activity,* not an accident, and certainly not a slip on a banana peel. Jack Trimpey and Guy Lamunyon wrote an article in which they define the terms *lapse* and *relapse,* and distinguish between them:

> **Lapse**: A short period of drinking/drug use (usually 24 hours or less). Recovery is easily regained following a lapse, and often brings with it an increased understanding of addictive voice recognition, of how and why the lapse occurred, and of how to prevent it from happening again.

Relapse: A relapse is a return to addictive alcohol/drug use, often lasting a day, a week, or more. A series of repeated lapses may be considered a relapse.[12]

Thus, slipping on a banana peel and falling down is a lapse; staying down is a relapse. A lapse is a mini-decision, a lapse of judgment, quickly corrected. A relapse is a mega-decision, a major setback, not so easily corrected, but still correctable. As Jack Trimpey notes, "relapses don't just happen. There is always a conscious element . . ."

The good news is that lapses (usually) and relapses (sometimes) are expected parts of the recovery process. A lapse is like a firm push on the break pedal of a car; it won't stop the car, but it will slow it down. A relapse is like slamming on the brakes and bringing the car to a screeching halt. Achieving sobriety is like quitting cigarettes; studies show that those who succeed have kept trying in spite of previous unsuccessful attempts to quit.

Traditionalists take a grim view of lapses and relapses. They insist that one drink—one lapse—puts an individual with 10 years of sobriety back to square one. That's unrealistic and cruel. To add insult to injury, they further insist that one drink will *inevitably* lead to one drunk. Traditionalists adamantly ignore the research data that refutes their assertion, and they persist in preaching a prophecy which is as false as it is self-fulfilling.

If you are an addict, you are free to use the two paragraphs above as an excuse to drink or drug. If you decide to so do, however, recognize right now that *you* are responsible for that decision. Be conscious of making it (or not making it). I'm supplying information here, not excuses to deliberately "slip" back into your old ways. As we both know, there is no such thing as an accidental drunk. You drink when you decide to drink, and quit when you decide to quit.

(For more information on relapses see *Relapse Prevention* by Alan Marlatt and J.R. Gordon.[13] See also Chapter 17 of *Rational Steps to Quitting Alcohol*, by A. Ellis and E. Velten.)

Moderate, Controlled, and Social Drinking

This is a subject that is easy to dodge, and often is, because it's considered too hot to handle. It's the fiery red flag of the addictions field. So, let's handle it.

Herbert Fingarette notes, "Controlled drinking has become the umbrella term for the notion that abstinence need not be the only reasonable goal for the heavy drinker seeking help."[14] The idea of controlled drinking is a legitimate area of inquiry, one that is supported by an ever-growing body of literature.

Moderate, or controlled, drinking[15] is the objective of perhaps several million people who either once had a drinking problem or who have become aware of an incipient problem and want to deal with it. (It's important to note, however, that the goal of moderate drinking is generally considered inappropriate for individuals whose patterns of consumption are or were chronic, and self- or other-abusive.)

Clinical interest in controlled drinking was initiated in 1962 by D.L. Davies in an article, "Normal Drinking in Recovered Alcohol Addicts," and later given impetus by way of the Sobells' research in the 1970s. Then Roger Vogler and Wayne Bartz wrote *The Better Way to Drink*,[16] and now we have the Sobells' new book, *Problem Drinkers' Guided Self-Change Treatment*,[17] a motivationally based, self-managed treatment for problem drinkers. And there have been many other responsible people in the addictions field who have supported the idea that problem drinkers can achieve moderate levels of alcohol consumption.[18]

A good case can be made for the concept of moderate drinking, but that is not the purpose of this segment. As one authority in the field put it, ". . . at this time global conclusions about the practicability of controlled drinking as a goal are premature."[19] And another authority states:

" . . . [The hottest issue is] whether problem drinkers can manage to reduce their drinking. The answer is clearly yes for some people; the question is under what circumstances this is the best goal to shoot for, and when abstinence is the preferable aim.[20]

We don't yet know enough about controlled drinking to determine whether it is or is not a viable alternative to total abstinence. The concept of moderate drinking is accepted and practiced abroad—in England, and Finland, for example. It is highly probable that the appropriateness of the concept is culturally related, and should thus be applied differentially.

It's a fact that many people have successfully returned to moderate drinking after solving a drinking problem. This has been clearly shown by a number of controlled studies, but we do not yet know with certainty how to distinguish those persons for whom this alternative may be a viable option. (Rational Recovery Systems Network, in view of this lack of definitive information, is against the notion of moderate drinking [for "alcoholics"] now and into the foreseeable future.)

The idea, however, is slowly gaining recognition and approval; yet it may not be widely accepted in the United States for another ten years. Traditionalists often refuse to even discuss the subject. The feasibility of the "controlled drinking" approach awaits further validation through research, especially research determining who is most likely to succeed (or fail) in controlled drinking programs.[21] In the meantime, my best advice to those who are considering controlled drinking as an alternative to abstinence is this: if your best judgment indicates it's reasonable, try it, after say a 30-day period of total abstinence; but be aware that all the facts are not in, that there is no consensus among authorities about its feasibility, and that there are risks involved in attempting it. Also, please remember that these risks involve possible adverse consequences out of all proportion to possible benefits. (Perhaps people are often more interested in proving that they are *not* alcoholics than they are in a return to moderate drinking.) Moderate drinking may be an idea whose time has not yet come, but we cannot ignore the data, as well as the growing numbers of thinkers in this field who feel otherwise.[22]

Audrey Kishline, for example, thinks that moderate drinking is an idea whose time *has* come, and since early 1993 has been doing something about it. She is a former member of A.A. and an intelligent, energetic woman of strong convictions. She left A.A. and joined Rational Recovery, and, although enthusiastic about RR, eventually left it in order to initiate her own program—one with a different orientation: controlled drinking. For the past three years she has successfully practiced moderate drinking, and is now developing a self-help support program called Moderation Management (MM) designed for problem drinkers (not chronic, heavy drinkers) for whom moderate drinking may be a viable alternative to total abstinence. Significantly, Kishline has established close contact with and has received the support of about 10 or so highly visible persons in the addictions field, in both the United States and Canada. I know Kishline personally, but as a member of RR's board of directors, I should emphasize that Rational Recovery, as a total abstinence program, is in no way associated with her project. (See "Sources of Information" in Appendix for details.)

National Council on Alcoholism & Drug Dependence

It's the information age, and facts on addiction and recovery are now available from libraries, bookstores, and dozens of other sources. The NCADD is such a source—but only for traditionalists. The NCADD is, in effect, an extension of the public relations departments of Alcoholics Anonymous, the AMA, and the treatment industry. It has, however, begun to show some signs of awareness of recent developments in the field.

Organized Religion and Addictions

Catholics, Jews, and Protestants have done a miserable job of caring for addicted members of their denominations. The example given in Chapter 7 regarding Calix is typical. It is unconscionable that the Catholic Church in the U.S.A. reaches a mere 1,000 of its possibly 2,000,000 addicted members. The Jewish organization JACS is in the same boat, as is the Protestant Institute for Christian Living. So what's their problem?

Not caring? They care, but they also share the biased view of that large segment of the general population that still perceives heavy drinking as always and necessarily related to weak moral character,[23] and even–God forbid–as a sin. Prejudice, even toward their own, is part of the problem. The other half of the problem is unadulterated ignorance. A spokesperson for the above-mentioned Big Three could explain it this way: "We're not in the sobering-up business. Let A.A. take care of that. Think of us as extensions of A.A. Each of us wants to handle the spiritual and religious part of recovery in a special way. We're grateful for what A.A. does, but at the level of theology we're far more qualified than a bunch of well meaning amateurs. A.A. can get them sober and keep them sober, but the body has a soul, and that's our concern. So, send us sober bodies with impoverished souls."

That position, taken by Catholics, Jews, and Protestants, is short-sighted, irresponsible, and no less than an unconscious dereliction of duty. It's untenable for two reasons: first, it *assumes* that A.A. is highly successful, an assumption which, as we have seen, is not valid; and second, it breaks the recovery process into two presumably unrelated halves—the rough work and the finish work. But the "rough work" includes a thorough indoctrination in a psychological and theological system that may not be compatible (especially in the case of Jews) with the "finish work" which is to follow. The shepherds haven't thought it through, and it's time they did.

Rather than limit their concern to the spiritual and religious aspects of recovery (after the hard part has been done by A.A.), it might be well for these groups to pick up the heavy drinker at his or her point of maximum vulnerability and need—that is, dead drunk—and initiate a carefully tailored program that caters to the needs of body, mind, and soul.

Privacy, Confidentiality, Computers, & Victims

Let's say that ten years ago you checked into a hospital or treatment center for detoxification or treatment, and that you paid out of your own pocket. You've been sober ever since. You apply for additional health insurance and are rejected, or your well-earned and overdue promotion to vice president doesn't come through, or you are not given security clearance on a sensitive government project. Could any of these events have anything to do with your old medical records which show "alcohol dependency" or "alcoholism" as the reason for that long-ago admission?

What loopholes—if any—are built into clause 2 of the standard hospital admission form which (in part) reads, "I authorize this hospital or treatment center to disclose all or any part of the medical record of myself . . . to such insurance companies, organizations, or agencies that may be concerned with the payment of hospitalization charges."? That is followed by, *in capital letters*:

THIS AUTHORIZATION IS GIVEN WITH FULL KNOWLEDGE THAT SUCH DISCLOSURE MAY CONTAIN INFORMATION WHICH MAY RESULT IN A DENIAL OF INSURANCE BENEFITS *OR WHICH MAY BE OTHERWISE HARMFUL OR INIMICAL TO ME* . . . (Emphasis added)

Did you actually *read* those admission forms you signed ten years ago, or did you give away fundamental personal rights, such as your right to confidentiality of information? Did you then or now have any control over that personal, revealing, and often sensitive information entered on those forms which you didn't read, were not encouraged to read, did not receive a copy of, and therefore know nothing about?[24] And how about all that fine print? Was what you signed simply a pressured compliance with a "routine procedure" or was it something that could come back to haunt you and hurt you? When, after ten years of sobriety, you applied for health insurance and were rejected, did that rejection have anything to do with a computer entry, accessible to dozens of agencies and thousands of people?

I wonder, but I don't know. The lack of confidentiality of medical records is worth thinking about, knowing about, and perhaps researching.[25] If you are interested, I am willing to coordinate my efforts with you, co-author with you, or ghost-write for you. If you have an "inside track" in this area, so much the better.

RR and Other Addictions

The purpose of this segment is to demonstrate that the principles of Rational-Emotive Therapy apply to problems other than substance abuse. The RR program applies with equal effectiveness to over-working, playing, shopping, and dozens of other activities, all of which have one thing in common—the *over* aspect. Thus, an innocent game of Bingo is just fine, but it's inadvisable to devote a major amount of time to it because that can interfere with one's responsibilities and other activities. Socrates might have said, "An unbalanced (unexamined) life is not worth living." Consider, if you will, the excessive consumption of food and its obvious physical, and not-so-obvious psychological effects. Because of mismanaging their food intake, millions of people lead miserable lives. A 1983 Harris survey found that 58% of us were overweight. By 1993 that figure had gone up to 66%.[26]

If you're overweight, you don't have to buy an expensive exerciser and walk your way to nowhere, or join a weight reduction club. As you may know from experience, once you've taken off those 10 or 20 pounds, the cycle usually begins all over again.[27]

At the club, you courageously subjected yourself to discipline, that is, *external* control. You were looked at, weighed to the ounce, judged, put under pressure, gently admonished with an occasional tsk-tsk, and rewarded with applause for every pound lost. And if you picked up two or three pounds during the week, it was easy to find some good excuse not to show up at the Tuesday meeting.

The good news is that with a little effort you can change, and can guarantee and accelerate that change with the help of a psychological tool kit of practical techniques. The best set of techniques for losing weight can be found in one little book, a common sense kind of book, that I guarantee will enable you to solve your weight problem. The book is titled *Fatness: The Small Book*[28] by Lois Trimpey of Rational Recovery Systems. (She used to be fat, isn't now, hasn't been for years, and will never be fat again, unless she chooses to become so.)

In an article published in the *Journal of Rational Recovery*, Trimpey named the cause of her problem: the irrational voice within her, the voice that prompted her to eat inordinately, the voice that made all those flimsy excuses to overindulge.[29] She called it the *Feast Beast*. In naming "it" she identified it as the destructive voice of non-reason and determined to defeat it. The Feast Beast whined, appealed to ego, judged, used faulty logic, assumed, ignored the facts, begged, cajoled, and used every dirty trick in the book. Lois countered and defeated its proposed arguments with CS-RR—Common Sense-Rational Responses. Here are two examples from the silent conversation that ensued:

Feast Beast: Salads are nice I suppose, but tasteless and have little substance. I work hard, and need *real* food to keep up my energy and get the work out.

Common Sense Rational Response: Nonsense. Salads are great, tasty, and there are dozens of them to choose from. And they are *real* foods, fresh and healthful, and loaded with energy. I'll stick with the facts.

Feast Beast: Food gives us strength. You can't argue with that one.

Common Sense Rational Response: You're right, but we're not talking about that either. I'm concerned with both my physical needs and my mental health. From experience, I know that an excess of food is harmful to both. Let's stick with the subject.

Lois's immediate *goal* was to lose weight and she did, but her *objective* went far beyond that. She not only successfully applied the principles of Rational Recovery, but wrote *Fatness: The Small Book* so as to help others. (Be sure, by the way, to note her segment on "Our Nutty Culture," and especially her remarks on peer pressure, peer dependency, and "Co-what?")

THIQ (TIQ) (tetrahydroisoquinoline)

Tetrahydroisoquinoline is a narcotic-like substance produced in the brain *after* ingestion of alcohol. It's also a word employed as a verbal club by those who use big words to intimidate others. Its use seems to salve the egos of those who prefer to impress rather than express, and to impose a view rather than share an opinion.

The following more detailed explanation of THIQ is an abbreviated version of comments made by J. Weisberg and G. Hawes:

> Alcohol breaks down, in part, in the body to poisonous[30] acetaldehyde which converts to acetate in the liver, and is then excreted from the body. The breakdown reactions metabolize, that is, absorb and transform, acetaldehyde, and function as pain killers. But acetaldehyde also reacts with the neurotransmitters–message-carrying neurons–in the brain. The acetaldehyde and neurons react to produce TIQs.
> . . . these substances also play a role in certain diseases such as Parkinson's disease, and have been shown to influence mood and mental illness (p. 10). *Since TIQs are narcotic-like substances it is necessary to drink much more alcohol in order to feel its effects.*[31] (Emphasis added.)

The simple fact is that in order to have a problem with THIQ you have to drink first. After reviewing all the intimidating technical material, Weisberg and Hawes note that *perhaps* THIQ is one factor in the compulsive drive to drink or take drugs, but that the available information does not necessarily indicate an underlying physiologic mechanism of alcoholism or drug addiction. Most of the books in the addictions field don't even index the term. An exception is *Recovering: How to Get and Stay Sober*, by L. Ann Mueller and Katherine Ketcham. The authors state:

> To summarize in one sentence [THIQ] is an early physiological susceptibility. Alcoholics have a built-in, inherited, uncontrollable reaction to alcohol that causes them to become addicted when they drink (p. 16).

The key word in that quotation is *susceptibility*, that is, vulnerability. The decision to take that first drink has nothing to do with THIQ, as the authors implicitly recognize. After the first drink, however, they claim that a chemical trigger is pulled and that the person has no further control over continued consumption. That allegation is unsupported by evidence. In the addictions field, THIQ has become a buzz word that is used persuasively, and often forcefully, to support the theory that the causes of heavy drinking are physiological or genetic rather than behavioral.

The THIQ hypothesis may, if and when it becomes established, have some merit. It could help to explain the pronounced tendency on the part of some people to continue drinking, once started, and thus serve as a warning to such people *not* to start.

Transactional Analysis

It would be nice if some people lived forever—Eric Berne, for example. But he died, and soon Transactional Analysis began to go into eclipse. I have included "TA," as the theory is known, in this chapter in the hope that it will become a more significant part of the addiction recovery process.

A brief explanation is in order. As Claude Steiner explained in *Games Alcoholics Play:* "The building blocks of the theory of transactional analysis (TA) are three observable forms of ego function: the Parent, the Adult, and the Child."[32] Steiner explains:

A. The *Child* ego state is essentially preserved in its entirety from childhood.
B. The *Adult* ego state is essentially a computer, an impassionate organ of the personality, which gathers and processes data for the purpose of making predictions.
C. The *Parent* is made up of behavior copied from parents or authority figures.

Steiner's little book provides an abundance of insights. For example, "withdrawal" is usually far more psychological than physical; he calls it *withdrawal panic.* And Steiner explains heavy drinking as a decision, not a disease. TA is an invaluable tool in the mental health field in general, and in the addictions field in particular.

The 12 Steps, Re-Ordered

Most people assume that there is a logical and sequential progression of the 12 steps, starting with number 1 and, building-block fashion, ending with number 12. The issue of order is not academic, because a differently ordered progression of steps could prove less confusing and more effective than the present order. So, in an attempt to be constructive, I have re-ordered the 12 steps, and have added a rational component to each.

The idea was inspired by an article by Jeffrey M. Brandsma (Associate Professor of Psychiatry at the University of Kentucky Medical Center in Lexington Kentucky).[33] I have borrowed from his article (and at times deviated from it) in the following presentation. In the spirit of serious fun, here is a re-ordered and consolidated (from a 12-step to a 9-step) program from a former member of A.A. for the benefit of those still within A.A.:

1) Step One, as is: "We admitted we were powerless over alcohol— that our lives had become unmanageable."

A good common sense start. To solve a problem we must recognize that we have one. No one is powerless, but anyone can *feel* powerless, that is, overwhelmed by circumstances, and without sufficient coping skills to manage them. "I'm powerless" is gut-talk, down-talk, real at the moment, but not realistic.

2) Step Two, as is: "Came to believe that a Power greater than ourselves could restore us to sanity."

This step assumes the existence of God (capital "P" in Power), as discussed above. Assumptions can be, but are not necessarily accurate. Without that capital "P," "power" would do nicely, since it would pertain to any source of help inside or outside of the person. As Brandsma points out on page 36, ". . . the thrust of this step and several others is to have people recognize and admit their psychological [inter]dependency . . ." And "restore us to sanity" can be interpreted only one way: you are now insane, a statement that is not at all nice, and just a wee bit judgmental. Some of the drunkest people I know are not insane. Things were more simple in Bill Wilson's pre-World War II day; it was assumed that everyone knew the meaning of the word *insanity.*

3) Step Eleven, repositioned: "Sought through prayer and meditation to improve our conscious contact with God as we understood Him, praying only for knowledge of His will for us and the power to carry that out."

It would seem that once a person has come to believe in Step Two's *Power*, that it would then be appropriate to follow the recommendations made in Step Eleven—pray, meditate, and seek conscious contact and direction from that Power. But the actual existence of this God, this Power, may be of no actual consequence in many cases. If a person truly believes that there is a God, then that God, for that person, is a *functional* reality, one that can be petitioned for assistance in any form, including a miracle. And who can doubt the benefits of meditation, if only for purposes of stress reduction.

4) Step Three, repositioned: "Made a decision to turn our will and lives over to the care of God as we understood Him."

This follows from Step Three above. Pray, meditate, establish contact, seek direction—then make the decision. It may be assumed that those willing to turn their power of will, their decision-making capability, over to God, do so conditionally—that is, with the understanding that God concerns himself only with those areas of behavior related to the consumption of alcohol.

5) Steps Four and Five, repositioned and combined: (4) "Made a searching and fearless moral inventory of ourselves"; and (5) "Admitted to God, to ourselves and to another human being the exact nature of our wrongs."

Good idea. Take a look at yourself and see what you see. No need to dwell on it because that can easily lead to guilt and garbage that you don't need. Just face it, but keep things in balance, and try to see something positive about yourself too. You're not *all* bad after all; maybe there's *some* good in you—maybe a lot of it. Keep it healthy. Hair shirts and public confessions went out with the Middle Ages. Step Five is a confessional step. I used to do it once a week in a confessional box[34] and it worked pretty well. I said my three Our Fathers and three Hail Marys and that was that—until the next time. (Had the Xerox copier been invented, I could have mailed in a list of the usual transgressions and saved both myself and the priest a lot of time.) As Brandsma points out, this step serves to reveal to ourselves the extent of our self-deceptions. Try substituting "self-defeating behaviors" for "wrongs" in the above step. See what you think. And admit to God? Again, the assumption. The non-believers must work out something for themselves here. Maybe honest self-assessment covers it, but "admit" suggests guilt, and guilt is unhealthy. To recognize your shortcomings is to declare that you are alive and human. All the perfect people have been either canonized or buried.

6) Steps Six and Seven, repositioned and combined: (6) "Were entirely ready to have God remove all these defects of character"; and (7) "Humbly asked Him to remove our shortcomings."

As they say, God helps them who help themselves. Step Six is, in its essence, a request for a miracle—that is, direct divine intervention in *your* case. Is your case *that* bad, or could you work at it a little harder, perhaps with a little help from God, your spouse, your therapist, and your friends? I have no wish to offend you, but I think that Step Six includes a touch of arrogance based on an exaggerated idea of self and the severity of one's problems. Among the several *billion* people who inhabit this earth, you may be the most important, and burdened with the world's worst problems, but I doubt it.

7) Steps Eight and Nine, repositioned and combined: (8) "Made a list of all persons we had harmed, and became willing to make amends to them all"; and (9) "Made direct amends to such people wherever possible, except when to do so would injure them or others." Combined: Made a list of all persons we had harmed and decided to make amends to as many of them as possible when prudent to do so according to one's best judgment.

Remember, some of those people never want to see you again and others have moved to Timbuktu or some foreign country like Texas. If your conscience bothers you and you still cling to guilt but want to get rid of it, write a check to the United Way and forget it. If that doesn't do it, write another check. You'll soon run out of guilt. But try to work from a motive of justice rather than guilt. Then forgive yourself. If you have any trouble doing that, write to me, and I will respond with a formal letter of forgiveness. It will start with the Latin *Absolvo te in nomine Patris et Filius et Spiritu sanctus,* and it will be embossed with the papal seal of the Vatican and the official seal of the American Humanist Association. I promise you Pope John Paul's personal signature, but if he is not available at the time, I will forge it.

8) Step Ten, as is: "Continued to take personal inventory and when we were wrong promptly admitted it." Brandsma says:

> This step cannot be criticized. A desirable outcome for all forms of therapy is for the client to develop, maintain, and practice self-monitoring capacities. To admit mistakes without self-downing is evidence that one is beginning to accept oneself as a fallible human being—a crucial change for a person with alcohol dependency.

9) Step Twelve, as is: "Having had a spiritual awakening as a result of these steps, we tried to carry this message to alcoholics, and to practice these principles in all our affairs."

"To carry the message" is a great idea. One of the sure signs of mental health is that point of personal development when a person recognizes the self as a part of the whole, rather than the center of a self-made universe. Activism is better than isolationism, and lots of people need help. So carry the message, volunteer to do something. Become a blood donor. Work with the disabled or the aged. Write a book or become an RR coordinator. Be a player, not a spectator. The world needs you.

Having dispensed with Wilson's redundancy and verbosity—his tendency to say things in three languages, all of them English—the twelve steps are thus distilled to nine. Here's a concluding statement from Brandsma:

> If one looks at these 12 steps carefully, one can infer the type of person that they are directed at. Thus "alcoholics" are people who are psychologically very dependent, down on themselves (depressed), use denial and distortion (self-deception), and are resistant to influence and change. Their drinking is in service of one of the aspects of this personality style [not "type"], not a disease. They are human like the rest of us, only more so in some respects.
>
> AA does provide a substitute dependency which is better than that of alcohol, but a more elegant outcome is desirable; that is, growth

toward more autonomy and responsibility with regard to one's dependencies. To the extent that AA is effective, it is because it has a program, offers fellowship, and meets dependency needs.[35]

---

1. The article appeared in Volume 5, Number 1, of a journal published in January, 1991 (pp. 1-12). A computer glitch deleted the names of the authors and the name of the publication, and I have not been able to retrieve or locate that information. (The initials AAAS might apply.)

2. Trimpey, J., and Comber, E. (1990). "A Reverse Bill of Rights", in *The Journal of Rational Recovery*. Vol.2, Issue 6: July/August; (pp. 17-20).

3. Horgan, J. (April, 1992). "D_2 or Not D_2: A Barroom Brawl over an 'Alcoholism Gene'," *Scientific American*, pp. 29, 32.

4. *The Truth About Addiction and Recovery* (p. 62).

5. Lester, D. (1988). "Genetic Theory: An Assessment of the Heritability of Alcoholism," in C.D. Chaudron and D.A.Wilkinson, eds., *Theories on Alcoholism*. Toronto: Addiction Research Foundation, (p. 17).

6. McMillin, C.S., and Rogers, R.L. (1992). *Under Your Own Power: A Guide to Recovery for Nonbelievers and the Ones Who Love Them*. New York: Putnam's Sons.

7. Eisenberg, A., Eisenberg, H., and Mooney A.J. *The Recovery Book*. (P. 389). New York: Workman Publishing.

8. RR–pp.42, 125, 569; SOS–pp. 44, 569; WFS–pp. 138, 570.

9. RR–pp. 13, 15, 53-54; SOS–11-12, 55-56.

10. Adler, C. and Plagenhoef, R.L. (1992). *Why Am I Still Addicted?: A Holistic Approach to Recovery*. Blue Ridge Summit, PA: Tab Books, div. of McGraw-Hill.

11. An article appeared in *Alcohol Alert*, No. 18, October 1992, and was reprinted in the *Oregon Alcohol and Drug Review*, February 1993. Title: "The Genetics of Alcoholism." Highly recommended.

12. Lamunyon, G., and Trimpey, J. (1991). In the *Journal of Rational Recovery*, Vol. 3, Issue No. 6; July/August.

13. Marlatt, G.A. and Gordon, J.R. (Eds.) (1985). *Relapse Prevention: Maintenance Strategies in the Treatment of Addictive Behaviors*. New York: Guilford.

14. For a recent review of the debates, see Rozien, "The Great Controlled-Drinking Controversy" in *Recent Developments in Alcoholism, Vol. 5* (1987).

15. The terms "controlled drinking," "moderate drinking," "moderated drinking," and "social drinking" are generally used interchangeably. They need precise definition, for reasons of effective communication. To my knowledge, no serious attempt has been made to do so. However, *controlled drinking* somehow suggests a previous pattern of "uncontrolled" or "uncontrollable" drinking; *moderate drinking* and *moderated drinking* both suggest a possible previous history of excessive consumption as well as a perceived risk associated with drinking; and *social drinking* suggests a light, harmless, and socially acceptable pattern of alcohol consumption, either with or without a previous history of alcohol abuse.

16. Vogler, R.E., and Bartz, W.R. (1985). *The Better Way to Drink: Moderation and Control of Problem Drinking.* Oakland, CA: New Harbinger Publications.

17. Sobell, L. and Sobell, M. (1993). *Problem Drinkers' Guided Self-Help Change Treatment.* New York: Guilford Publications.

18. Hunt and Azrin, 1973; Pomerleau; Pertschuk; Adkins, & Brady; Popham & Schmidt; Silverstein; Nathan; Taylor; Sobell and Sobell; Marlatt and Reid; Cahalan; Garlington; and Kissin. All of the above (and many not listed here) render a degree of support to the Vogler/Bartz thesis, some enthusiastically, others with reservations. Peele, Brodsky, and Arnold (see bibliography) provide a long list of researchers who support the Vogler/Bartz concept.

19. Fingarette, *Heavy Drinking*, p. 127.

20. Peele, S., Brodsky, A., Arnold, M. (1991). *The Truth About Addiction and Recovery.* (p. 233). New York: Simon and Schuster.

21. It is difficult to track the success/failure rate of those who have tried to moderate their drinking patterns because their efforts are made, for the most part, on an individual basis. The Kishline project may, if records are maintained and then evaluated by outside agents, add a significant dimension to what we know about the feasibility of the concept.

22. In 1983 Bill Talley (previously mentioned) inaugurated American Atheists Addiction Recovery Groups (AAARG), later changed to Methods of Moderation and Abstinence (MOMA). It failed, I think, not so much because his ideas lacked merit, but because his timing was off (i.e. too early), and because of administrative and financial problems within the organization. For an excellent pro/con discussion on this subject see *Controversies in the Field of Addictions*, edited by Ruth Engs, Chapters 23 and 24 (by John Wallace and Martha Sanchez-Craig, respectively; see bibliography.)

23. *Weak moral character* is a tough judgmental term with strong religious overtones. The fact is, however, that some people are indeed weak and undisciplined, which does affect their behavior.

24. On those rare occasions when I have checked into a hospital (not the passive "have been hospitalized") I have told the admission clerk "I want a copy of everything I sign here," and "I want to see your Patient's Bill of Rights." Do it pleasantly, but firmly. It makes a difference. Your health, money, and rights are at stake.

25. See: 1) *Your Medical Rights*, Library Call Number (LCN) 362.1; 2) *Take This Book to the Hospital with You* (1991 update), LCN 362.11; 3) *The Great White Lie* 362.11. All good books, but No. 2 by C.B. Inlander and E. Weiner of the Peoples Medical Society is an excellent starting point. Also, there are 105 entries under "Medical Records" in the Info-Track magazine information retrieval system of your public library. A surprising 16 of these concern the *lack of confidentiality* of medical records.

26. Knight-Rider Newspapers release of March 18, 1993.

27. Organizations such as Weight Watchers do, however, serve a good purpose. Self-discipline is not that easy, and sometimes help is needed. Becoming a member is a sign of a personal commitment toward a goal. In Weight Watchers and similar commercial establishments, positive attitudes, physical conditioning, and healthy

dietary issues are stressed. The atmosphere is friendly and the personnel are usually well trained.

28. The next edition, to be published in 1994 by Delacorte, will be titled *Taming the Feast Beast.*

29. Trimpey, Lois. (1992). *The Journal of Rational Recovery.* Vol. 4, Issue 5, May/June. (pp. 27-28).

30. The ingestion of disulfiram (Antabuse) blocks the body's natural breakdown of highly toxic acetaldehyde. Poisons build up and harmful results are produced —on rare occasions, death.

31. Weisberg, J. and Hawes, G. *A Health Guide for Addicts, Alcoholics, and Their Families.* New York: Franklin Watts.

32. Steiner, C. with foreword by Eric Berne. (1971). *Games Alcoholics Play.* (p. 3). New York: Ballantine Books.

33. In *Rational Living*, Spring, 1976, Vol II, No. 1 (pp. 35-37).

34. Now called a "reconciliation room," but it's still a box.

35. Brandsma, p. 37.

15

The Future

"Predictions are dangerous" they say, "especially the ones about the future." Well, yes. Not even the World Future Society can gaze into a crystal ball and predict what is to come. But certain trends involving social and political structures, institutions, lifestyle changes, geopolitics, etc. are discernible. Here I attempt to state, in terms of probability, what *may* happen within approximate time limits. It's a dirty job, but somebody has to do it.

The End of the "Drug War"

It will end soon because it hasn't worked and has been a severe economic drain. We have spent tens of billions of dollars in the last decade on police actions against those who import and use drugs such as heroin and cocaine, from which fewer than 10,000 people die each year. But over 500,000 Americans die each year from diseases related to the consumption of alcohol and tobacco.

Nadine Strossen, President of the American Civil Liberties Union (ACLU), notes an eerie similarity between the "drug war" posture of the Reagan/Bush administrations and that of Clinton and friends.[1] Clinton inherited that mess and must tolerate it, for now. But that will change. The director of the Office of National Drug Control Policy (ONDCP) will not repeat the $45 billion dollar mistake of Reagan/Bush and "drug czar" William Bennett, and in time, the ONDCP may simply be dismantled. Monies will be redistributed into effective recovery programs. Educators concerned with causation and prevention will replace police squads and armed confrontations. The new "drug czar," Lee Brown, will work with a 16% hike in monies tagged for prevention-based programs. Look for "benign neglect" of Reagan/Bush police-state strategies until after the 1996 presidential election; then expect rapid change. **Time: 1997**

The Contraction of Alcoholics Anonymous

There are five major reasons A.A. will "contract":

First: Communal A.A. functions, to at least some extent, as an *ex officio* outpatient program of Institutional A.A., and receives from it about 30% of its membership (A.A. statistic). As Institutional A.A. comes under increasing scrutiny (on performance) from the government and insurance companies, and as clients become aware of the many alternatives to A.A., referrals to A.A. will abate, slowly at first, then quickly. Other self-help support programs will receive referrals at A.A.'s expense.

Second: All other factors aside, the growth in membership of the independents will occur at the expense of A.A. At some point that drain will level off, and membership in A.A. will stabilize at perhaps 500,000 members. These changes will occur as a result of vigorous recruitment efforts by the independents, and because research findings demonstrating the ineffectiveness of A.A. will become better known. As social agencies and the courts become more aware of the independents, they will no longer automatically assign all alcohol-related cases to A.A. Such assignments now represent a possible 10% to 15% of current A.A. membership (with full cooperation from A.A.).[2] Also, as mentioned earlier, court assignments *exclusively* to A.A. will be declared unconstitutional on a state-by-state basis. (This trend, as we have seen, has been established. The issue will never reach, or need to reach, the Supreme Court.)

Third: As A.A. continues to expand into the world market, its lack of organization (and proud of it!) will vitiate its efforts even as its operational expenses increase. A.A. currently operates on a budget of over $10 million dollars a year, about 75% of which comes from the sale of books and other literature—with over half of those sales being to institutions, many of which are having severe financial difficulties. The market is already saturated with A.A. books and literature, and as the market (especially the institutional market) dries up, the sale of A.A. literature will decrease at an alarming rate.

A.A. insists that it is a mirror-reflection of the A.A. of the 1930s, and to a large extent it is. Its failure to accept new knowledge (e.g., the benefits of using disulfiram) and to adopt new techniques is certain to reduce its membership and influence. As Dr. John Norris, a non-alcoholic physician, friend of Bill Wilson, and for many years chair of A.A.'s General Service Board said: "If anything is going to destroy A.A., it will be what I call the 'tradition lawyers.' They find it easier to live with black and white than they do with gray. These bleeding deacons—these fundamentalists—are afraid of and fight any change."

When an organization fails to adapt to changing conditions, it assures itself of diminishment, even non-existence. A.A. is heading toward a vegetative state unless it changes its ways. I predict that it won't change a thing. I find that rather sad.

Fifth: As Ernest Kurtz and others observe, the religious nature of A.A. must be characterized as essentially liberal, as distinct from conservative or fundamentalist. During times of accelerated change, people seek out religions that provide structure—not ambiguity—in their lives. As John Naisbitt pointed out in *Megatrends,* "They need something to hang on to, not something to debate."[3] They want answers, not questions. Thus the strict and demanding Southern Baptists grow in numbers, as do the Mormons and the Seventh-Day Adventists, and they do so during a 30-year decline in membership of virtually all of the major old-line denominations such as Catholics, Lutherans, and Methodists. The passionate (and sometimes perverse) electronic hucksters draw members and cash from established denominations, as do the innumerable independent churches, as do the philosophies and religions of the Far East. Virtually all futurists agree on this issue. As a "liberal" religion, A.A. will suffer the fate of the more formal, established denominations.

Sixth: The final reason for the diminishment of Alcoholics Anonymous has been covered elsewhere in this book, but in a nutshell it is this: A.A. has not worked well, it simply has not done the job. Things that don't work don't last. (For an opposing viewpoint see *Alcoholics Anonymous: Cult or Cure?,* by Charles Bufe.[4])

Time: 1998-1999

The Expansion of Alcoholics Anonymous

I consider this a very distant possibility.[5] A.A. may take 10 years or so to act on its membership problem (the "Comments" document indicates a *deep* concern), but there may be a source of new life and growth available to it. The (admittedly faint) possibility is this: A.A. would offer itself as a coordinating agency to all independent self-help support organizations. It would function as an umbrella organization concerned with *all* recovery programs, and each of the former independents—now integrated into A.A.—would contribute to the support of A.A.

A.A. would appoint a department head for each program and publish a monthly magazine containing contributions from each of the self-help organizations. A.A. would handle publishing on a contractual basis, and would manage traveling representatives, regional gatherings, annual meetings, and a host of other functions. It would actively seek grant monies and, as a structured and funded organization, tackle the alcohol and drug problem in the United States. It is probable that A.A. could do that job better than any government agency or any other self-help support program now in existence.

A.A. could ask Washington for $50 million a year, a sum that represents a penny compared to the billions now spent on drug-related problems. The United Way did the job in its field, and A.A. could do it in the addictions field. The emergence of A.A. as an umbrella organization is a possibility *now* and into the *near* future, but as the independents grow in stature and influence, this opportunity will gradually vanish. Knowing A.A., I must admit that the probability of this happening is comparable to the probability of my winning the lottery. But it's a nice idea. **Time: Soon or never.**[6]

The Merger of Women for Sobriety, Men for Sobriety, and Rational Recovery

The only thing that separates them now is lack of contact. The WFS/MFS organizations contend that alcoholism is causally related to something genetic or physiological. RR has no problem with that. (If it's genetically caused or a disease, don't drink; if it's a behavior, don't drink.) Both organizations endorse the power of self-control over that first drink. The unifying element among WFS, MFS, and RR is an orientation toward mental health. **Time: 1996**

Addiction Activities by Mainline Religions

As mainline religions continue to diminish in numbers and influence, they will make a serious effort to bring back to their churches those addicted persons who have strayed from them. A church with 40 million members may well have one million addicted ex-members. When this fact is noted and its implications appreciated, we will see increased participation by mainline religions in the addictions field. The major religious bodies may soon come to view the home front as being almost as important as their foreign missions.

This book may alert mainline religions in the United States to their dereliction of duty, and reveal to them a major opportunity in the addictions field. Fundamentalist churches will not take advantage of this opportunity because they have no therapeutic program to offer. They simply condemn heavy drinking as sinful and encourage church participation as a remedy for it. That's like reducing quantum theory to checkbook mathematics. **Time: 1997**

Help for the Courts and Probation Officers

Judges and probation officers are highly skilled professionals who are overworked and who operate on low budgets. When they discover the independents, they will quickly avail themselves of these new, cost-free, and more effective sources of help—assuming that such professionals are able to break their emotional ties to A.A. and objectively evaluate its performance. **Time: 1995**

A New National Perspective on Addictions

In the United States we tend to think that our 12-step traditional system is the world standard. It isn't. If anything, we are out of step with thinking in most parts of the world. The disease notion, related to private medicine (for profit), is the key to that. But private medicine (at least as practiced today) is on its way out, and with it will go the nonsense about drinking as a disease. **Time: 1996**

The Emergence of the American Council on Alcoholism

This will coincide with the decline of the National Council on Alcoholism and Drug Dependence, but the rise of the ACA will not be related to the diminishment of the NCADD. The ACA will rise because it takes a less partisan approach to addiction problems, stays up to date with current research findings, and is better funded. The NCADD will diminish as it, the voice of traditionalism, is overwhelmed by changes taking place in the addictions field. Its position is that of a lobbying and public relations arm of A.A., and what happens to A.A., Communal and Institutional, will happen to NCADD. Even now its position is tenuous, and it operates on a shoestring budget. It will—assuming no change of direction—shrink into a shadow of its former self. **Time: 1997**

Increased Professional Educator Involvement

Within the past year, Rational Recovery developed a highly signifi-cant credential: it issued a CRREd. certification—Certified Rational Recovery Educator designation—to two experienced persons holding Masters degrees in education. As the disease notion fades, and as the medical industry is assigned limited responsibilities, non-medical professionals such as mental health workers, therapists, clinical psychologists, and social workers, will eventually assume control of the addictions care system. The role of the educator will be especially significant in the area of prevention.[7] This approach is already well advanced in several European countries.
Time: 2000

Chiropractic and Naturopathic Involvement

Chiropractic and naturopathic physicians will enter the field of addictions and will stress a *holistic* approach to recovery.
Time: 1998

A New, Nontraditional Magazine

Someone will soon start to publish a high quality magazine catering to nontraditional thinkers. It will be a counterpart to tra-ditionally oriented magazines such as *Professional Counselor*, and it will be a smashing success. **Time: 1995**

Conclusion: I formally predict that all, some, or none of these predictions will come true.

1. *Civil Liberties*, Winter Issue, 1992-1993, page 17.

2. The triennial A.A. surveys consistently avoid mention of any numbers or percentages relative to court referrals to A.A. The 10% mentioned is an estimate. No hard data is available at this time. Given the percentages of people *assigned* to A.A. by social agencies, the courts, and the treatment industry, it has been argued that A.A. is, in a real sense, force fed, and thus dependent to an astonishing extent upon outside agencies for its existence.

3. Naisbitt, p. 240.

4. The following paragraph is quoted (p. 120) from C. Bufe's *Alcoholics Anonymous: Cult or Cure?*: "Despite ideological fossilization, it seems a foregone conclusion that A.A. will continue to expand both in the United States and abroad, not because it's an effective treatment for alcoholism—it isn't—but because its criteria for membership (that is, the criteria for 'alcoholism') grow ever broader; because it's developed a symbiotic relationship with the alcoholism treatment industry; because its religiosity and implied political quietism fit snugly into the existing social order; because it addresses (however inadequately) oftentimes real problems for which, all too frequently, no free or inexpensive alternative treatment is readily available; because it's widely and uncritically promoted in the media; because it provides relief from isolation and loneliness; and because it provides a quick and easy escape from the 'torture' of critical thinking and individual decision-making—in other words, A.A. provides a substitute dependency, a quick and easy escape from the personal struggle necessary to achieve true independence from alcoholism."

5. I have presented both sides of the question, but am convinced that A.A. is headed for tough times.

6. The idea may not be so far fetched. When survival is at stake strange things sometimes happen. In this instance it would mean a virtual revolution in the A.A. program. The notion is, I freely admit, a flight of fancy, but is not entirely fanciful.

7. Alvin Toffler also extols the future role of the professional educator in the U.S. in facilitating the transition from an industrial-based economy to an information-based one. There will soon be a scarcity of qualified teachers, Masters level and above, who will then command authority in their field and have increased control of the conditions under which they work.

Appendix

- Sources of Information and Help
- The Educational Format of RR (Indiana Chapters)
- Clarinda Correctional ACLU Article Text
- Definitions of Alcoholism by the Author

Sources of Information and Help

Alcoholics Anonymous World Services
   475 Riverside Drive, New York, NY 10115
   Phone: 212-870-3400; Communications to:
   Grand Central Station, P.O. Box 459, New York, NY 10163
   Fax: 212-870-3003; TTY: 212-870-3199
American Council on Alcoholism
   5024 Campbell Blvd., Suite H, Baltimore, MD 21236
   Phone: 800-527-5344
American Ethical Union
   2 West 64th Street, New York, NY 10023
   Phone: 212-873-6500
American Humanist Association
   7 Harwood Drive, Box 146, Amherst, NY 14226
   Phone: 716-555-1212
Anxiety Disorders Association of America
   6000 Executive Blvd., Suite 200, Rockville, MD 20852
   Phone: 301-231-9350
Association for the Advancement of Behavior Therapy
   15 West 36th Street, New York, NY 10018
   Phone: 212-279-7970
Cult Awareness Network
   2421 West Pratt Blvd., Suite 1173, Chicago, IL 60645
   Phone: 312-267-7777
Diagnostic Counseling Services
   P.O. Box 6178, Kokomo, IN 46904-6178
   Phone: 317-459-5464.
   [*The Compass*—diagnostic tool for professionals]

Drug Policy Foundation (Publishes the *Drug Policy Letter*)
4455 Connecticut Ave., N.W., Suite B-5,
Washington, D.C. 20008-2302
Fax: 202-537-3007

Forest Hospital
Forest Health Systems, Inc.
555 Wilson Lane, Des Plaines, IL 60016-4794
Phones (24-hours): 708-635-4100 (Margo Reiner or other)
and 800-866-9699 (Ask for Addictions Dept.)

Hampstead Hospital
East Road
Hampstead, NH 03841
Phone: 603-329-5311

Institute for Rational-Emotive Therapy
45 East 65th Street, New York, NY 10021
Phone: 212-535-0822
Phone: (Materials orders): 800-323-4738
Fax: 212-249-3582

National Council on Alcoholism and Drug Dependence
12 West 21st Street, New York, NY 10010
Phone: 212-206-6770

Rational Recovery Systems Network
P.O. Box 800, Lotus, CA 95651-0800
Phones: 916-621-2667 and 916-621-4374
Fax: 916-621-2667 (call first)

Unitarian-Universalist Society for Substance Abuse Education[1]
223 West Springfield Street
Boston, MA 02118
Phone: 617-259-0758

Educational Format of Rational Recovery

The educational format of RR can vary from chapter to chapter. The one presented below is used by Indiana chapters of RR. It reflects Rational Recovery's essence as an educational program.

PART ONE: Meetings, An Introductory Statement: In RR we recommend attendance at a minimum of one meeting per week, with two preferable, and three maximum. We do not substitute dependency on meetings for dependency on alcohol or drugs. Individuals assess their own needs and make their own judgments.

PART TWO: Meetings, Types of

A. General: The principles of RET ("Round Robin" participation with subsequent crosstalk at every meeting)

B. AVRT and the BEAST

C. Open discussion on selected subjects

1) Willpower
2) Higher Power
3) Disulfiram (Antabuse)
4) Alcoholics Anonymous, positive/negative
5) Institutional experiences
6) Religion, God, spirituality, and recovery
7) Codependency
8) "Near-beers" (e.g. Sharps)
9) Moderate, controlled, social drinking
10) Other self-help groups
11) When to graduate, and how to prepare for it
12) "Alcoholism"—definition(s) of
13) Disease/decision
14) Anonymity
15) Drunkalogs
16) A.A.-bashing/RR-bashing
17) THIQ (TIQ)
18) Family/friend/spouse participation in recovery
19) Court mandates
20) RET's concept of variable worth
21) Sponsors: good/bad idea, and why
22) Ritual as a part of structure
23) Gender-oriented meetings (for men, for women)
24) Suicide: understanding/handling thoughts concerning
25) Lapse/relapse
26) ABC's of RET
27) A-B-C-D-E spreadsheets (RET)
28) Drinking (drugging) as an occupational hazard
29) RR's relationship to professionals
30) Battling the BEAST, techniques
31) Big plan vs. day at a time
32) Communication skills
33) Letting go of resentment (Judith Rae worksheet)
34) Decreasing anxiety, quickly and effectively
35) Dealing with trauma
36) Decreasing vulnerability to criticism
37) Grief resolution

38) Decision making
30) LFT: Low Frustration Tolerance
40) Procrastination
41) Addictive Voice Recognition Training
42) Volunteer work and post-recovery
43) _____

D. Tapes:
    1) Audio (with discussion)
    2) Video (with discussion)

E. Speaker meetings:
    1) Inside: journey and progress (not to be confused with drunkalogs), special presentations by graduates
    2) Outside: a professional speaking on her/his area as it relates to heavy drinking (e.g. nutrition, bio-feedback, Transactional Analysis.)
    3) Advisor presentations (evaluation of group progress, and educational).
    4) Graduate presentations (Silver Dollar Club).

F. Small Book meetings (by chapter, or portions thereof)

G. RR slogans (all six in one meeting)
    1) Bring the mind, the body will follow
    2) Just say "know!"
    3) Learn to think or drink and sink
    4) We're concerned with thriving, not just surviving
    5) We don't give up alcohol; we get rid of it
    6) You act the way you feel and you feel the way you think

H. Planning Sessions: one-half of a meeting, devoted to proposed changes, meeting structure, and other practical matters.

PART THREE: Educational Material: Includes the full range of RR publications, 20 magazine articles, *The Small Book* and the Big Book, selected works by Albert Ellis, and at least five additional books, to be completed before "graduation" from RR.

Clarinda Correctional ACLU Article Text

The ACLU affiliate is co-plaintiff in a lawsuit charging that the Clarinda [Iowa] Correctional Facility's mandatory drug abuse treatment program, known as "The Other Way" (TOW), is religiously biased and violates the First Amendment's Establishment Clause. The program, patterned after the 12 steps of Alcoholics Anonymous, requires inmates receiving treatment to profess belief in a "Higher Power" as a first step. Unlike the AA program, however, inmates cannot choose their deity but must accept God as the "supreme being." Inmates unwilling to comply are expelled from the program and denied parole or work release.

The lawsuit also charges that TOW discriminates on the basis of religion in violation of the First Amendment's guarantee of free exercise and the Equal Protection Clause of the Fourteenth Amendment, and that another requirement of the program—that inmates confess past sins to counselors—may violate the Fifth Amendment's prohibition against self-incrimination.

Program participants are compelled to attend religious lectures and pursue Bible studies in order to advance. Non-[believing] inmates report being ignored and ridiculed. Said affiliate legal director Randal Wilson: "This program violates our most basic freedom—the right of personal conscience."

The suit seeks, in addition to a finding that the TOW program is unconstitutional, that Clarinda [be required to] provide a substance abuse program free of religious indoctrination.

Definitions of Alcoholism and Alcoholic
by the author

Alcoholism pertains to the effects of heavy and prolonged drinking on the mind-body, effects so severe that a person subject to them has become unable to rectify his or her condition without professional assistance or institutional treatment. Thus *alcoholism* may be viewed as a stage beyond problem drinking.

Problem drinking is a name applied to a self-determined pattern of activity, based on a set of values, beliefs, and learned behaviors, adopted in order to deal with reality in general and problem resolution in particular. The term may be considered a description representing a point on a continuum of alcohol consumption at which that consumption is causally related to mental, physical, home, and/or job problems.

Alcoholic refers to a person judged by professionals to meet the diagnostic criteria (see above) for alcoholism—a person whose deteriorated mental and physical condition is such that self-help, independently or with the aid of a group, offers relatively little chance of recovery; an "alcoholic" is thus a person who, in high probability, will not recover without professional assistance. Like the problem drinker, the alcoholic will experience mental, physical, home, and/or job problems.

Problem drinkers are *not* to be equated with *alcoholics.* The former place relatively high on the scale of alcohol consumption, but they do not progress inevitably or even probably toward full-blown alcoholism. They not only shift their positions on the alcohol-consumption scale, but often undertake the process of self-recovery, either by achieving abstinence or by moderating their drinking patterns. Thus, most of those whom we call "alcoholics" are not alcoholics as such, but problem drinkers positioned somewhere along the scale of alcohol consumption (based on John Craig's diagnostic tool, *The Compass*).

Heavy drinkers are individuals who place relatively high on the scale of alcohol consumption, but whose drinking does not neces-sarily adversely affect their lives or the lives of others. Thus, *heavy drinkers* are not necessarily *problem drinkers.*

Addendum: *The causes of problem drinking and alcoholism are the same.* The causes are many and interactive, and can be categorized as psychological, social, cultural, and physical, all in proportions that vary with the individual. Neither problem drinking nor alcoholism can be understood as an isolated phenomenon; instead, both are manifestations of some other underlying problem(s).

---

1. Established in 1986 as the U.U. Society for Alcohol Education, by the Rev. Farley Wheelwright, D. Min., an AHA (American Humanist Association) certified Counselor. It was reconstituted and renamed (as indicated), in June 1993, with a new board of directors. Its new president is Mary Rogers (617-259-0758) (Massachusetts).

Bibliography

Andrews, L. (1987). *To thine own self be true: the rebirth of values in the new ethical therapy.* Garden City, NY: Anchor Press/Doubleday.

Bazell, R. (1990). "The drink link." *The new republic,* May 7, pp. 13-14.

Beck, A.T. (1976). *Cognitive therapy and the emotional disorders.* New York: International Universities Press.

Beck, A.T. (1991). "Cognitive therapy: a 30-year retrospective." *American psychologist,* Vol. 46, pp. 382-389.

Bernard, M. E. (1986). *Staying rational in an irrational world: Albert Ellis and rational-emotive therapy.* Carlton, Victoria, Australia. McCulloch Publishing (in association with The Macmillan Company of Australia). Secaucus, NJ: Carol Publishing Group.

Bufe, C. (1991). *Alcoholics anonymous: cult or cure?* With introduction by Albert Ellis. San Francisco: See Sharp Press.

Burns, D.D. (1980). *Feeling good: the new mood therapy.* New York: William Morrow.

Cahalan, D. (1988). "Implications of the disease concept of alcoholism," *Drugs and society,* Vol. 2, pp. 49-68.

Christopher, J. (1988). *How to stay sober: recovery without religion.* Buffalo, NY: Prometheus Books.

Christopher, J. (1989). *Unhooked: staying sober and drug-free.* Buffalo, NY: Prometheus Books.

Christopher, J. (1992). *SOS sobriety: the proven alternative to the 12-step programs.* Buffalo, NY: Prometheus Books.

Craig, J. *The compass.* Diagnostic Counseling Services, Inc., P.O. Box 6178, Kokomo, IN. (Diagnostic instrument for determining extent of substance abuse.)

Crawford, T. and Ellis, A. (1989). "A dictionary of rational-emotive feelings and behaviors." *Journal of rational-emotive and cognitive-behavior therapy.* Vol. 7(1), pp. 3-27.

Danysh, J. (1974). *Stop without quitting.* San Francisco: International Society for General Semantics.

Diagnostic and statistical manual of mental disorders, 3rd revision (1987) Washington, D.C.: American Psychiatric Association.

Dryden, W. (1990). *Rational-emotive counseling in action.* London: Sage.

Dryden, W. and Gordon, J. (1991). *Think your way to happiness.* London: Sheldon Press.

Eisenberg, A., Eisenberg, H., and Mooney, A. (1992). *The recovery book.* New York: Workman Publishing.

Ellis, A. (1957). *How to live with a neurotic: at home and at work.* New York: Crown. (Rev. ed., 1975, North Hollywood, CA: Wilshire Books.)

Ellis, A. (1962). *Reason and emotion in psychotherapy.* New York: Lyle Stuart. (Paperback edition, Secaucus, NJ: Citadel.)

Ellis, A. (1963). "Showing the patient that he is not a worthless individual." *Voices*, Vol. 1(2), pp. 74-77. (Revised and reprinted, 1985, *Showing clients they are not worthless individuals.* New York: Institute for Rational-Emotive Therapy.)

Ellis, A. (1971). *Growth through reason.* North Hollywood, CA: Wilshire Books.

Ellis, A. (1971). "Emotional disturbance and its treatment in a nutshell," *Canadian counselor*, 5, 168-171. (Revised and reprinted, 1974, New York: Institute for Rational-Emotive Therapy.)

Ellis, A. (1973). *Humanistic psychotherapy: the rational-emotive approach.* New York: McGraw-Hill.

Ellis, A. (1974). *Technique for disputing irrational beliefs (DIBS).* New York: Institute for Rational-Emotive Therapy.

Ellis, A. (1980). "Discomfort anxiety: A new cognitive-behavioral construct. Part 2." *Rational living*, Vol. 15(1), pp. 25-30.

Ellis, A. (1983). *The case against religiosity.* New York: Institute for Rational-Emotive Therapy.

Ellis, A. (1985). " Intellectual fascism." *Journal of rational-emotive therapy*, Vol. 3(1), pp. 3-11. (Reprinted, New York: Institute for Rational-Emotive Therapy.)

Ellis, A. (1988). *How to stubbornly refuse to make yourself miserable, about anything—yes, anything!* Secaucus, NJ: Lyle Stuart.

Ellis, A. (1991, August 16) "Rational recovery systems: alternatives to A.A. and other 12-step programs." Paper presented at the 99th Annual Convention of the American Psychological Association. (*Harvard Mental Health Newsletter*, 1992.)

Ellis, A. and Dryden, W. (1987). *The practice of rational-emotive therapy.* New York: Springer.

Ellis, A. and Dryden, W. (1990). *The essential Albert Ellis: seminal writings on psychotherapy.* New York: Springer.

Ellis, A. and Dryden, W. (1991). *A dialogue with Albert Ellis: against dogma.* Stony Stratford, Milton Keynes, England: Open University Press.

Ellis, A. and Grieger, R. (Eds.) (1977). *Handbook of rational-emotive therapy, Vol. 1.* New York: Springer.

Ellis, A. and Grieger, R. (Eds.) (1986). *Handbook of rational-emotive therapy, Vol. 2.* New York: Springer.

Ellis, A. and Harper, R.A. (1975). *A new guide to rational living.* North Hollywood, CA: Wilshire Books.

Ellis, A., McInerney, J., DiGuiseppe, R., and Yeager, R. (1988). *Rational-emotive therapy with alcoholics and substance abusers.* Elmsford, NY: Pergamon.

Ellis, A. and Schoenfeld, E. (1990). "Divine intervention and the treatment of chemical dependency." *Journal of substance abuse*, Vol. 2, pp. 459-468, 489-494.

Ellis, A. and Vega, G. (1990). *Self-management: strategies for personal success.* New York: Institute for Rational-Emotive Therapy.

Ellis, A. and Yeager, R. (1989). *Why some therapies don't work: the dangers of transpersonal psychology.* Buffalo, NY: Prometheus.

Engs, R. (1977). "Let's look before we leap: the cognitive and behavioral evaluation of a university alcohol education program." *Journal of alcohol and drug education*, Vol. 22(2), pp. 39-48.

Engs, R. (1979). *Responsible drug and alcohol use.* New York: MacMillan.

Engs, R. (1981). "Responsibility and alcohol." *Health education.* January/February.

Fillmore, K.M. and Sigvasrdsson, S. (1988). "A meeting of the minds—a challenge to biomedical and psychosocial scientists on the ethical implications and social consequences of scientific findings in the alcohol field." *British journal of addiction,* Vol. 83, pp. 609-611.

Goodwin, D.W. (1988). *Is alcoholism hereditary?* (2nd ed.). New York: Ballantine.

Hauck, P. A. (1973). *Overcoming depression.* Philadelphia: Westminster.

Hauck, P. A. (1974). *Overcoming frustration and anger.* Philadelphia: Westminster.

Hauck, P. A. (1991). *Hold your head up high.* London: Sheldon.

Inlander, C.B., and Pavalon, U.I. (1990). *Your medical rights: how to become an empowered consumer.* Boston: Little, Brown and Company.

Jellinek, E.M. (1960) *The disease concept of alcoholism.* New Haven, CT: College University Press.

Kaminer, W. (1992). *I'm dysfunctional, you're dysfunctional: the recovery movement and other self-help fashions.* Reading, MA: Addison-Wesley.

Katz, S. and Liu, A. (1991). *The codependency conspiracy: how to break the recovery habit and take charge of your life.* New York: Warner Books.

Kirkpatrick, J. (1978, 1st ed). *Turnabout.* New York: Doubleday. (1990 ed.: Bantam Books.)

Kirkpatrick, J. (1986). *Goodbye hangovers, hello life.* New York: Doubleday.

Kissin, B. (1983). "The disease concept of alcoholism," in R.G. Smart et al. (Eds.), *Research advances in alcohol and drug problems,* Vol. 7, pp. 93-126. New York: Plenum Press.

Knaus, W. (1974). *Rational-emotive education.* New York: Institute for Rational-Emotive Therapy.

Knaus, W. (1982). *How to get out of a rut.* Englewood Cliffs, NJ: Prentice-Hall.

Knaus, W. (1983). *How to conquer your frustrations.* Englewood Cliffs, NJ: Prentice-Hall.

Lattimer, D. "Going to church the 12-step way." *San Francisco chronicle,* December 17, 1990.

Lega, L., et al. (speakers). (1985). *Thinking and drinking: an RET approach to staying stopped* (video cassette). New York: Institute for Rational-Emotive Therapy.

Low, A. A. (1950). *Mental health through will-training.* Glencoe, IL: Willett Publishing Co.

Marlatt, G. A., Demming, B., and Reid, J. B. (1973). "Loss of control drinking in alcoholics: an experimental analogue." *Journal of abnormal psychology,* Vol. 81, pp. 223-241.

Marlatt, G. A. and Gordon, J. R. (Eds.) (1985). *Relapse prevention: maintenance strategies in the treatment of addictive behaviors.* New York: Guilford.

Marlatt, G. A. and Rohsenow, D. (1980). "Cognitive processes in alcohol use: expectancy and balanced placebo design." In N. K. Mello (Ed.), *Advances in substance abuse: behavioral and biological research.* Greenwich, CT: JAI.

Maslow, A.H. (1978). *Toward a psychology of being* (2nd ed). New York: Delacorte.

Maultsby, M. C., Jr. (1971). "Rational-emotive imagery." *Rational living.* Vol. 6(1), pp. 24-27.

Maultsby, M. C., Jr. (1984). *Rational behavior therapy.* Englewood Cliffs, NJ: Prentice-Hall.

Maultsby, M.C., Jr. (1978). *A million dollars for your hangover.* Lexington, KY: Rational Self-help Books.

Maultsby, M. C., Jr. and Ellis, A. (1974). *Technique for using rational-emotive imagery.* New York: Institute for Rational-Emotive Therapy.

McMillin, C. and Rogers, R. *Under your own power: a guide to recovery for nonbelievers and the ones who love them.* New York: Putnam's Sons.

Meichenbaum, D. (1977). *Cognitive-behavior modification.* New York: Plenum.

Meichenbaum, D.H. and Cameron, R. (1974). "The clinical potential of modifying what clients say to themselves," *Psychotherapy: theory, research and practice,* Vol. 11, pp. 103-117.

Merry, J. (1966). "The 'loss of control' myth," *Lancet,* Vol. 1, pp. 1257-1258.

Miller, P. M. (1976). *Behavioral treatment of alcoholism.* Elmsford, NY: Pergamon.

Miller, W. R. and Munoz, R. F. (1982). *How to control your drinking: a practical guide to responsible drinking* (Rev. ed.) Albuquerque, NM: University of New Mexico Press.

Miller, T. (1986). *The unfair advantage.* Manlius, NY: Horsesense, Inc.

Naisbitt, J. (1982). *Megatrends: ten new directions transforming our lives.* New York: Warner Books.

Oei, T.P.S., Lim, B., and Young, R.M. (1991). "Cognitive processes and cognitive behavior therapy in the treatment of problem drinking," *Journal of addictive diseases,* Vol 10(3), pp. 63-80.

Peele, S. (1989). *Diseasing of America.* Lexington, Massachusetts: Lexington Books.

Peele, S. (1990). "Second thoughts about a gene for alcoholism." *The Atlantic monthly,* August, pp. 52-58

Peele, S. and Brodsky, A., with Arnold, M. (1991). *The truth about addiction and recovery: the life process program for outgrowing destructive habits.* New York: Simon & Schuster.

Pittman, B. (1988). *A.A. the way it began.* Seattle, WA: Glen Abbey Books.

Rae, J. *Daily rational reflections.* (To be published in Winter 1993.)

Ragge, K. *More revealed: a critical analysis of alcoholics anonymous and the 12 steps.* Henderson, NV: Alert Publishing.

Robertson, N. (1988). *Getting better.* New York: William Morrow.

Seligman, M. E. P. (1991). *Learned optimism.* New York: Knopf.

Room, R. (1983). "Sociological aspects of the disease concept of alcoholism." In R.G. Smart, et al. (Eds.), *Research advances in alcohol and drug problems,* Vol. 7, pp. 47-91. New York: Plenum Press.

Schaler, J.A. (1991). "Drugs and free will," *Society,* Vol. 28(6), pp. 42-49.. September/October.

Sichel, J. and Ellis, A. (1984). *RET self-help form.* New York: Institute for Rational-Emotive Therapy.

Smith, S.L. (1991). *Coping through self-control.* New York: Rosen Publishing Group.

Sobell, L. C. and M. B. (1993). *Problem drinkers' guided self-change treatment.* New York: Guilford Publications.

Steiner C. (1971). *Games alcoholics play: an analysis of life scripts.* New York: Ballantine Books.

Szasz, T.S. (1972). "Bad habits are not diseases." *Lancet,* July 8, 1972, pp. 83-84.

Szasz, T.S. (Rev. ed., 1985). *Ceremonial chemistry: the ritual persecution of drugs, addicts, and pushers.* Holmes Beach, FL: Learning Publications, Inc.

Tate, P. (1993). *Alcohol: how to give it up and be glad you did, a sensible approach.* Altamonte Springs, Florida: Rational Self-Help Press. (Foreword by Albert Ellis.)

Tessina, T. (1991). *The real thirteenth step: Discovering confidence, self-reliance, and autonomy beyond the 12-step programs.* Los Angeles: Jeremy P. Tarcher.

Trimpey, J. (1992) "The structural model of RR vs. the disease model of A.A." *The journal of rational recovery*, Vol. 5(2), pp. 13-16.

Trimpey, J. (1992b, rev. ed.). *The small book: a revolutionary alternative for overcoming alcohol and drug dependence.* Revised ed. includes introduction by Albert Ellis. New York: Delacorte. (Orig. ed. 1989 by Lotus Press.)

Trimpey, J. (1993-94). New book in progress, with probable title of *The cure: AVRT*, by Delacorte.

Trimpey, J., Velten, E., and Dain, R. (1992). "Rational recovery from addictions." In W. Dryden and L. Hill (Eds.), *The fundamentals of rational-emotive therapy.* Stony Stratford, England: Open University Press.

Trimpey, L. (1990). *Rational recovery from fatness: the small book.* Lotus, CA: Lotus Press. (To be published by Delacorte in 1994 as *Taming the Feast Beast.*)

Vaillant, G.E. (1983). *The natural history of alcoholism: causes, patterns, and paths to recovery.* Cambridge, MA: Harvard University Press.

Vaughan, C. (1984). *Addictive drinking: the road to recovery for problem drinkers and those who love them.* Penguin.

Velten, E. (1986). "Withdrawal from heroin and methadone, with rational-emotive therapy." In. W. Dryden and P. Trower (Eds.), *Rational-emotive therapy; recent developments in theory and practice*, pp. 228-247. Briston, England: Institute for RET (UK).

Vogler, R.E. and Bartz, W.R. (1982). *The better way to drink: moderation and control of problem drinking.* New York: Simon and Schuster. (Paperback ed. 1885, by New Harbinger Publications, Oakland, CA.)

Wessler, R. A. and Wessler, R. L. (1980). *The principles and practice of rational-emotive therapy.* San Francisco: Jossey-Bass.

Wolfe, J. L. and Brand, E. (Eds.). (1977). *Twenty years of rational therapy.* New York: Institute for Rational-Emotive Therapy.

Woods, P. J. (1990). *Controlling your smoking.* Roanoke, VA: Scholar's Press.

Yankura, J. and Dryden, W. (1990). *Doing RET: Albert Ellis in action.* New York: Springer.

Young, H. S. (1974). *A rational counseling primer.* New York: Institute for Rational-Emotive Therapy.

Index

AAARG (see American Atheists
Addiction Recovery Groups)
AAATP (see American Association of
Addiction Treatment Providers)
A.A. (see Alcoholics Anonymous)
A.A. Membership Survey 64
A.A. The Way It Began 57f
A-B-C (RET), 129, 130, 161
Abstinence 46, 90, 95, 98, 106, 108,
117, 137, 138, 204
ACA (see American Council on
Alcoholism)
ACLU (see American Civil Liberties
Union)
ACOA (see Adult Children of
Alcoholics)
Acupuncture 140
Addiction
costs 3, 173
definitions 34, 35, 37, 99
Addiction Research Foundation 168
Addictions Roundtable 4
Addiction Voice Recognition Training
121–124
Addictive Drinking 190, 195f
Adler, Alfred 108
Adler, Carol 201, 215f
Adult Children of Alcoholics 175–177,
193f, 194f
Adult Children of Alcoholics 176
Agnostic(s) 53, 59f, 85, 159

AHA (see American Hospital
Association)
AIDS 75
Al-Anon 91, 106f, 183
Alateen 183
Alatot 183
Alcohol Alert 215f
Alcohol Health Research World 105f, 107f
Alcohol: How to Give It Up 134f
Alcoholic(s) 5, 18–22, 25f, 46, 52, 72f,
173, 229, 230
definition 18–21, 116, 118, 119,
229, 230
population estimates 62
Alcoholics Anonymous 1, 3, 7, 17, 21,
22, 27, 29, 31, 36, 38, 40–72, 74,
77–80, 83–87, 89–96, 99–107, 109,
119, 124, 125, 131, 135f, 137, 142,
143, 149–163, 166, 167, 169, 170,
180, 181, 183, 185–189, 193–196,
198, 204–206, 211, 219–225
as corporation 41, 56f
as charismatic healing group 43,
44
as/as not cult 40, 185–189
effectiveness 61–72, 135f, 140,
141, 147
"Final Report" 56f, 57f
finances 42, 57f, 219
General Service Board 56, 69, 70,
186, 219

General Service Conference 56f, 57f
General Service Office 43, 59f, 69
as identity transformation organization 43, 44
literature sales 42, 43, 143, 219
meetings 42, 45, 53
membership 56f, 62, 64–67, 143, 219, 224
membership surveys 64–67, 72f, 143
as modified temperance society 43, 45
mottoes and slogans 41, 44, 45, 68, 128, 149, 189, 195f
organizational aspects 42, 43
preamble 38
as quasi-religious society 43, 46 55, 56, 81
rituals 45
Alcoholics Anonymous (see Big Book)
Alcoholics Anonymous Comes of Age 47, 55, 57f, 58f
Alcoholics Anonymous: Cult or Cure? 24f, 41, 47, 56f, 64, 65, 185, 187, 189, 194f, 220, 224f
Alcoholics Anonymous Grapevine, Inc. 42
Alcoholics Anonymous World Services, Inc. 42, 71f
Alcoholics Victorious 28, 70, 83, 86–89, 100
Alcoholism 14, 16–25, 52, 90, 91, 99, 103, 116, 118, 134f, 136–140, 199–201, 229, 230
Alcoholism & Addiction 26, 28, 31f
Alice in Wonderland 16
AMA (see American Medical Association)
American Association of Addiction Treatment Providers 17, 24f, 62, 195f
American Association of Behavior Therapists 131
American Atheists Addiction Recovery Groups 86, 89, 216f
American Civil Liberties Union 79, 218, 228, 229
American Council on Alcoholism 29, 30, 222, 225
American Ethical Union 225
American Health 172, 174f
American Hospital Association 17, 62, 75, 149
American Humanist Association 214, 225, 230f
American Medical Association 17, 19, 22, 23f, 24f, 61, 74, 103, 115, 116, 133f, 138, 169, 177, 178, 193, 195f, 196f, 205
American Psychiatric Association 20, 177
American Revolution 71
American Society of Addiction Medicine 18, 148, 195f
American Stock Exchange 143
Anarchy 133f
Andrews, Lewis 195f
Angel Island 12
Anonymity 31f, 125
Antabuse (see Disulfiram)
Antipsychotic Drugs 141
Anxiety Disorders Association of America 225
Aquarian Conspiracy 105f
Arnold, Mary 72f, 118, 125, 216f
ASAM (see American Society of Addiction Medicine)
Aspirin 9
Autonomy 37
AV (see Alcoholics Victorious)
Aversion Therapy

electric shock 140
nausea 140
AVRT (see Addiction Voice
Recognition Training)
B., Jim 55
Barrett, Clarence 14
Bartz, Wayne 203, 216f
Bashing
A.A. 70, 71, 180, 181
RR 180, 181
Beast, The 122–124, 130, 179, 190
Beattie, Melody 184, 194f
Belladonna 57f
Bennett, William 77, 218
Berne, Eric 18, 23f, 74, 162, 167, 195f,
210
Better Way to Drink 203, 216f
Bible 71, 89, 229
Bible Belt 9
Big Book 24f, 25f, 28, 41, 42, 44, 50–
54, 59f, 68, 72f, 81f, 126, 142, 151,
159, 160, 167, 180, 181
Bittner, Vernon J. 87
Bibliography of Alcoholism 57f
Black, Claudia 20, 24f
Black's Law Dictionary 19
British Journal of Addictions 24f
Bottoms (high/low) 181, 182
Box 459 72f
Branching Out 165f
Bradshaw, John 184
Brandsma, J. 186, 211, 212, 214, 217f
Brief Advice/Feedback 139, 141
Brodsky, Archie 38f, 72f, 96, 118, 125,
172, 200, 216f
Brown, Lee 218
Buddha 37
Bufe, Charles 9, 14, 19, 22, 24f, 41, 47,
56f, 64, 65, 71f, 125, 185, 187, 189,
194f, 195f, 220, 224f
Burns, David 106f, 124, 125, 164

Bush, George 77, 218
Caffeine 9
Cahalan, Don 14, 44, 57f, 63
Cain, Arthur 85, 105f
Cain, J.W. 98
Calix 28, 70, 83, 84, 86, 89–91, 93, 100,
105f, 106f, 206
Carroll, Lewis 16
Catholic Bulletin 87
Catholic Church 55, 58f, 89–91, 105f,
133f, 205, 220
Central Beliefs of Alcoholism 115, 119
Ceremonial Chemistry 81f, 133f, 194f
Chalice 90
Chardin, Teilhard de 9
Chavetz, Morris 21, 24f
Chemical trigger 39f, 117, 133f, 200,
209
Chicago, Illinois 163
Children's books 182, 183
Chiropractic physicians 223
Christopher, Jim 19, 23f, 27, 31f, 96,
99, 106f
Circle K Corporation, 76
Civil Liberties 81f, 224f
Clarinda (Iowa) Correctional Facility
79, 228, 229
Clinton, Bill 77, 218
Cocaine 218
Cockrell, Kete 178
Codependency 183–185
Codependency Conspiracy 34, 38f, 168,
174f, 183, 184, 193f, 194f
CODESH (see Council for Democratic
and Secular Humanism)
Cognitive Therapy/Relapse
Presentation 140
Coleman, Wim 35, 39f
Comber, Edwin 198, 215f
Comments on A.A.'s Triennial Surveys
64–67, 71f, 135f, 147, 180

Committee on Governmental Affairs 139

Community Reinforcement Approach 139, 141

Compass, The 134f, 225, 230

CompCare 145f

Comte, August 107f

Confidentiality 125

Confrontational Counseling 140, 141

Confucius 7

Consulting Psychologists Press, Inc. 164f

Consumers' Research 145f

Controlled drinking (see Moderate drinking)

Controversies in the Addictions Field 29, 30, 216f

Cory, G. 144f

Costello, Mary 90

Council for Democratic and Secular Humanism 100

Course in Miracles 35

Court Mandated Offenders 77–80, 127, 188, 219, 224f

Covert Sensitization 139

Craig, John 118, 133f, 230

Craig, Phyllis 118, 133f

Crosstalk 42, 99, 111, 169

Cult Awareness Network 225

Cults 185–189

Cured Alcoholic 105f

Daily Rational Reflections 124

Delacorte Press 132

Delirium Tremens 171, 191

Denial 116, 147–149, 189, 190, 195f

Dependency 33, 34

Des Moines, Iowa 79

Detoxification 99, 142, 190, 191, 195f

Diagnostic and Statistical Manual of Mental Disorders, 3rd Revision (see *DSM-III-R*)

Diagnostic Counseling Services 225

Dickinson, R.D. 105f

DiGuiseppi, Raymond 151

DiMattea, Dominic 193

Disease concept of alcoholism 3, 17, 18–24, 99, 103, 107f, 115–118, 136, 137, 148

Diseasing of America 12, 63, 172

Disulfiram 99, 107f, 139, 140, 178–180, 217f

Doctrine of variable worth 114

Doroff, David 44, 57f

Dorsman, Jerry 14, 63, 125

Downs, Cathy 78, 81

Drinking patterns 11, 229, 230

Driver education programs 77, 78

Driving Under the Influence 190

Drug and Alcohol Abuse 195f

Drug Policy Foundation 226

Drug War 77, 218

Drunkalogs 125

Dry drunk 36, *178*

DSM-III-R 20, 24f, 134, 150, 151, 177

DTs (see Delirium Tremens)

DUI (see Driving Under the Influence)

Durkheim, Emile 45

Eagles Clubs 41

EAP Digest 193, 196f

EAPs (see Employee Assistance Programs)

Editorial and Management Offices of Vatican City 105f

Educational lectures/films 140

Edwards, M. 59f

Eisenberg, Eileen 200, 215f

Eisenberg, Howard 200, 215f

Elks Clubs 41

Ellis, Albert 23f, 35, 75, 85, 106f, 108, 110, 114, 125, 127, 129, 132, 133f, 155, 161–164, 202

Ellis Island 12
Ellison, Jerome 86
Employee Assistance Professional
    Association 192
Employee Assistance Programs 76, 77,
    192, 193, 195f, 196f
Employee Assistance Quarterly 192
Employee Counseling of Indiana 193
Encyclopedia Britannica 20
England 11
Engs, Ruth 27, 29, 30, 125, 216f
Epictetus 108
Episcopalian Church 58f
Escape from Freedom 58f
Estes, Ken 145f
Ethics 68, 69, 126, 178, 197–199
Evangelicalism 46, 48, 49
Everyday Detox 195f
Facts About Drinking 164f
Facts on Alcohol Related Birth Defects 23f
Family members 160
Fatness: The Small Book 112, 208, 217f
Federal Aviation Administration 109
Feeling Good 124, 164
Feit, M. 192, 195f
Ferguson, Marilyn 86, 105
Fingarette, Herbert 20, 24f, 26, 27, 35,
    39f, 62, 75, 125, 133f, 137, 144f,
    191, 203, 216f
Fish, George 65, 66, 71f
Forces of Change in Addictions Field
    academic 74, 75
    cultural 75
    economic 75–77
    legal 77–80
    professional 80
Ford, Henry 138
Forest Hospital 144f, 150, 163–165,
    199, 226
Four Noble Truths 37
Fox Bill 89

Fox, Lucia Brown 9
Fox, Vince 1, 3, 4, 109, 133f, 134f, 212
Frankl, Viktor 15f, 171, 174f
Free Inquiry 96, 99, 106f
Freethought Today 61
Freud, Sigmund 108, 122, 174f
Freudianism 85
Fromm, Erich 58
Future Shock 15f
Games Alcoholics Play 23f, 195f, 210,
    217f
Genetic predisposition 199, 221
Gerstein, Joseph 155, 164f
Gitlow, Stanley 200
Glasser, William 34, 144f, 162, 167
God 6, 17, 22, 25f, 33, 44, 45, 47–49,
    51, 53–55, 59f, 60f, 87, 88, 104,
    119, 135f, 152, 153, 159, 167, 174f,
    178, 198, 211–213
Gold, Mark 22
Good Morning America 109
Goodwill *41*
Goodwin, Donald 63, 177, 194f
Gordon, J.R. 202, 215f
Gore, Al 77
Granberg V. Ashland County 56, *79*
Grapevine 28, 39f, 58f
Great Depression 83
Great White Lie 216f
Greil, Arthur 43, 46, 57f
Group Psychotherapy 140
Gurion, J. 172, 174f
Hampstead Hospital 144f, 150, 162–
    165, 199, 226
Handbook of Nonsexist Writing 59f
Harper's 86
Harvard University 24f, 46, 81f, 131
Hawes, G. 209, 217f
Hawkins, David 35
Hazelden 144f
Heavy drinker (definition) 230

Heavy Drinking 24f, 26, 39f, 62, 133f, 137, 191, 216f
Helping Ourselves 104f
Hemingway, Ernest 75
Hester, Reid 27, 125, 195f
Higher Power 6, 17, 22, 25f, 41, 45, 48–50, 53, 54, 97, 104, 112, 119, 124, 154–156, 159, 163, 174f, 178, 198, 211, 212, 229
Holosko, M. 192, 195f
Horgan, John 199, 215f
Horvath, Tom 164f
Hoskins, Ray 36, 39f
How to Quit Drinking Without A.A. 63
How To Stay Sober 31, 99, 106f
Hypnosis 140
IBM 42
ICL (see Institute for Christian Living)
I'm Dysfunctional, You're Dysfunctional 44, 57f
Indiana 97
Indiana Medicine 178
Indiana State Medical Association 178
Indiana University 78, 134f
Indianapolis, Indiana 4, 32f, 59f, 144f
Inlander, C.B. 216f
Inside an Emotional Health Program 195f
Insight psychotherapy 140, 141
Institute for Christian Living 87, 88, 206
Institute for Rational-Emotive Therapy 132, 151, 193, 196f, 226
Institute for Spiritual Research 35
Insurance industry 75–77
Intellectualism 147–149
Interdependence 33
Iran 12
Ireland 11
Is Alcoholism Hereditary? 63, 194f
Israel 11
It Will Never Happen to Me 24f

JACS (see Jewish Alcoholics, etc.)
JAMA (*see Journal of the American Medical Association*)
Jampolsky, Lee 35
Jehovah's Witnesses 188
Jellinek, E.M. 39f
Jesus of Nazareth 60f, 87, 88, 90
Jewish Alcoholics, Chemically Dependent Persons and Significant Others Foundation (JACS) 28, 70, 84, 86, 91–93, 100, 105f, 206
Journal of the American Medical Association 131, 144f, 194f, 200
Journal of Rational Recovery 61, 83, 131, 134f, 146, 175, 193f, 194f, 215f, 217f
JRR (see *Journal of Rational Recovery*)
Jung, Carl 35, 108
Kaminer, Wendy 14, 44, 57f
Kansas, University of 177
Karney 162, 163
Katz, Ben 14
Katz, Stan 34, 168, 174f, 183, 193f, 194f
Keller, Mark 20, 24f
Keller, Ron 87
Kentucky, University of 211
Ketcham, Katherine 106f, 209
Keyes, Ken Jr. 82
Kipling, Rudyard 16
Kirkpatrick, Jean 27, 68, 75, 93, 100,, 102, 103, 105f, 106f, 125
Kishline, Audrey 96, 204, 216f
Knaus, William 1, 121, 123, 134f
Knight-Rider Newspapers 216f
Knights of Columbus 173
Krier, Beth Ann 194f
Kurtz, Ernest 14f, 24f, 46–50, 55, 58f, 59f, 60f, 133f, 195f, 220
Lamunyon, Guy 146–149, 164, 201, 215f

Lanier, Dan 193, 196f
Lear's 109
Length of sobriety 59
Lester, David 200, 215f
Levant, Oscar 171
Librium 99
Life Process Program 72f, 118, 172–174
Lions Clubs 41
Little Prince 68
Liu, Aimee 34, 168, 174f, 183, 193, 194f
Locke, John 16
Lord's Prayer 142, 149
Los Angeles Times 194f
Loss of ontrol 20, 117, 133f
Lotus, California 108, 164, 226
Low, Abraham 122
Ludwig, Arnold 21, 22, 24f, 62
Luff, Ellen 79
Lutheran Church 47, 87, 220
Lyon, Mark 175, 176
Man's Search for Meaning 171, 174f
Marital therapy 139, 141
Marlatt, Allan 125, 215f
Martin, Father 142
Martin, Forrest 149, 152, 155, 165f
Maturing out (see Spontaneous recovery)
Maultsby, Maxie 110, 125, 133f, 162
Maxwell, Milton 58f
McDonald, Matthew 165f
McInerney, John 151
McMillin, Chandler Scott 200, 215f
Meacham, John 79
Medicaid 116, 199
Medical Basis of Psychiatry 116
Medicare 116, 199
Megatrends 82, 84, 220
Men for Sobriety 28, 84, 85, 93–96, 106f, 107f, 120, 134f, 137, 167, 221

Mensa Bulletin 61
Methodist Church 220
Methods of Moderation and Abstinence 105f, 216f
Mexico 11
Meyer, John 79
MFS (see Men for Sobriety)
Milam, James 22, 106f, 200
Milgram, Gail 148
Millennarianism 188
Miller, William 27, 59f, 74, 125, 139–141, 195f
Milwaukee Sentinel 175
Mind control 188
Minneapolis, Minnesota 88, 89
Minnesota Model 144f
Minnesota State Addictions Department 144f
MM (see Moderation Management)
Moderate drinking 96, 202–204, 215f, 216f
Moderation Management 28, 72f, 84, 96, 106f, 167, 204
MOMA (see Methods of Moderation and Abstinence)
Moon Is Down 75
Mooney, Alan 200, 215f
Moral Re-Armament (see Oxford Group Movement)
More Revealed 34, 38f, 63, 188, 194f
Mormon Church 220
Mueller, L. Ann 209
Myers-Briggs Type Indicator 152, 164f, 165f
N.A. (see Narcotics Anonymous)
Naisbitt, John 82, 84, 105f, 224f
Narcotics Anonymous 77, 80, 106f, 109, 193
Nation, Carry 46, 58f
Nation, The 86
National Academy of Sciences 69

National Clerical Conference on Alcoholicsm 21, 24f
National Council on Alcoholism and Drug Dependence 17, 18, 22, 23f, 24f, 59, 75, 144f, 148, 169, 177, 178, 193, 195f, 205, 222, 223, 226
National Institute on Alcohol Abuse and Alcoholism 185
National Self-Help Clearinghouse 59f
Natural History of Alcoholism 63, 144f
Naturopathic physicians 223
NCADD (see National Council on Alcoholism and Drug Dependence)
Neil, Scott 26–28, 30f
Neipris, Jeff 91
New Covenant 89
New Life Program 94, 100–102
New Mexico, University of 139
New Realities 35
New Testament 8
New York Stock Exchange 143
New York Times 28, 68, 109
New York University 81, 131
Newman, John Henry 47
Newsweek 28, 68, 109
Niebuhr, Reinhold 45
Nixon, Richard 200
Norris, John 219
North Carolina 13
Not-God 14f, 24f, 46, 58f, 133f, 195f
Office of National Drug Control Policy 218
Office of Technology Assessment 137, 144f
ONDCP (see Office of National Drug Control Policy)
Oregon 79
Oregon Alcohol and Drug Review 215f
Orwell, George 148
Osler, Sir William 141
Oxford Group Movement 39f, 47, 55, 58f
Oxford Movement 47, 58f
Oxford University 47
P., Hank 55
Paraprofessionals 142, 145f, 160
Parker, Jim 191
Parkinson's Disease 209
Patient's Bill of Rights 143, 216f
Paul VI, Pope 89, 105f
Peck, Scott 35, 39f, 110, 133f
Peele, Stanton 12, 38f, 63, 72f, 74, 75, 96, 118, 125, 172, 200, 216f
Penny gin 11
Pepsi-Cola 9, 39f
Perls, Fritz 122
Perrin, P. 35, 39f
Philadelphia Inquirer 176, 177
Pietism 46–48
Pittman, Bill 57f
Plagenhoef, Richard 201, 215f
Powerlessness 48, 53, 72f, 88, 99, 148, 167, 211
Powershift 7, 15f
Prentice, A.C. 194f
Preventive Medicine 22
Prince George's Journal 63
Privacy rights 206, 207
Probation officers 80, 222
Problem drinker (definition) 230
Problem Drinkers Guided Self-Change Treatment 168, 174f, 216f
Problem drinking (definition) 229, 230
Professional advisors 120, 121
Professional Counselor 223
Prometheus Books 99
Protestant Reformation *71*
Psychodrama 141
Psychology Today 92
Pyschotropic Medication 140
Purdue University 78

Quarterly Journal of Studies on Alcohol 58f
Ragge, Ken 14, 34, 38f, 63, 71f, 125,
    188, 194f
Rational Emotive Therapy (RET) 1,
    106f, 108, 109, 113, 114, 132, 141,
    145f, 155, 160, 167, 207
*Rational-Emotive Therapy with Alcoholics
    and other Substance Abusers* 151, 161
Rational Living 217f
Rational Madness 36, 39f
Rational Recovery 4, 27–29, 32f, 38,
    68, 70, 80, 81f, 83–85, 87, 96, 102,
    103, 106f, 107f, 108–134, 137, 149–
    153, 155–165, 167, 169, 170, 173,
    174f, 180, 181, 185, 190, 194f, 198,
    200, 204, 207, 208, 215f, 221, 223,
    226–228
Reagan, Ronald 77, 218
Real 13th Step 36, 39f
Reality Therapy 34, 141, 144f, 167
Reason 68
Recent Developments in Alcoholism 215f
Recidivism 77, 155
Recovering 209
Recovery Book 200, 215f
Recovery Centers of America, Inc. 145f
Recovery management
    traditional institutional 136–145
    nontraditional institutional 146–
    165
    w/private therapist 166–168
    w/self-help group 166, 168–170
    self-managed 136, 166–175, 230
Reiner, Margo 163, 164
Reissman, Frank 59
Relapse 201, 202
Relapse Prevention 202, 215f
Religion 12, 46, 47, 49, 56, 87–89, 119,
    120, 205, 206, 221, 222, 229
Republican Party 13
Resistance 147, 148

RET (see Rational-Emotive Therapy)
Road Less Traveled 35, 39f, 133f
Robertson, Nan 22
Rogers, Mary 230f
Rogers, Ronald 200, 215f
Room, Robin 125
Rozien, Ron 215f
RR (see Rational Recovery)
RR Residential 150, 164
Rudy, David 43, 46, 57f
Rutgers Center for Alcohol Studies
    200
Sacramento, California 150, 164
St. Meinrad's Abbey 133f
Salvation Army 41
Sanchez-Craig, Martha
Sanders, Donna 176
Sardo, Susan 163
Schaef, Anne Wilson 37, 39f, 184, 194f
Schaler, Jeffrey 14, 63, 96, 117, 125,
    133f
Scientific American 199, 215f
Search, Lynaea 9
Secular Organizations for Sobriety 23f,
    27, 28, 70, 84, 85, 96–100, 103,
    106f, 107f, 120, 137, 200, 215f
Secular Sobriety Groups (see Secular
    Organizations for Sobriety)
Sedona, Arizona 35
Seefeldt, Richard 175, 176
Self-control training 139
Self-help movement 82, 104f, 105f,
    168–170
Serenity Prayer 45
Seventh Day Adventist Church 220
Shabaz, John 56, 79
Shuckit, M. 195f
Sifford, D. 176, 177
Small Book, The 4, 23f, 53, 113, 117,
    122, 124–126, 130, 133f, 134f, 151,
    155, 158–160, 164, 167, 170, 171,

174f, 228
Smith, Dr. Bob 57f, 58f, 159
Sobell, Linda 96, 168, 174f, 203, 216f
Sobell, Mark 96, 168, 174f, 203, 216f
Sobering Thoughts 103
Social drinking (see Moderate
    drinking)
Social Security 199
Social skills training 139, 141
Society 117, 133f
Sociological Analysis 57f
Sonnernstuhl, William 195f
SOS (see Secular Organizations for
    Sobriety)
SOS Sobriety 106f
Southern Baptists 220
Sparks, Dr. Robert 69, 70
Spener, Rev. P.J. 47
Spirituality 22, 23f, 31f, 49, 56, 58f,
    59f, 92, 103, 153, 178
Sponsor(s) 33
Spontaneous Recovery 136, 167, 172,
    173
Stafford V. Harrison 79, 81f
Statistical Abstract 105f
Stedman's Medical Dictionary 22
Steiner, Claude 18, 23f, 28, 74, 195f,
    210, 217f
Steinhardt, David 92
Stress Management Training
Strossen, Nadine 218
Sturdevant, Boyd 193
Swaggart, Jimmy 181
Szasz, Thomas 74, 75, 81f, 133f, 177,
    194f
Take This Book to the Hospital with You
    216f
Talley, Bill 105f, 216f
Tate, Phillip 1, 14, 114, 134f
*Techniques for Using Rational-Emotive
    Imagery* 133f

Temperance Movement 13
Tennant, F.S. Jr. 137, 144f
Tennyson, Alfred Lord 73
Tessina, Tina 14, 36, 39f
Theories on Alcoholism 215f
*Theory and Practice of Counseling and
    Psychotherapy* 144f
THIQ 209, 210
Third Wave 15f
Time Magazine 24f, 137, 143, 144f
TIQ (see THIQ)
To Thine Own Self Be True 195f
Toffler, Alvin 7, 13, 15f, 81, 224f
Toronto, Canada 168
TOW Program 79, 228, 229
Towns Hospital 44, 57f, 58f
Transactional Analysis 85, 141, 145f,
    167, 210
Treatment centers 41, 43, 64, 75, 78,
    136–165
Trimpey, Jack 1, 14, 19, 23f, 27, 28, 35,
    53, 68, 75, 108–110, 112–114, 117,
    120–125, 128, 130–133, 149, 151,
    152, 162–164, 167, 169, 170, 179–
    181, 190, 193f, 194f, 198, 199, 201,
    202, 215f
Trimpey, Lois 28, 108–110, 112, 132,
    163, 185, 208, 217f
Trow, Gene 105f
Truth About Addiction and Recovery 38f,
    118, 174, 215f, 216f
Turnabout 101
Twelve-Step program(s) 3, 43, 77, 80,
    81, 91, 92, 97, 146–148, 150, 152,
    154–158, 188, 198
Twelve Steps 41, 48–50, 53–55, 87, 142,
    153, 154, 157–159, 211–214, 228
Twelve Steps for Christian Living 87
Twelve Traditions 56f, 68, 106f, 142
Twerski, Benzion 92
Under Your Own Power 215f

Understanding America's Drinking Problem
14f, 57f, 63
Understanding the Alcoholic's Mind 24f,
62
Unhooked 31f, 106f
Unitarian-Universalist Church 109,
133f
Unitarian-Universalist Society for
Substance Abuse Education 226,
230f
United States Constitution 71, 228
First Amendment 78, 79, 199, 229
Fifth Amendment 229
Fourteenth Amendment 229
United States Supreme Court 21, 22,
24f, 79
Urtz, Kay 87
*U.S. Journal of Drug and Alcohol
Dependence* 79
U.S. News & World Report 62
USA Today 116, 133f
Utah 11
Vaillant, George 63, 137, 138, 144f,
159
Vatz, R.E. 133f
Vaughan, Clark 190, 195f
Velten, Emmett 1, 14, 85, 112, 114,
127, 129, 155
Vestibule Inpatient Program 149–165
Veterans Administration 77, 80, 81,
109
Vietnam 12
VIP (see Vestibule Inpatient Program)
Vogler, Roger 203, 216f
Volstead Act 46
Wall Street Journal 24f
Wallace, John 216f
Washingtonian Society 39f, 46, 47, 58f
Washington Post 28, 68
Weber, Max 45
Webster's Dictionary 19, 24f, 38f, 71, 110

Weight Watchers 216f
Weinbert, L.S. 133f
Weiner, E. 216f
Weisberg, J. 209, 217f
Wells, H.G. 128
West, James 200
WFS (see Women for Sobriety)
Wheelwright, Farley 230f
When AA Doesn't Work for You 1, 85,
112, 127, 129, 135f
When Society Becomes an Addict 39f, 194f
Why Am I Still Addicted? 200, 215f
Will, George 76
Willis, Cean 131
Wilson, Bill 17, 21, 22, 23f, 24f, 44, 45,
46, 47, 50, 54, 55, 57f, 58f, 60f, 69,
70, 105f, 133f, 159, 186, 211, 219
Wilson, Randal 229
Wisconsin, University of 175
Woilitz, Janet 176
Women for Sobriety 27, 28, 68, 70, 84,
85, 93, 96, 100–104, 105f, 106f, 120
134f, 137, 167, 200, 215f, 221
WordPerfect 5.1 36
World Health Organization 18
Yeager, Raymond 151, 155, 161
Your Medical Rights 216f
Zeldin, Cindy 8

Addendum

When I wrote this book I was a member of the board of directors of Rational Recovery (RR). In 1994, however, RR combined its for-profit Rational Recovery Systems, Inc. and its not-for-profit Self-Help Network into a single for-profit corporation. It also changed its program from one based on Albert Ellis's principles of mental health (Rational Emotive Behavior Therapy—REBT) and education to a "structural model" of addiction based on an alleged neuro-physiological component.

I found that notion unacceptable, as did the majority of RR's board of directors. We resigned from RR and established Smart Recovery (or SR), an acronym for Self Management And Recovery Training. SR is an abstinence-based program, though not a 12-step program. SR understands dependency—chemical and psychological —on alcohol and other drugs, as a behavior subject to change; this is in contrast to the traditional "alcoholism as a disease" position.

SR is, in essence, the *old* Rational Recovery, and it retains the familiar tenets of Drs. Ellis, Velten, Prochaska, Norcross, DiClemente, Burns, Marlatt, and other cognitive-behavioral therapists.

For further information contact:

Rational Recovery, P.O. Box 800, Lotus, CA 95651; phone 916-621-2667. Contacts are Jack Trimpey, President; Lois Trimpey, Vice-President; Linda Mallard, Office Manager (all at above address/phone number).

Smart Recovery, 35000 Chardon Road, Willoughby, OH 44094; phone: 216-975-0515; Fax: 216-975-3394. Contacts are Randy Cicen, Executive director; Shari Allwood, Office Manager; Vince Fox, 5351 E. 9th St., Indianapolis, IN 46219, (phone 317-357-8905); Philip Tate, Editor, *Smart Recovery: New and Views*, 240 Lake Destiny Trail, Altamonte Springs, FL 32714 (phone 407-788-4242); Joe Gerstein, 521 Mount Auburn Street #200, Watertown, MA 02172 (phone 617-891-7545).

To Order Another Copy of
Addiction, Change & Choice

call

1-800-356-9315

(for credit card orders)

- -

Please send me ___ copies of *Addiction, Change & Choice* at $16.95 each ($14.95 + $2 P/H). I've enclosed a check or money order for $ _____.

Print Name _____

Address _____

City_____**State**_____**Zip**_____

Send to: **See Sharp Press, P.O. Box 1731, Tucson, AZ 85702-1731**

If you enjoyed *Addiction, Change & Choice*, you'll also enjoy

Please send me ___ copies of *Alcoholics Anonymous: Cult or Cure?* at $11.95 each ($9.95 + $2 P/H). I've enclosed a check or money order for $ _____.

Print Name _____

Address _____

City_____State_____Zip_____

Send to: **See Sharp Press, P.O. Box 1731, Tucson, AZ 85702-1731** or call 1-800-356-9315 for credit card orders.